Missing: The Oregon City Girls

NEW  HORIZON PRESS

Dear Reader:

We proudly present the newest edition to our internationally acclaimed true crime series of *Real People/Incredible Stories*. These riveting thrillers spotlight men and women who perform extraordinary deeds against tremendous odds: to fight for justice, track down elusive killers, protect the innocent or exonerate the wrongly accused. Their stories, told in their own voices, and in their own words, reveal the untold drama and anguish behind the headlines of those who face horrific realities and find the resiliency to fight back...

Missing: The Oregon City Girls tells the inside story which captured national interest of two young girls who vanished and the private investigator, a step-grandmother to one, who unlocks the deadly secret that stalks a community.

The next time you want to read a crackling, suspenseful page-turner, which also is a true account of a real life hero illustrating the resiliency of the human spirit - look for the New Horizon Press logo.

Sincerely,

Dr. Joan S. Dunphy
Publisher & Editor in Chief

Real People/Incredible Stories

Missing:
The Oregon
City Girls

A Shocking True Story
of Abduction and Murder

Linda O'Neal
Philip F. Tennyson
&
Rick Watson

New Horizon Press
Far Hills, New Jersey

Linda O'Neal, Philip F. Tennyson & Rick Watson
Missing: The Oregon City Girls
A Shocking True Story of Abduction and Murder

Cover Design: Wendy Bass
Interior Design: Eileen Turano

Library of Congress Control Number: 2005924252

ISBN: 0-88282-268-3
New Horizon Press

New Horizon Press books may be purchased in bulk quantities for educational, business, or sales promotional use. For information please write to New Horizon Press, Special Sales Department, PO Box 669, Far Hills, NJ 07931 or call 800-533-7978.

www.newhorizonpressbooks.com

Manufactured in the U.S.A.

2010   2009   2008   2007   2006   /   5   4   3   2   1

Dedication

This book is dedicated to Ashley Pond and Miranda Gaddis whose lives and travails poignantly inspired its contents. Ashley and Miranda, we will never forget your tragedies which have galvanized our determination to prevent evil child predators from tarnishing the innocent.

Table of Contents

Authors' Note

The point of view of this book is based on the experiences and work of Linda O'Neal and reflects her perceptions of the past, present and future. The facts about the murder of Ashley Pond and Miranda Gaddis recounted in this book are true to the best of her knowledge and recall. Some of the names have been changed and identifying characteristics altered to safeguard the privacy of individuals. The personalities, events, actions and conversations portrayed in this book have been taken from Linda O'Neal's memory, extensive personal interviews, police and FBI reports, court documents, including trial transcripts, letters, personal papers, research, press accounts and the memories of some participants. Quoted testimony has been taken from pre-trial transcripts and other sworn statements. Some minor characters and scenes are composites and some conversations have been reconstructed.

Prologue

T he emergency line beeps in rhythm with the flashing red indicator. The woman in the communications control room opens the line, "Dispatch."[1]

A soft-spoken female voice stumbles a bit trying to focus. "Yes. Um, how do I go about filing missing persons and what's the…what's, you know, the stipulation on how to go about doing it?"[2]

The twenty-something single mother sitting at her station says, "Okay, well, there isn't really a time frame. They used to say twenty-four hours on things like that, but there isn't really a time frame. You can start with me. I can have a deputy call you back and you can get a report filed that way. Is this an adult or a child?"

"A child."

"Okay. That's a runaway. That's something a little bit different."

"Okay."

"And this is your daughter, or son?"

"My daughter."

"How old is she?"

"She's twelve. She would never run away though." The woman's voice wavers as her restraint starts to crumble.

"Okay. You don't think she would ever run away?"

"No, I know she wouldn't."

"Just a minute please." The dispatcher switches between lines and addresses a radio transmission coming in behind the call. "Fifty-two fourteen…Yeah, we have a potential runaway, suspicious circumstances." The dispatcher quickly examines her caller-ID display and then resumes. "Newell Creek Village, off Beavercreek Road. Stand by for further." She switches back, "Okay, ma'am, I'm back. Go ahead…How long has she been missing?"

"Well, she left for school this morning, and I have contacted all her friends and none of them saw her at school. And she has dance after school. She wasn't at dance so she's been missing since this morning."

"Where does she go?"

"Gardiner Middle School. This is so out of character for her. She always calls and informs me of everything."

"Well, if you'll tell me what she was last seen wearing…"

"Um, you know, I didn't get up with her this morning, but I know that she…she was wearing blue jeans, Tommy Hilfiger blue jeans. I'm pretty sure she was 'cause they're not here. I looked….and white Skechers…"

"Okay, what's her name?"

"Ashley, A-S-H-L-E-Y Pond, P-O-N-D."

"Last seen wearing blue jeans."

"Yeah. And white Skechers, like sneakers, you know? And ma'am, I have no idea what shirt she was wearing. I didn't get up with her this morning."

"Hold on a moment ma'am." The dispatcher turns her attention back to the officer standing by on the radio. "Fifty-two fourteen, we have a twelve-year-old possible runaway, Ashley Pond, last seen wearing blue jeans, white Skecher shoes…"

The radio speaker vibrates with the officer's response. "I know the address…"

There is no time to register her surprise. The dispatcher continues, "…That's correct, apartment 228."

She then turns her attention back to the caller. "What color jacket does she have?"

"She normally wears sweatshirts. It probably would be, um, she only wears a blue sweatshirt, so she probably would be wearing a blue sweatshirt or some type of sweatshirt. She doesn't like coats."

"Okay."

"We looked at what ones are missing. There's—yeah, I think she's wearing her blue sweatshirt. Let me ask her sister real quick. She might remember.

"Honey? Hon, do you remember what shirt Ashley was wearing this morning, or what she was wearing?"

A child's voice replies, "I didn't see her this morning."

The distraught woman on the phone returns to her conversation with the dispatcher. "But she...because she got up at 7:00 and said... and thought she was late getting up for school, and I fell back to sleep."

She asks the child again, "So you didn't see her at all, huh?"

Getting a shake of the head in response, she says into the phone, "Okay, yeah, cuz I remember her getting up this morning and thinking she was late and she wasn't. And then I fell back to sleep. So, she doesn't remember, but I know she most likely...is wearing some type of sweatshirt."

"Just a moment please."

"Thank you."

The dispatcher takes yet another police radio transmission. "Fifty-two sixteen...you're 10-7 at nineteen-thirty hours." She shifts back to the caller. "Just a moment please, okay?"

"Okay. Are you trying to do two things at once?"

"Yeah, about ten things, actually. What is your name?"

"Lori, L-O-R-I."

"Your last name?"

"Pond, P-O-N-D."

"Okay, just a moment here. Okay, we've got an officer on the way out there."

CHAPTER ONE

Missing Person

Attractive, thirty-four-year-old Oregon City Police Detective Viola Valenzuela-Garcia catches the assignment. Following procedure, her first move at 9:30 AM takes her to Gardiner Middle School where the missing child attended the seventh grade. Garcia's plan is to individually seek out Ashley's friends and acquaintances since she prefers the informality of one-on-one interviews. In the school counselor's office, she conducts her first interview with thirteen-year-old Miranda Gaddis, Ashley's neighbor and classmate. After brief small-talk, Garcia gets right to the point. "So in your opinion Miranda, where is Ashley right now?"

"I believe that she took off, ran away."

"Why would she do that?"

"She told me her life sucked, big time. She was real mad at her mother, Lori Pond."

"Was she close to her mom?"

"I don't think so. You see, Ashley's mom has a drinking problem, and a lot of the time she is really awful to Ashley." Miranda rolls her tongue piercing around in her mouth.

"Can you think of a specific example of this?"

"Ashley told me she locks her out of the house for hours sometimes. And she grounds Ashley a lot for no good reasons. Just before Christmas I had a long talk with Ashley about her problems and stuff. You know what she said? She told me she wanted to run away, just get far away from all the stuff going on around her."

The policewoman looks up from her notes and says, "A lot of adolescents are going through a tough period of adjustment. When most kids talk about getting away, they usually have some destination in mind. Maybe a friend's or relative's place. Somewhere safe, maybe. Did Ashley ever confide in you about that?"

"Not really."

"Now I know you've already told me about Ashley having problems with her mother, but setting that issue aside for a bit, can you think of any other reasons Ashley would have for taking off?"

Miranda's expression changes and she looks suddenly sad. "Yeah... She hates living where she lives and she hates the way most of the other kids have been treating her. She gets a lot of grief tossed at her every day. I mean, she is kind of rude and snobby a lot of the time, but they're really mean to her."

"When did this all start?"

"When Ashley told everybody that Mallori Weaver's father had been touching her and stuff. But in the end it was never proven. The kids that thought she was lying got pretty mad at her. It caused a lot of hassles for awhile."

"Miranda, think hard for me; is there anybody you know of that could or would want to hurt Ashley?"

The girl is quiet for a moment as she studies the floor, thinking. She looks up. "Her mom's new boyfriend Dave lives there with them, but I don't think Dave would ever hurt her. She actually likes him. He's nice and buys her stuff. If you ask me, her real problem is Lori, her mom."

Ironically, the second student to confer with Garcia in the counselor's office is twelve-year-old Mallori Weaver. Mallori is one of Ashley's closest friends and is the daughter of the man that Miranda Gaddis had spoken of. Garcia smiles when she asks, "How close are you to Ashley Pond?"

"Not so close now, but last year we were like sisters. My dad took care of her lots a times and in fact, Ashley even lived with us for a long time. She was like part of the family."

Garcia nods. "So when was this? When was she a part of your household?"

"It was during sixth grade, and then that summer. She moved back to her mom's at the beginning of seventh grade."

"During the time she lived with you, how did she get along with your dad?"

"Great, really great. My dad was very nice to Ashley. He bought clothes for her. He even bought her a bike. He fed her and everything. And after all that, I can't believe that she'd turn around and lie the way she did about him. It wasn't fair."

"A lie? What type of lie?"

"Just a few days before seventh grade started, she all of a sudden starts telling people that my dad had tried to rape her or something. After that he kicked her out and she had to go back to live with her sisters and her mom."

"Mallori, do you remember any times in the past when Ashley ran away or mentioned running away?"

The child ponders a moment before responding. "Yeah, I think so. In fact I remember she did run away, for a few hours anyway."

"Who found her?"

"Her mom and my dad found her behind the Foster Farms building. She hadn't been gone that long. But that's the only time I know about her running away."

The detective makes a few notes. "Can you think of any reasons that Ashley would take off without telling anyone first?"

"If she ran away, I think it was because of Lori. Ashley couldn't stand being home with her mom because of her mom's drinking problem and the way it made her act."

"You said you and Ashley had been close."

"Yes."

"I'm sure then that you must have confided a lot with each other like good buddies often do."

"Sure."

"Can you tell me any other reasons Ashley was unhappy?"

"Well…we both are on the dance team. We have dance practice every day after school to get ready for the competitions. Now, the rule is if you miss one practice you can still compete. But if you miss a second time, then you can't. Ashley found out on Tuesday that she isn't going to the next competition. She missed two practices. It made her very unhappy. The next day, yesterday, Wednesday, she was gone."

"Thanks, Mallori, for all your help. It's a big job when somebody goes missing so mysteriously like this. But I'm sure we'll find Ashley." The detective pauses and looks into the young girl's eyes. "By the way, is there anything else you want to tell me about Ashley? Anything you can think of that I should know about?"

"Well," she pauses and then goes on, "I guess so. There was something weird. It was around ten o'clock that same day she disappeared. Wednesday. Lori's boyfriend, Dave, came over to our house looking for Ashley. While he was there, I asked him about dropping Ashley off at school when she was late, but he said he hadn't ever been dropping her off at school. What was weird about it was Ashley had told me that Dave was giving her a ride to school on the days she'd missed the bus. And Ashley missed the bus a lot."

"You live next to Newell Creek Canyon don't you?"

"Uh-huh."

"And a lot of your friends, like Ashley and Miranda, live in the apartments adjacent to the canyon, is that right?"

"Sure."

"Are there special places in Newell Creek Canyon where kids hang out?"

"Yeah."

"Would you be able to show me where they are, if we went there together?"

"You mean right now, during school?"

"Yes."

"Sure. I can show you, if you think it'll help."

"Okay, one little formality. I'll have to call your parents to secure parental permission."

"I live with my dad."

"I see. And what's his name?"

"Ward, Ward Weaver the third."

"Do you have his work phone number?"

Within minutes Garcia calls the man's employer and has Mallori's father on the phone. "As you may know Mr. Weaver, Ashley Pond disappeared yesterday and I'm in charge of finding her. I've been interviewing kids here at school trying to find some leads. I just had a nice chat with your little girl and she has indicated she knows places in the canyon where some of the neighborhood youngsters hang out. May I have your permission to take her away from school for a while to point out some of these places? Then I'll bring her right back to finish up her school day."

Weaver's response is quick and polite. "Yeah, I heard last night that Ashley was missing. Of course you have my permission. Anything I can do to help, count me in."[1] He proceeds to rattle off details about his knowledge of Ashley Pond. There had been quite a bit of trouble between Ashley and her mother, so the girl had practically lived with the Weaver family for several months last year. Weaver speculates, "Because of family problems, maybe Ashley simply ran away. In any case, I had no contact with her today or yesterday and, in fact, she hasn't been around my house for several months."

"Why not?"

"Well the hard truth is when Ashley gets in situations over her head, she has the nasty habit of shooting off her mouth making false accusations against people out of anger. I really feel sorry for the child and I hope you find her real soon. She needs professional help. But when you do find her, you need to check out her living situation. Her mom drinks a lot and hangs around with a rough crowd. It wouldn't surprise me at all if one of 'em is involved in whatever happened. But if I can ever be of help, feel free to call on me, any time. I wish I had more information for you."

Detective Garcia thanks the talkative fellow for his comments. "I'll get Mallori back to the school as soon as we get done at the canyon. It shouldn't take that long. Call me, sir, if you should think of anything else."[2]

CHAPTER TWO

Be On the Lookout

For seventeen years Philip Tennyson has operated a videotape service. He rents cameras, makes copies of tapes and shoots and edits videos. Philip conducts his business from a converted garage-office attached to the small home he shares with his blended family, including his wife Linda, a high-profile Portland private investigator, her twenty-year-old son Jonathan and Philip's thirteen-year-old son, Damon. Linda works mostly for defense attorneys. She's earned a reputation for dogged, detailed investigations, especially homicide cases. Since marrying Philip, six years before, she has moved her office to their house, taking over a spare bedroom and two-thirds of the dining room table. The kitchen separates her office from Philip's equipment-laden video studio.

On January 10, Philip is sitting at his editing bay examining a clip depicting groups of dancing teenage girls. The video office door swings open as his wife Linda O'Neal blows in, cell phone to ear. She's drenched from a pounding rain and clutches a waterlogged bag of groceries, half covered by a tattered umbrella. She is vigorously defending an issue. "I understand your instructions, but it's not my fault," she informs the attorney on the other end of the line, "and I will do it, but I'm telling you, the so-called witness doesn't know a damn thing." She hangs up, ponders the case she's working on a moment and then plasters a kiss on the top of Philip's head before she blasts on through the tiny editing suite into the adjoining kitchen.

Linda calls out to her husband, "Have you finished my surveillance tape yet?"

He shouts a reply toward the kitchen, "I've been working on it, but the guy with the dance team tape wants forty copies at ten bucks a piece. I'm doing your surveillance tape for love, so guess which project comes first?"

While putting the groceries away, Linda hears Philip's telephone ring repeatedly. "Philip, catch your phone," she yells.

"I'm right in the middle of an edit. I'll get it in just a minute." Finally, he picks up and Linda hears him talking to Maria, his eldest daughter by a previous marriage.

Linda meanders toward the editing cubicle.

"Have you seen my niece, Ashley, in the last day or two?" Maria asks sharply.

"No, we haven't seen Ashley." Philip asks, "Why?"

Maria abruptly requests to speak with Linda. Philip shrugs and hands over the phone.

"What's going on?" Linda asks.

"Ashley didn't come home from school last night and we're calling everyone we can think of. So far, no one has seen her."

Linda reflects for a moment. "Didn't she drive Damon crazy on some camping trip you guys went on last year?"

"She did pester him a lot, huh? Ashley's a pistol. She's got a definite attitude, no arguing there."

"So what happened, you think she ran off?"

"No, I really don't think so, Linda. Ashley spent last weekend here with her cousins and we all had a great time. She was fine when we took her home to her mother. She was in a good mood and wouldn't have run away."

Linda and Philip hadn't seen much of his step-grandchild.

"Is she more sophisticated than other twelve-year-olds?" Linda has unconsciously switched into her private investigator's voice.

"Not really. She's on the dance team and she's involved with other activities at school."

"Do you think she has an older boyfriend?"

"No, Ashley isn't into boys. After her problems with her father, she isn't really into the boyfriend thing. Remember she won't even be thirteen until March 1. Lori called the police yesterday, but the first thing they think is runaway. I'm really getting worried. Can you help?"

"I've got a friend who works for Clackamas County. If Ashley is still missing by tomorrow, I'll get a hold of my friend and see what I can find out. In the meantime, widen the scope of the calls. Call everyone you can think of. She may just be hiding out in plain sight. Don't worry, we'll find her. These types of disappearances are really very common, especially with teenagers who are troubled or feel misunderstood. Ninety-five percent of the time the kids turn up."

Maria seems unconvinced, but thanks Linda for her advice and hangs up.

Philip looks up at his wife. "Yeah, but what happens to that other five percent?"

His brow furrowed, her husband looks apprehensive and Linda suddenly has a gut feeling there may be good reason.

■

By this time, Viola Valenzuela-Garcia has spent hours interviewing people as she searches for clues to the whereabouts of Ashley, but she's disappointed. Nothing useful comes forth. Then a call from Gardiner Middle School produces what seems to be a solid lead. Mallori Weaver had approached the vice principal with information she claimed was provided by "Uncle Paul" to the effect that he had actually seen Ashley roaming around a shopping mall. Clackamas Town Center is a large regional mall some four miles from Oregon City. Uncle Paul is Paul Myers, her dad's closest friend.

Responding to the tip, Detective Valenzuela-Garcia is handing out flyers and continues searching for Ashley while she patrols the main walkways of Clackamas Town Center.[1] Earlier in the day she had issued a BOLO, "Be On the Look Out," alert for white female juvenile, five-feet-five inches, one-hundred-three pounds, brown eyes, long brown hair, date of birth 3/1/89, last seen wearing blue jeans and white sneakers.[2]

Garcia enters a costume jewelry store and soon begins fingering some garish earrings attached to a central display case. The bespectacled female clerk bids adieu to a departing customer and turns her attention to Garcia. "Sell many of these?" the lady cop asks, holding up a particularly outrageous pair.

The clerk laughs. "Not to anyone over the age of twelve. What can I do for you, officer?"

Garcia hands the clerk a copy of the flyer. "Have you seen this girl? We received a credible tip that she is hanging out in the mall somewhere."

The clerk stares for a moment at the portrait of a smiling Ashley that dominates the flyer before shaking her head.

Resuming her surveillance of the main walkway, Garcia next stops a young man sporting a Mohawk and a black goatee. She hands him a flyer. "There's a missing girl and we think she was around the mall today. Please take a look at this picture. Have you seen her?"

"Nope," he says disinterestedly as he turns and walks away, scuffing the tiled floor with the hobnailed heels of his work boots.

Later, while at a table in the food court, Garcia is munching French fries next to her stack of flyers. She notices a skinny teenager walking near the second floor railing. Her heart pounds as she examines the photo of Ashley on the flyer. She takes a longer look at the girl near the railing who suddenly notices the attention and darts into a passing crowd of teenagers exiting from a nearby movie theatre. Garcia rushes into the group and scans, her head turning quickly from side to side. But it is too late. Whoever the girl was, she is gone. The detective resumes her random interviews, hoping one will ultimately lead to a meaningful clue about the disappearance of Ashley Pond.

Garcia next contacts Ward Weaver at his job site, only a short drive from the mall. Her goal is to unravel more information about the supposed sighting of Ashley by Paul Myers. Ward Weaver cheerfully admits that Paul Myers is indeed his close buddy and further explains that Myers had told him that he had seen Ashley at the mall after her disappearance. Garcia gets Myers's phone number from Weaver.

Watching him, Garcia finds Weaver's attitude strangely unaffected by the disappearance of his daughter's friend. She reports, "While I was there talking with Ward Weaver, he seemed very distracted and his behavior was inappropriate, considering the topic of discussion. I was discussing the fact that Ashley Pond was still missing and rather than seeming concerned or upset, Weaver instead was laughing and being flirtatious as he talked with me. This seemed very incongruous with the fact that Mr. Weaver said he cared for Ashley like his own daughter."

Once Garcia has Myers on the phone, she describes the efforts surrounding the tip that had supposedly originated from him.

"There must be some misunderstanding, ma'am," he says. "I told them I had seen the girl at the mall all right, but when I seen her it was before she went missing, not after. Somebody got it all wrong. I talked to my friend Ward just this morning and evidently our conversation was incorrectly communicated to his daughter Mallori, who then must have told the Gardiner Middle School folks. Like a damned rumor getting spread, things get turned around. I hope this puts you straight on the matter."

CHAPTER THREE

Searching for Clues

Linda O'Neal is in her kitchen cooking pasta. The television news on in the background is focusing on Ashley's disappearance. While several graphics rotate, the news anchor's voice reports, "Oregon City Police were called to the apartment Ashley Pond shares with her mother and two sisters six times last year. In two of the cases, anonymous callers asked police to check on the welfare of a child who had been locked out of the apartment. In two other instances, the state's child protective services asked police to check on the welfare of the children." Linda begins to mull over Ashley's possible state of mind at the time the girl disappeared, asking herself where the teenager might be.

Watching the newscast, Linda realizes her step-granddaughter's disappearance is not going to be easily solved. Linda begins to formulate a "To-Do" list and she decides to call her stepdaughter to organize a meeting of interested parties. The goal is to stimulate a proactive approach in the search. She dials Maria's number. It rings four times before a young voice answers. "Hello?"

"Hi, is your mom home? This is Linda O'Neal."

"No, she and Tony are at Bingo."

"Is this Suzie?"

"Uh-huh."

"Suzie, maybe you can help me. As you probably heard, I'm trying to help find your cousin, Ashley. Your mom told me she spent last weekend with you guys."[1]

"Yeah, she did."

"Well, did she seem upset or tell you something was wrong?"

"About what?"

"Anything that explains why she might run away from home."

"Well, Ashley talked about certain things that bothered her. I just don't have a good memory, I mean, I don't remember exactly, but I know she did tell me things about her mom and the babysitting. She had to watch the kids all the time. She had to take care of her younger sisters. When you're only twelve, it's hard. I used to have to do that with my sister and brother when both Mom and Dad had jobs. I'd watch them for hours and hours, so I kind of know how it feels. But Ashley was doing it and trying to take care of her mom at the same time."

Linda responds thoughtfully, "That's difficult, but in divorced situations, even so-called normal kids sometimes have to assume too many responsibilities."

Linda, surprised by Suzie's words, suddenly finds herself immersed in memories of her own mother's emotional problems resulting in mood swings that kept her family walking on eggshells. The more she heard about Ashley's life, the greater a sense of kinship she felt. She had been that girl wanting to leave, wanting something better. In that moment it becomes clear to her that she will do everything in her power to find the girl.

Linda's attention is jerked back as Suzie continues, "Like, Ashley'd say her mom gets out of control some times, and she'd always be watching the kids. Like, taking care of them while her mom was passed out in the bedroom or something. I think Ashley came over to our house so much mainly to get away from everything and stuff. She always wanted to spend time with me and I feel bad now, because I never really did much. I mean, like, everybody knows she can really be obnoxious. That's just Ashley. You know? She told me stuff about when her mom was drinking and stuff."

Linda looks down for a moment, thinking, and then says, "Lori's going to have her fourth baby in a few months. So maybe Ashley meant that she was taking special care of her mom to help with the pregnancy."

"Linda, Lori needs help and everybody knows it. That's more than kids should have to deal with."

"Well, I'm sure that is very hard for Ashley. What do you remember most about her?"

"She's lots of fun, but she has an attitude. Everybody knows Ashley has an attitude. Some people don't want to deal with her, but she's great to hang with."

Linda smiles, "I can see you liked her—attitude and all. Do you have any idea where she could have gone, Suzie, any idea at all?"

Suzie sighs, "No, not really. My mom called every one of her friends and they haven't seen her either."

"I know. She's doing a great job, your mom. How are you holding up through all of this?"

"I just wish I would've spent more time with Ashley. That's what bugs me the most."

"It's a very natural reaction when someone special drops out of our lives. We all feel that way, Suzie, and we're going to find her. I promise. Thanks for sharing with me, Sweetheart. Could you have your mom give me a call when she gets back, okay?"

"Okay, Linda. I will. Bye."

■

Two days later Linda has organized a get-together with Philip, his daughter Maria, her husband Tony, and their daughter Suzie. Linda's new intern, twenty-one-year-old Allison, is with her.

She is not making good time, caught in late afternoon freeway congestion. Linda is at the wheel of her green sedan, switching frantically from lane to lane and fearing she may be late for her own meeting. Intern Allison sits quietly in the passenger seat listening to the radio speakers blasting a Doobie Brothers tune that entices Linda to join in. Her cell phone intrudes on the moment. After muting the Doobies, she picks up.

"Linda O'Neal Investigations…speaking."

"This is Bob Raymond. I represent Jack Jordan in a post conviction relief and I'm wondering, do you still have the case files?"

Linda slowly merges into the right lane. "It was 1995, wasn't it?"

"Wow! I'm surprised you remember that. Do you still have your investigative notes on that case?"

"Yeah, hold on." Linda swerves her car into the emergency lane and brakes. Getting out while ignoring the whizzing traffic, she and Allison open the trunk and rearrange several paper grocery sacks, each stuffed with thick manila file folders. "There it is." Linda spies one sack labeled "1995" and roots through the contents. Allison stares in bewilderment watching the private detective extract the documents before returning her attention to the cell phone caller. "Yeah, I've got my hands on them this moment. Do you need this stuff right now? Or can it wait until the end of the day? I'm on my way to an important appointment."

"No, the end of the day is fine. You've got my fax number."

Linda hangs up her cell phone and offers a comment to her intern. "There you go Ally, the most significant issue in the investigation process: good records, easily accessible."

Soon they are back on the road and arrive at her stepdaughter's house. Maria lives with her husband Tony in a sprawling one-story ranch nestled in a Portland suburb. Their daughter Suzie stands in the front yard waiting for Linda. After hiking a block from the closest parking spot, Linda approaches carrying a large briefcase with Allison a few steps behind. The teenage girl grabs the handle. "Let me help you with that, Linda."

"Why thank you, Suzie. Is your mom in the house?"

"I think so. And if you're looking for my grandpa, he's in the house too." She giggles.

Linda follows the girl through the front door. Philip stands near the grey stone fireplace holding court with Tony and Maria. "Yeah, your mother and I used to run the gut in Salem in my old Plymouth. Everybody saw us coming. Remember that old car, Maria? You were just a baby when I finally got rid of it. It just wore out, I guess. But I sure loved it. It had a pull down shade over the back window, a big floor shift and a windshield that cranked out with a tiny knob." He chuckles.

Linda approaches and hugs Maria before touching her intern's arm. "I want you all to meet my newest sleuth-in-training. She just started interning with me this week. This is Allison. She just graduated from the College of Legal Arts. She was my best student last term. And she's real interested in helping us find Ashley, whatever it might take."

Tony says, "We're all ready to follow your lead, Linda. But Lori and her mother and the rest of that side of the family aren't too high on us doing our own investigation. The cops told them to let them handle it. They don't want anybody else sticking their nose in it and all, I guess."

Linda takes her briefcase from Suzie. "I can understand that. But let's have our meeting and then we can figure out what, if anything, we can do to help the situation, not hurt it."

Allison asks, "How do her mother and grandmother fit in the picture?"

Linda expounds. "Philip was married to Lori's mother and they had two kids, Maria and Jon. They got divorced and Lori's mother got married again and had two more kids. One of them, Lori, had a child—well several children—one of whom is Ashley Pond, the girl who's missing. I don't really know a lot of these people well, but my husband is involved in all their lives."

Within minutes, most are assembled around the fireplace. Linda stands in front of smoldering coals and her voice is strong and firm. "I'm here to create an effective investigative structure. With everyone's cooperation, we can inject more energy into the challenges ahead. Maria feels the police don't seem to be looking for Ashley. I have agreed to donate some of my time to the case, but remember, I'm a private investigator; all of my work will be done in addition to what the cops may or may not be doing. So, Lori and her mother have nothing to fear from that standpoint. My trails may cross the paths the police are following. They may not. But I can promise all of you, we will sooner or later find Ashley."

From her briefcase, Linda retrieves her unofficial copy of the police report. "The police are treating the disappearance as a 'suspicious circumstances incident, no crime scene, no witnesses, probable runaway.' Now this was partly due to the fact that the Pond family had domestic disturbances causing police visits over the past year."[2]

Maria scowls. "That's not fair," she says. "Most of those police visits didn't even involve Lori or the kids."

"Fair or not, you've got to understand how the police view situations. And the fact is, in their experience, regardless of who was actually making the disturbances, they had been dispatched several times to quell situations." For emphasis Linda holds up a folder and thumps the side with her hand. "It's all here, every call and when you read through it, if you're a cop, you're going to get the idea that Ashley was much more likely to be a runaway than a kidnap victim."

Maria shakes her head. "Well, I still think it isn't fair."

"It may not be, but I found out that the detective charged with handling this case just entered Lori's 9-1-1 call into evidence. And they wouldn't have done that unless there were some inconsistencies."

Maria shakes her head. "I want you to talk to Ward Weaver."

Linda is puzzled. "You've never mentioned him before. Who's Ward Weaver?"

"Ward Weaver is the father of one of Ashley's friends. And Ashley told me that he tried to have sex with her. I talked to one of Ashley's school friends and she was really freaked out about it."

"Who?"

"Miranda Gaddis. She goes to school with Ashley and is on the dance team with her. And she lives at Newell Creek with a bunch of sisters. Anyway, you know what she told me? She said that she had once seen Ward Weaver stop Ashley from leaving his house by pressing his body up against her, even though Ashley wanted to leave. He just held her there. That's what she said."

"Maybe Mr. Weaver tried to compromise Ashley, sexually. Maybe it was all a big misunderstanding. Investigating the disappearance of a person requires asking a lot of tough questions and demanding answers that are not easy to come by." Linda writes on her pad. "I promise I'll dig into this Weaver fellow's background and try to find out if the police have found anything on him, but we need to keep an open mind so we can gather any pertinent evidence."

"Can we at least go over to his place and see if there are any clues?"

"No, no, no, not now," Linda replies quickly. "Remember, as of today there is no evidence that officially connects this guy to any crime. If we traipse over there, we might contaminate the place if it is a crime scene. We've got to keep our investigation totally legal and above board. If we don't, I can't be involved. I cannot afford to lose my license. In most investigations you have to chase down dozens of leads to get the solution. It's almost a mathematical equation. Rarely does it turn out to be the first guy you're suspicious of. Too pat. Right now, Ashley Pond is a straw in a tornado."

Suzie taps Linda's arm. "What do we do next?"

"Well, the first thing we need to do is establish a list of every adult that may have had any kind of contact with her. And Maria, those friends of Ashley that you called, you need to call each of them again, every three days until we find Ashley. We also need to find out if any of Ashley's acquaintances are missing or have run away, because first time runaways usually take off in pairs. Now, most of what we will be doing is drudgery and most of it will lead nowhere. But, there is no other way to conduct a missing person's investigation except with diligence. That's what it's going to take."

Allison raises a hand. Linda smiles. "What's on your mind?"

"What's your best guess, Linda? Do you think Ashley ran away?"

"I certainly hope she did, because that would be the best of all possible scenarios to lead to her safe return. Another possibility: maybe an adult had something to do with her disappearance. But the least likely scenario—and that's what can give us a positive basis for hope—the least likely is a stranger abduction. From what I've been told, Ashley is a feisty, energetic child. The odds that some stranger grabbed her and forcefully took control of her are slight. And that's good for us too, because you must all realize, in stranger abductions, the odds of finding the victim alive are cut in half in three hours and then cut in half again in eight hours."

Tony interrupts. "We were told there would be a TV news story about Ashley. They said five o'clock, and it's five o'clock. Maybe we ought to watch it."

Linda nods. "Definitely."

The group shifts to the nearby family room and focuses attention on the fifty-inch big screen TV in the back. Within minutes the male anchor introduces Ashley's story. "Today marks the seventh day since twelve-year-old Ashley Pond mysteriously disappeared from the Newell Creek Apartments in Oregon City. News Channel 15's special correspondent, Pinski Brown, has the details. Pinski?"

Pinski Brown is walking up the hill near Pond's apartment to the school bus stop. This is the place Ashley disappeared from and Brown comments that there were no eye witnesses. She says, "Local law officials tell us that they see this case as most likely a possible runaway under suspicious circumstances. Experts in the field, however, inform us that time is the enemy in disappearance cases. If the disappearance is a stranger abduction, the odds of finding the victim alive are dramatically reduced if the person has been missing a week. But at this point, they believe she most likely is a runaway, not a kidnap victim."

The TV screen juxtaposes a series of brief shots showing police passing out flyers, knocking on doors and talking to citizens. "Today marks the seventh day—the seventh consecutive day that has passed with no sign of the missing seventh grader. During the past seven days, police have canvassed the neighborhood, stopped commuters and interviewed dozens of passersby, so far, all to no avail."

Ashley's photo abruptly dominates the screen. Brown continues, "This case has baffled the local authorities as they have virtually nothing to go on. So, anybody out there, if you know anything at all about the disappearance of Ashley Pond, please call the *Crime Stopper* number at the bottom of your screen. They urgently need your help in solving this mystery. Back to you, Bill."

"And there you have it, the latest on the missing Oregon City girl." Tony switches the news off.

"Alright," Linda says, "let's try to give them the help they need."

CHAPTER FOUR

Runaway or Missing Person?

O regon City was the first incorporated city west of the Mississippi River. Established in 1829, by Dr. John McLoughlin, as a lumber mill near Willamette Falls, it was later designated as Oregon's territorial capital and was known as the end of the Oregon Trail. Now it is a working class suburb of Portland.

Under gray skies on the outside steps of the Oregon City Municipal Building, Police Detective Gary Harris and Chief of Police, Gordon Huiras, surrounded by a cadre of uniformed officers, are holding a press conference about Ashley Pond.[1] While several TV cameras record the moment, Detective Harris explains to the assembled reporters that they have changed their minds in the missing child case. Whereas they had been leaning toward a runaway theory, they now consider Ashley missing and in danger, because: First, she did not take clothes or money with her. Second, she has been missing more than a week. And third, she has failed to make any contact with her friends or family members.[2]

A crime reporter asks Detective Harris, "Is there any truth to a circulating rumor that many local residents and members of the family have provided you with some tips about possible suspects?"

Harris nods. "We looked at those reports and lots of people mentioned in those reports have already been talked to. Nothing indicates that they had anything to do with the disappearance."

A female TV reporter next asks, "If you're now entertaining a theory of foul play, do you currently have any suspects?"

"We are looking closely at adults who know the girl to determine whether they had anything to do with her disappearance. There are four to six adults that have our attention."

The reporter begins writing on her note pad. "Can you give us some names?"

Harris shakes his head solemnly. "You know I can't do that. These are only persons of interest at the moment and their privacy must be respected."

Another reporter shouts his query. "Have you been able to search the entire apartment complex for Ashley?"

"We did get into the primary places we wanted to get into, along with the area around the complex. We have also searched Lori Pond's apartment. Ms. Pond consented to the search and nothing was found that can be linked to her daughter's disappearance."

A female reporter gets her turn. "How about computers that Ashley might have used? Anything there?"

"The Pond family computer is currently being examined by a forensics computer expert. Her email correspondence is being carefully evaluated at this time."

The crime reporter interrupts with a follow-up. "What about chatrooms? Any chance Ashley may have met someone online and had a rendezvous?"

"As of now we are still awaiting a conclusive report on that." Detective Harris then indicates his boss. "I'd like to introduce our Chief of Police, Gordon Huiras, who has a brief statement."

Huiras, a stocky man in his early forties whose graying hair is destined to become even grayer as this case indelibly marks his life states, "Because of the shifting nature of our evolving hypothesis in this case, today we've asked the FBI to join with us to expand our search for Ashley Pond. Coordinating the resources from the Clackamas County Sheriff's Department, the Oregon City Police and the Oregon State Police, the FBI will centralize all aspects of the investigation. It's the very best way to maintain maximum efficiency.

They will coordinate all leads. Time is of the essence here. With their assistance we are launching a new, more intensified search beginning immediately. Every location will be reexamined with fresh eyes seeking more subtle clues. That's the agenda for now." Huiras hesitates a moment. Then, after glancing at his fellow officers standing soldier-like, he offers a final comment. "Of course we will strive to always keep the media fully informed as developments arise, but that's where we are at this moment, exactly ten days since the girl went missing. Thank you very much."

Later that afternoon, dog handler Marty Neiman of Search-One-K-9 Detection, his dog Klause and a Clackamas County Sheriff's Deputy are scouring the area surrounding the Newell Creek Apartments.[3] The dog sniffs garage doors and then the edge of the wooded area leading to the apartment complex. His nose sweeps across the damp ground rhythmically, but detects no new scents. Next, the group leads Klause up the hill where they encounter the sight of Ward Weaver's half-acre yard, its overgrown lawn and seedy tool shed beckoning for their attention. After the deputy confers with the dog handler, the men saunter onto the Weaver property, Klause wagging his tail. The deputy approaches the front door and knocks.

Seconds later, Weaver swings it open and when he notices Klause, calls out a friendly greeting. "Here boy! Come here. That's a good dog." Klause enjoys the attention and licks Weaver's face. He grins. "What a neat animal. Is there something I can help you guys with?"

Marty pulls the leash to separate Klause from Weaver. The deputy removes his gloves. "Good afternoon, sir. We are conducting a search for the missing girl, Ashley Pond. We would like your permission to search the property with a dog."

"What's his name?"

"Name?"

"Your search dog, what do you call him?"

Marty smiles and interjects, "Klause, and it won't take very long, because he's very quick."

Weaver chuckles. "A quick sniffer, huh? Sure, go ahead guys. Have old Klause sniff away all you want, but only outside. I don't want any dogs in my house. Now I've got to get back inside. I'm helping my daughter with her math homework." He quickly but gently closes the door.

The men conduct their search, but find nothing outside the house. The old storage shed reveals tattered boxes of assorted junk enmeshed in sticky cobwebs, but no discernable clues about the missing child. Marty and the deputy follow Klause on a new journey as he leads them down Beavercreek Road toward a store, but the trail goes cold.

■

Days tick by without a sighting. The morning of January 23, Detective Viola Valenzuela-Garcia is handing out over 1300 flyers to commuters. She is standing in the middle of Beavercreek Road during the morning drive, holding a huge life-sized poster of Ashley Pond.[4] Stopping cars, she stares the driver and passengers in the eyes until they roll down the window and take a flyer. All the while she is silently pleading for help in solving the case which is slowly eroding her soul. The thought of her own twelve-year-old child is never far from her mind. The rain is incessant as each of the cars' tires throws sheets of slimy road water in her direction.

At the same moment, fifty feet away, Portland's Channel Two reporter, Anna Song, is holding a microphone, standing near the spot where the local school bus will soon be retrieving the Newell Creek group of Gardiner Middle School students. Song's cameraman has her image in close, with a dozen youngsters clustered in the background chatting noisily. With tape still rolling, Song approaches the group who react with giggles and awe. She holds her mike out. "Pardon me, do any of you want to talk about Ashley Pond on TV? Come on, here's your chance."

A five-foot-four slender girl with lovely tied-back blonde-streaked hair steps up and offers her comments. "It's really hard to believe that happened to one of your friends or something. It's just really different and really sad."

Song becomes intrigued and follows up. "Were you pretty close to Ashley? Was she a close friend of yours?"

"We were friends."

"Did she ever talk about problems at home?"

"Yes. I knew her like from the third or second grade. And yeah, she did."

"What do you think actually happened that morning?"

"Wednesday?"

"That one morning when she basically disappeared. Did she talk about running away?"

"Yeah, she told my little sister about a week before she did it; she told her she was thinking of running away."

Song pauses a moment and asks a final question of the talkative student. "What do you think happened that morning?"

The teen giggles nervously. "I have no idea what happened. Really, I have no idea what happened. I just know she disappeared. Ran away or got kidnapped or something. But she's been gone for so long, it seems like she got kidnapped or something."

The young TV reporter looks searchingly at her. "Can I have your name?"

"Sure. Miranda, Miranda Gaddis."[5]

On schedule the yellow, belching colossus rolls up behind the students and within sixty seconds all have boarded. They crowd around the windows watching Song wave to them as the bus lurches its way down Beavercreek Road, soon disappearing from view. Song is buoyant. "I think we've got some good stuff here, Wally," she says to her cameraman as he disassembles his gear.

■

More days pass without a sign of Ashley. On February 5, Philip is away shooting a corporate video. Linda O'Neal is sitting at her dining room table that doubles as a communications hub for her home office. The table is littered with boxes of files, a computer, a fax machine and a thirteen-inch TV. Linda is typing up a routine case report. Her phone rings and she picks up. "Linda O'Neal Investigations. Can I help you?"

A twittering female voice nervously inquires, "Is this Linda O'Neal?"

"Yes."

"Do people hire you to investigate things?"

Linda laughs. "That's right. My job is to get to the bottom of the issue and provide a coherent report. Are you in need of an investigator?"

The caller hesitates and then hastily explains. "This is a bit hard to accept, but hear me out and then let me know if you might be of assistance. My husband, Rob, is a psychic."

Linda rolls her eyes and glances at her watch. "Oh really? And who are you?"

"My name is Pamela, and what I'm about to tell you is gospel. We're from California. Do you remember the Polly Klaas kidnapping murder?"

Linda feels a strange tingle at the back of her neck. "Yes. Her dad, Mark Klaas, started the missing child non-profit group."

"Well, Rob and I were on the search team of volunteers looking for her and Rob helped find Polly. He got a vision. He heard Polly and led the police to where she was in a shallow grave by a freeway. And now he has information about another missing girl. He can hear her, too. He really feels strongly that he can help, but the Oregon police are much more difficult than the ones in California. Because it's from a psychic, they won't even return our calls. So we need help, and Rob thinks a private investigator is the way to go."

"And what missing girl would that be?"

"Ashley Pond."

Linda is so stunned she drops her phone.

"Hello? Hello? Are you still there?"

"Yes, I'm sorry. I'm still here. How did you get my number?"

"To be honest it was totally random, but when your husband's a psychic, perhaps nothing is totally random." She laughs. "He just opened up the yellow pages, ran his finger across and stopped and said, 'This one.' It was you."

"What do you want an investigator to do for you?"

"Well, Rob has been drawn to a particular house in Molalla and somehow he's made a connection from Ashley's bus stop, where she disappeared, to this creepy old house. Rob got such a strong reading there. We want the place fully investigated. Rob is convinced that the answer to Ashley's disappearance will be found in this strange house. It's surrounded on all sides by twenty or thirty acres of thick woods. So we want to hire you to, well, first investigate it, then, if you find anything, get the police to follow through. Maybe they'll listen to you. They laugh at us."

"Okay. I think I can help you, but I need a couple of days to check you out. Give me a phone number." Linda writes on a nearby pad. "Yes. Okay Pamela, I will call you back. Yes. Thanks."

Later that day, Linda sits behind the customer counter in her husband's video studio. She is minding the store for him while he is on a video shoot. She is carefully adding figures from a bank deposit with an electronic calculator when Philip enters, burdened with several large equipment cases slung over both shoulders. He greets her warmly. "Did Mrs. Porter pick up the duplicate DVDs of her daughter's wedding?"

Linda rises and begins to assist him with untangling the straps and overlapping bags. "She did, and she is such a sweetheart. She wanted me to tell you how excited they all were at the showing. They especially loved the reception stuff. She said you got an extreme close-up of her dad crying like a baby during his toast. It broke them all up."

"Yeah, that's always been my motto, 'give 'em more than they ask for.'" He begins to dismantle his main camera. "How's your day going? Did that scumbag Juan ever plead out on that assault?"

"Hell, he wants a trial. And he's going to go down big time. I can't verify one of his so-called witnesses. That case is a mess." She hesitates nervously. "Philip, I had the strangest phone call today about Ashley."

"Ashley? I thought you said you were stalled on ideas. Maria told me you told her to keep checking her friends. You still believe she ran away, don't you?"

"I don't know what to believe after this call. It was from a psychic, or at least her husband is. She swears he helped find Polly Klaas with his instincts. But it's so bizarre she would call me out of the clear blue about Ashley."

"They have a connection to Ashley?"

"They can't get the cops to listen to their theories and they thought a licensed detective could serve as a go-between. Their connection is...I'm not sure. And they called me totally at random. They were just looking through the phone book and chose my name. Isn't that the weirdest thing?"

Philip finishes with the camera and gingerly slips the parts into its case. He snaps the locks shut, approaches Linda and embraces her. "Sweetie," he whispers tenderly, "in my opinion, getting involved with psychics would only undermine your credibility. I mean, come on! Psychics?"

"But I'm telling you, they called *me*. Out of fifty or a hundred detectives in the yellow pages, they called me. It gives me goose bumps. And let's face it, I've got nothing whatsoever to go on in this case. Neither have the police. It's been over three weeks, and there are no substantive clues. Would it hurt to check out what the psychic has to say, at least?"

■

Linda can't get the psychic's comments out of her mind. More time passes and there is no news. As crazy as it seems, she feels a visit to the Oregon City school bus stop to explore the psychic's tip is warranted. So, at eleven the following Saturday morning, Linda drives along Beavercreek Road before making the left turn leading to the vast Newell Creek complex that stands below the canyon's ridge. Linda notices a wide bus stop right at the turn and makes a U-turn, lurching her car to an abrupt halt right where the bus would stop. After turning the engine off, she sits and absorbs...what? She's not sure of what to expect, yet this is the very spot from which the child had vanished. There must be some clue. She spends the next several minutes examining the surroundings: the busy street with cars whizzing by, the winding road that leads to the apartment complex, the small house across the way. The gray apartments down the road from a forested gully. Where children used to play there are only forgotten toys and lonely bikes. In her rearview mirror she notices a pair of teenaged girls, one model-tall and blonde, one petite and brunette, strolling up the hill from the apartments. When they get close she hails them, "How's it going girls?"

They both smile and standing several feet away, give her eye contact. The taller one says, "Fine."

"Can I ask you a question?"

"Sure."

"Is where I'm parked the spot where the school bus to Gardiner Middle School stops?"

"It sure is. That's our bus. We both go to Gardiner."

"Is that right? You don't happen to know the little girl that disappeared do you, Ashley Pond?"

The blonde girl with a blue backpack and neon green shirt says, "Yeah. We knew her. But why do you want to know?"

"I'm a detective and I've been asked to find her."

The bubbly blonde takes a few steps and leans into the driver's window. Linda notices she's chewing gum and wearing floral perfume. "Wow, you're a detective, huh? I'm afraid somebody snatched her. What do you think?"

"Maybe the same thing."

"She's my friend. We're in seventh grade and on the same dance team together. We were supposed to do a competition soon." The girl looks at Linda seriously and says quietly, "Instead, I'm going to do a new routine I designed myself—for her."

"You don't think she's coming back."

"She's been gone now for weeks. She either ran away or was kidnapped, what else could it be?"

"This is the bus stop where your friend was heading the morning she went missing, right?"

The girl nods.

"Where do you think she would have gone from the bus stop?"

The girl shrugs and gestures widely with her right arm until her hand sweeps toward the lone house across the sidewalk.

Linda frowns sympathetically, "I'm sorry your friend is missing. I'm doing my best to find her."

"Well, she's got to be somewhere, but nobody knows where, not even the police."

The short brunette approaches the other teen and complains, "Come on, let's get to the store."

"Go ahead," Linda says, "it was nice talking to you."

The pair of teens wave to Linda and resume their journey. Linda shouts a final question that causes them to stop and turn. "What's your name? For my detective notes, who are you?"

The tall, talkative one smiles. "Miranda Gaddis."

CHAPTER FIVE

Another Blow Strikes

More days pass with no new information forthcoming about Ashley. Customers' cars surround a crowded suburban Barry's Restaurant. A green sedan is one of those cars and its owner, Linda O'Neal, is comfortably seated inside the restaurant across the table from her longtime friend. Ginger is a tall, slender and attractive forty-something woman who works in the administration offices for the Clackamas County Sheriff's Department. Off and on, for years the two have shared mutual gossip gleaned from their respective situations. Privileged information can be a most useful commodity for a private investigator, so valuable sources must be tended.

Chicken Cordon Bleu floating on a bed of crispy lettuce is being carefully set onto the table by a smiling senior citizen waitress. "Can I get you girls anything else?"

Linda smiles warmly. "Yes, an extra plate. We're going to share." After the waitress departs, Linda examines her companion. "You look really good, Ginger. Been working out?"

"It's the kick boxing. Tuesday and Thursday nights."

"Kick boxing?"

"Oh, yeah. Linda, those twenty-something studs are very effective instructors. You ought to give it a try. Want to come with me next time?"

"Do you have to wear one of those funny costumes?"

"It's not a costume, silly. It's just appropriate sports attire."

Linda chuckles nervously. "Well, I don't think so. It's really not my style. I'm not prancing around in some leotard and thong! Besides, every spare moment I get is being dominated by a tragedy on my husband's side of the family."

Ginger touches the top of Linda's hand. "I'm so sorry. What happened?"

"Philip's step-granddaughter is missing and I'm trying to help the family because, well frankly, so far, the police have dead-ended."

Ginger is confused. "The missing girl is your husband's what?"

"Yeah, I know, you practically need a program to keep up with this cast of characters." Linda pauses. "It's like this. Philip was married as a teenager. His wife was the mother of his first two kids, now in their thirties. They divorced. Then his ex-wife had two more kids by her next husband. One of those girls grew up and had kids of her own. Her oldest is the girl who disappeared, Ashley Pond."

Ginger sighs, "So you're trying to find Ashley Pond too. Every investigator in Clackamas County is looking for her. Boy, has that case turned into a circus. It's getting bigger and bigger, especially since the FBI took over."

"Yeah, and that puts you right in the center ring."

"Too bad it's in a tiny car filled with a bunch of clowns." Ginger shakes her head.

Linda glances around as if to detect potential eavesdroppers. When she is satisfied, she asks, "Any good suspects?"

"We can't go there, Linda. With the Feds involved we've been warned that leaks will not be tolerated. These guys are fanatical. I mean people could lose their jobs."

"Okay, we won't talk about the case, but there's nothing to keep us from gossiping about our mutual friends and my in-laws." They laugh. Linda resumes. "For instance, do you know if anybody's been driving over to Molalla a lot lately?"

"Molalla. Molalla. That rings a bell somewhere. Let me think a minute. As a matter of fact, I believe some detective was pursuing a lead from Molalla, a guy from West Linn police. Detective, uuh, Jay, I think it is. Jay Weitman."[1] [2]

"What about Molalla got him riled?"

"Can't go there, Linda. The best I can do is maybe just confirm information you have. Do you want to tell me what your Molalla connection is?"

Linda pauses to consider the implications. "No, I really don't. I don't have enough to go on yet. I was just hoping…Oh well." Linda's expression tightens as she prepares to plead. "Come on old friend. Give me something here. If it was the other way around, I'd spring. How about Lori Pond? Is she getting close scrutiny?"

Ginger smiles. "Oh Linda, you know how to work me so good. Okay. But don't push me. Naturally, they've all got eyes on Lori Pond. The profilers always say look to the immediate family. A lot of focus right now is on her, her background, who she has hung around with, all the police calls to her apartment."

"She has a lot of snakes in the closet, from what I hear, but is there any real evidence?"

"All I know is there's a lot of hours being invested in looking at Lori Pond. And of course, Lori Pond says it's some guy named Ward Weaver."

"Is there any evidence against Lori, like assaults or violence?"

"You tell me. The other day a detective was showing our boss a bunch of photos they took at Pond's apartment and there must have been five or ten different places where a hole got punched. I'm talking about the doors and the walls. Many, many holes. And when they asked Lori about one of the biggest ones, I think it was in the bathroom door, she admitted to causing the damage herself. She said every hole had an accidental cause and none came about because of any fighting. She said that big bathroom hole happened when she had to kick it in because Ashley locked herself in and wouldn't come out. And another one was when they were playing, not fighting. She said not one was caused by fighting."[3]

Linda beams. "Cool. Thanks, Ginger."

"For what? We just talked about your in-laws." She laughs.

■

A telephone call no matter what time of day or night can be a jarring experience. But if you're a private investigator working on a group of perplexing cases, when a phone rings you can't ever be sure who it might be. So every time, Linda is compelled to answer, no matter how occupied she might be. After all, this one might be an emergency. Dropping her case file to the table, she answers and it is, indeed, an emergency. It is her mother, and her mother is very agitated. Linda tries to be soothing. "Calm down Mother. Calm down. Now what did you say was the problem?"

"I told you. I'm at the beauty parlor. I just had my hair done, like I do every other Wednesday. And I got in my car to go home and it wouldn't go. It just wouldn't. So I need for you to come and get me and take me home."

"Can't you call Dad? He's a lot closer. I mean, Mother, I'm twenty miles away."

"Nonsense! Your father is home, but don't be silly, Linda. How could he come and get me? I've got the car."

"What do you think is wrong with the car?"

"I have no idea. It just won't go."

"Where did you say you were?"

"I'm at the beauty parlor. Come and get me, right now." Her mother hangs up the phone. Linda grimaces.

Philip is in his editing cubicle slaving away on a wedding video. He glances up when he hears the familiar footsteps approach from behind. "Well, well my lovely, I thought you were doing internet chores. Getting bored?"

"My mom's car broke down at the beauty shop. I've got to go on a rescue mission. Want to come along, be my sidekick?"

"I would Sweetie, but Dr. Peters is coming in at 3:00 to lay down his voice-over on his childhood home movies. He's coming all the way from Corvallis, so..."

"Okay, I guess I'm flying solo on this one."

Soon she is driving along the freeway westward from Portland towards the suburban city of Hillsboro. Linda attempts to keep the car at the speed limit, fifty-five miles an hour, but occasionally she slips up and pushes a bit faster. It is during one of those slip-ups, near

Beaverton in afternoon rush hour, that the right rear tire blows. It takes a quarter of a mile and about a pint of adrenaline to bring the car to a safe stop in the right emergency lane. Three solid lanes of bumper-to-bumper traffic fly by. The collage of SUVs, pickups and sedans provides a blurry backdrop to her plight as she opens her trunk and struggles through mountains of possessions in search of the spare tire.

By the time the motorcycle cop pulls in behind her, Linda has deposited several dozen items in various stacks behind the car. She also has jacked the rear wheel high into the air and has successfully substituted the spare for the flat.

She is in the process of lowering the car back to the ground when she sees him climbing off the big cycle. "Hello," she greets the helmeted officer. "You've arrived just in time to put a man's touch on a situation where it counts the most."

The policeman seems confused. "Excuse me?"

Linda chuckles. "The lug nuts. There's no way a lady can give that extra oomph when tightening those. Wouldn't you agree, officer?" She hands him the four-way wrench.

After tightening the nuts, he notices the many teetering piles of recently stacked items from the car's trunk. "Let me help you with that," he offers kindly. He retrieves several grocery sacks stuffed with file folders and hands them to Linda who hastily arranges them. He suddenly becomes alarmed and touching the front of his holster, he shouts, "A gun! Lady, are you in possession of a firearm?" Before Linda can respond the officer bends over and picks up a clear gallon sized Ziplock plastic bag with a .357 snub nosed revolver clearly visible inside along with a pair of speed-load clips.

"Oh, I'm terribly sorry about the gun, sir. But I have a permit to carry it, although I must confess that gun mostly just stays in the trunk. I'm a licensed private investigator." She pulls some documents from her crowded purse and attempts to give them to him. In order to take possession he hands her the plastic bagged revolver. Linda comments while he inspects the papers. "You can see everything is on the up-and-up. Now if you'll excuse me, I am on an emergency trip to Hillsboro. My mother's having a crisis. Her car broke down at the beauty parlor and I need to rescue her. I guess I've got a lot on my plate today."

The policeman removes his sunglasses and ponders. "How old is she?"

"It's not polite to ask a lady's age, but what the hell! She's seventy, going on twelve, if you know what I mean." Linda laughs and looks at her watch.

He smiles. "It's probably just a dead battery or something like that. Do you have jumper cables?"

"No, but if I can't get it started I'll just call a tow truck. For God's sake, that's what she should be doing. I don't see why…"

The officer smiles warmly. "I have a mom just a little younger than yours, and sometimes they just need a little TLC. It's going to be okay, ma'am, it really is."

Linda is touched. "Thanks for saying that, sir. It's very kind."

"It's the truth, ma'am."

Linda returns to her re-packing. "Can you hand me that?" She points to a round, white plastic object attached to folding legs.

The young policeman makes a face as he gingerly picks up the strange item. "What the heck is this?" he inquires.

Linda puts her hand over her mouth in mock embarrassment. "It's a folding port-a-potty. You tie these little plastic bags on the wire frame there. You see, you guys, when you're on stakeout and nature calls, just lean up beside the car. But what's a girl to do?" Linda giggles, takes the toilet seat from the officer and tucks it into the crammed trunk on top of some crushed file sacks.

Moments later she is back behind the wheel ready to roll. The friendly state patrolman approaches with a final comment. "Okay ma'am, best of luck to your mother and you."

Lydia's Lovely Look Salon is an integral component of Linda's mother's weekly regimen. For decades, she has been having the same style done before making a customary stop at the local supermarket during the journey home. Today's car trouble is the first break in that routine for more than thirty years.

When she pulls into the parking lot of the beauty salon, Linda notices that the building and signs are exactly the same as the last time she had her hair done at Lydia's for high school graduation. Linda was salutatorian, and had gone for the latest "Bond Girl" style. She also remembers the graduation card her mother had given her for the occasion—the one that contained a gift certificate for an introductory session at Weight Watchers. Her parents' charcoal Taurus sits nestled right in front of the shop's main entrance in the only designated "handicapped" spot. Linda briefly peers through the driver's window then enters the shop where she discovers her mother near the front window chatting with a few salon employees and their customers.

Her mother turns and sees her. "Linda, I was just telling them about your grandpa's place, the house I grew up in, in Iowa. Remember my grandpa's house was just up the path on the little rise?"

"Yes Mother, I remember." Linda picks up her mother's nearby purse and hands it to her. "Give me your keys. I'm going to check out your car and see if I can get it started."

She surrenders the keys then turns her attention to her interrupted Iowa story, while her daughter goes outside and gets into the sedan. Linda inserts the ignition key and turns it clockwise. To her surprise the engine fires up and idles smoothly. Next she engages the transmission by shifting it into "reverse," and backs up a few feet, then forward. She shrugs, shakes her head, shuts the engine off, restarts it, revs the motor for a few more seconds, then shuts it off again and gets out of the car.

When Linda is back inside the shop she walks over to her mother, "Mom, the car is fine. I thought you said it broke down."

"No, no, I said it wouldn't go."

"Well it started just fine for me, so there's no problem. Here's your keys." Linda hands the keys back, leaves the building and heads for her car. She stops when she hears a familiar voice calling her, only this time it is tinged with desperation. "Linda, please. Wait! Help me."

"But I just tried it and the car is fine."

"But Linda, maybe I'm not fine. I didn't say the car wouldn't start. I sat in it and I couldn't make it go. I was sitting there and I couldn't remember where I was going or even how to make the car move. Can you help me, please?"

For an instant Linda is at a loss for how to respond. During all of the preceding years her mother has always been a forceful presence, always self-assured and determined. This new version of mom, a frightened apparition, the ghost of the strong female who had always dominated every person she was in contact with is unsettling. For several moments Linda stands in the parking lot watching her mother's perplexed expression, anxiously wondering just what she should do. Finally she takes her mother by the hand, leads her to her car and assists her getting into the passenger seat. "I'll take you home, and then bring Dad back to get your car."

It is the scenario every adult child dreads: when parent and child exchange roles. For Linda it is particularly agonizing. During the five minute ride Linda is shocked at the silence. Her normally gregarious, talkative parent doesn't utter one word until she sees her own house as they pull into the driveway. "Goodness," she then exclaims, "I think it must be time to get dinner started."

While driving her dad back to the shop to fetch the car, Linda expresses her concerns. "I think you need to get Mom to a doctor, Dad. I don't know what's going on, but she may have had a small stroke or it may be a deteriorating mental condition. This could be a signal that something is seriously wrong."

Linda's father shakes his head. "Look, your mom goes to the doctor more than any woman her age. She's sees her doctor at least once a week, and he says she's fine. Don't worry, she's okay. She's just a little high strung. She's fine. Really, she's fine. Everything will be okay."

When they get back to the house, Linda watches her mother fixing dinner and for a short while the older woman appears to be functioning. Linda, still apprehensive, bids her parents good-bye.

During the traffic-infested journey from her parents' home, Linda uses her cell phone to discuss her concerns about her mother with her younger sister. "It was so weird. I mean, you know how Mom usually acts. I don't ever remember her asking for help from anybody. She always tells everybody else how it's going to be. She never asks for help, and today she was almost begging me."

Her sister is startled. "That definitely doesn't sound like Mom."

"She knew there was something wrong with her, at least at that moment. Later, once she was in the kitchen fixing dinner, she seemed normal. But I'm telling you, when she realized she'd forgotten how to drive, she was asking me for help. I was blown away. And when I told Dad about it, he just laughed it off. He says she's just fine. He thinks it was just a little stress. What do you think? You've had a lot more contact with her than I have the last few years. Have you noticed her acting strangely?"

"Well she seems focused on the long ago past. She's been talking a lot about her growing up years—a lot of stories about the farm, her nine brothers and sisters and meeting Dad. I have noticed that lately."

"She's past seventy now, and a lot of diseases like Alzheimer's kick in then. Sis, somebody needs to get hold of her doctor and talk with him. I mean, if she had some sort of stroke, it needs to be checked out. Something needs to be done here."

"What makes you think it's so alarming?"

"Remember Aunt Betty? Well, you were pretty young, but she had a small stroke and it became the starting point for the big decline for her. She went through several episodes of wigging out and it got worse and worse. They finally had to put her in some nursing home and she didn't last very long there at all. I'm telling you, this could be serious. Something has to be done and you should do it. You've always been closer to her than me."

"It should be up to Dad, shouldn't it?" her sister asks.

"I don't think he can make the call to her doctor and get the ball rolling." Linda waits for her sister to reply.

"You're the firstborn child Linda, you do it. Besides, you were the one she called when she thought she needed help."

For a few moments neither sister comments, both reflecting on the issue. Eventually, Linda's sister consents to telephoning the doctor.

When she finally arrives home, Linda looks for Philip and as usual, he is in his editing suite manipulating video images. When he notices her, he pauses the machine, stands and embraces her. "No tragedies while you were gone. I took one call on your business line. It was from Barnett. He said not to worry about the Espinoza trial after all. He's pleading out. Did you get your mother's car fixed?"

Linda sighs, "There was nothing wrong with her car. She couldn't remember how to drive, and she has been driving for more than fifty years."

"That sounds like a job for her doctor, not you."

Linda bites her lip and then goes on. "That's the next step. Sis is calling about an evaluation."

Philip looks pensively at his wife and decides to say nothing, seeing the conflicted emotions play plainly on her face.

Linda sighs heavily, "I need to get back to the search for Ashley."

The FBI task force watches Lori Pond and her boyfriend, Dave Roberts, all day on March 1, trying to find out whether they were involved in Ashley's disappearance.[4] The date would have been the girl's thirteenth birthday.[5] The couple lead the police to a birthday gathering the family holds as a remembrance.

When Linda finds out, her comment to Allison is abrupt. "Well, at least they are looking, even if it is right out of the manual. They haven't given up on her. But most of them still think she's hiding out somewhere. I'm not so sure."

The campaign to secure inpatient evaluation for their mother consumes a tremendous amount of Linda's sister's time the next ten days, mainly because she has to find a facility within modest driving distance from her parents' Hillsboro home. Their dad is firm on that requirement, because he will be making many visits to his wife and feels ill equipped to drive great distances because of his advancing age. Finally a bed becomes available at Forest Grove Hospital six miles away. Resistive at first, their mother eventually acquiesces because the hospital stay will help soothe all the family's anxiety. She's checked in on a Monday afternoon by her two daughters and their dad, each of whom commits to a visitation regimen. Dad will come every morning and every evening. The sisters will pop in whenever their schedules permit.

On Friday, March 8, while Linda's sister watches the Dayroom TV at the hospital, Linda and her mother are engaged in another conversation about Grandpa's Iowa farm.

"Did I ever tell you about that homemade wine he used to make down in the cellar? It's so funny Linda, because we could always tell when he'd been in that cellar, because he'd always have a big grin on that face of his when he came into the room."

Linda's sister interrupts, very excited. "Linda, Linda, didn't you say you were working on a case involving Ashley Pond?"

Linda feels her heart beating more quickly. "Is there some news?"

"Look! They're talking about her on TV."

A female reporter is shown speaking into a handheld microphone with the Newell Creek Apartments clearly visible in the background.

"Ashley Pond disappeared from this location exactly two months ago. And incredibly, a second teenaged girl has also disappeared from the same location under similar circumstances. Miranda Gaddis, a friend and classmate of Ashley's, disappeared this morning from the Newell Creek Apartments on her way to the school bus stop, the exact stop Ashley was headed for when she went missing on January 9. Police sources say she may have run away, or she may have met with foul play. But as of now, they have no witnesses and no crime scene."

As she stares up at the screen, Linda feels sadness and guilt ripple through her. Another girl missing means that the chance that Ashley will return is next to nothing. It means that she was most likely taken—it means that Linda had failed, and a little girl has paid the price. Aghast, the PI begins weeping softly while her puzzled mother tries her best to understand why her daughter's upset. "Linda, what's the matter with you?"

Linda lapses into a muttering monologue as she rocks her head back and forth, tears streaming down her cheeks. A nearby nurse hears her and rushes in to offer comfort. "No, no, no. Oh God! No. Not

Miranda, too. It's crazy. I just met her. She was so alert and perky. I've got to get back to work! Oh this could have been so different. If I had really worked on the Ashley Pond case, I might have prevented this. She was so lovely, so spunky. Maria asked me for help, but I wasn't sure what to do. Now I am. A third girl is not going to disappear if there's anything in the world that I can do to prevent it."

CHAPTER SIX

Two Girls Lost

On March 8, 2002, at about 5:30 PM, Oregon City Detective Greg Fryett receives a telephone call from his boss, Lieutenant Jarvis. "You won't believe this Greg, but a second juvenile girl has turned up missing at the Newell Creek apartments. We need you to take charge. Valenzuela-Garcia has been handling Ashley Pond's case, so you'll coordinate with her. Both girls live at the same apartment house, so you'd better get over there and see what you can find out."

Fryett brings in every available reserve officer to do extensive canvassing of the entire apartment complex. While his assistants ring doorbells, Fryett interviews the latest missing girl's mother, Michelle Duffey.

With her other children sitting nearby, Michelle tries to explain the unexplainable. "I don't think Miranda would leave. She's friends with Ashley Pond and she was very upset over Ashley's disappearance. My oldest daughter had been staying with the dance team coach. My youngest daughter was here this morning though. She left for school at about 7:10 on the early bus, the one that arrives at about 7:20. Then I was at home alone with Miranda until I left for work at 7:30. The last thing I heard when I left was Miranda locking the door behind me. I heard the clicking of the deadbolt. Then I went to work and I got back home about 2:15 in time to be here when my younger girl arrives, usually about 2:20."

At the conclusion of his interview with Duffey, Fryett searches the apartment for signs of forced entry but doesn't find any. His conclusion? It appears as though Miranda Gaddis left the apartment on her own with her books and backpack. He also determines there had been no caller ID phone calls recorded.

Fryett visits with every occupant of Building 1, the building that contains the Gaddis unit, but the interviews prove fruitless. Nobody has seen anything suspicious.

By this time, rain is falling steadily and Fryett, accompanied by Sergeant Lisa Nunes, trudges up the hill to the school bus stop. A lone residence nearby attracts the detective's attention. It's the only single family house in the apartment dominated neighborhood.

Night has fallen, but his curiosity prods him to survey the place. They walk through overgrown grass and notice a run-down shed near the rear of the half-acre yard. In the darkness they make their way to the front door and knock. A moment later the door swiftly swings open revealing a five-foot-eleven-inch, white male in his late thirties who throws his arms high in the air. With a broad smile he attempts to charm the policemen when he shouts, "I give up, officers. Take me away."

Fryett is not amused. "Another neighborhood girl is missing. Fourteen hours have elapsed. She's thirteen-years-old and her name is Miranda Gaddis. May we come in?"

The man opens his front door and gestures for them to enter. Fryett notices a young girl sitting on a nearby couch. He explains to the man, "We're looking for any information about Miranda. Have you seen her?"

The man plays with his reddish mustache then shakes his head. "The last fourteen hours? No, I certainly haven't seen her. But I do know her. She's a friend of my daughter Mallori."

The detective opens his notebook and removes the cap from his ballpoint with his teeth. "Can I have your name?"

The smiling man shrugs. "Sure. Ward, Ward Weaver III."

"Mr. Weaver, is that child on the couch your daughter?"

"Yes she is. Her name is Mallori and like I said, she is friends with Miranda and Ashley."

"Would you mind if I had a word with her?"

"No, not at all. Mallori, come over here. The officer wants to ask you some questions."

Mallori obeys and soon is standing next to her dad. Fryett smiles before he asks, "Can you tell me what your day was like today, Mallori?"

"Sure, well, I didn't go to school today, because I was sick."

"What time did you get up? Was your dad still here then?"

"I didn't sleep here last night. I slept at my mom's. I haven't been here all day."

"So you weren't in school today?"

"There was only a half day of school anyway, so I didn't go."

"You haven't seen Miranda?"

"No, I sure didn't. I saw her yesterday, but I wasn't even around to see her today."

"Your dad says she's friends with you; is that true?"

"Yes."

"Does she visit you here in the house?"

"Sure, we hang out here sometimes."

"Mr. Weaver, let me ask you something. Did Miranda come to your house this morning looking for Mallori?"

Weaver shakes his head. "Oh, no. She didn't."

"Was there anyone else in your house this morning?"

"No, just me and Mallori live here now. Nobody else."

"Would you have any objections if I just looked around your place a bit? It's just routine."

"Sure, go ahead. Help yourself."

Fryett and Nunes carefully examine room after room, not even sure exactly what they hope to find. The bedrooms and the closets are first, but they seem fine. The bathroom is next, nothing suspicious there. A pass through the living room and dining room doesn't reveal anything either. The kitchen is the only room left, but it too yields no clues.

"Could you show me around the backyard while Nunes stays inside with your daughter?" Fryett asks.

Weaver agrees and leads Fryett out the kitchen door to the rear of the house. Though the night is dark, Fryett notices the outbuilding again, but a cursory inspection fails to arouse any suspicions. At the end of the visit Fryett and Nunes shake Weaver's hand and politely thank him for his cooperation.

Weaver says, "Glad to help, and if I can be of any further help, feel free to call on me any time. I wish I had more information for you."

Detective Fryett thanks the talkative witness for his comments and hands him a business card. "Call me sir, if you should think of anything else."[1]

In these first twenty-four hours after Miranda vanishes, few clues surface. However, soon an explosion of FBI activity erupts. Agents from all over the country quickly swarm the makeshift command center above an Oregon City firehouse, swelling the total of official investigators past seventy. A separate agent is assigned responsibility for each building in the huge Newell Creek Apartment complex. Some inhabitants are interviewed as often as three times in three days. As days pass, the pressure intensifies as authorities become almost desperate to squeeze out a meaningful lead that can break open the baffling mystery.

More days pass and the FBI task force ratchets up its reward fund to fifty thousand dollars. This money is to be awarded to the provider of the one meaningful tip that solves the mystery. Linda wonders if the FBI investigators are following the wrong tips and ignoring the helpful ones. She knows that sifting through mountains of useless information eventually changes attitudes. And the "no crime scene, no witnesses" mantra only adds to collective confusion.

■

Harry Oakes, a man on the outside looking in, has been a search dog trainer for years and paid his dues to the profession.[2] But for mysterious reasons, the established dog handlers in the area have never accepted Harry as a legitimate member of their profession. His dog, Valorie, is just as smart as theirs. *Perhaps*, he thinks, *I'm too outspoken when I think the established handlers get it wrong.* When the authorities refuse to allow Oakes to join their official search for Ashley, he calls the girl's mother, Lori Pond, and offers to search for her daughter. She is ambivalent, but she meets with Oakes and Valorie on the morning of March 7. After he briefs her about his techniques, she is impressed enough to cooperate. "I need a personal item," he tells her matter-of-factly, "for a good scent…shirt or pants, something like that. Preferably something that hasn't been washed. Anything she would have worn recently."

Lori surrenders a pair of knee socks that Oakes carefully places into a plastic bag. He thanks Lori for letting him volunteer his expertise and promises he'll be returning to conduct a private search.

Incredibly, the very next day, March 8, Miranda Gaddis disappears from almost the exact same location as Ashley. Oakes knows that the FBI and the Clackamas County Sheriff's Department will be all over that whole area. But it doesn't mean that he can't search too. After all, he has secured the permission of the first missing girl's family.

Harry and his dog Valorie thoroughly search the Newell Creek Canyon on March 10. For hours and hours they methodically prowl back and forth across every square foot of the rugged terrain. Just before dark, while she crawls under some thick foliage at the bottom of a steep canyon below Beavercreek Road, Valorie finally releases one, enthusiastic alert. She howls and howls. Oakes makes note of the location, realizing that it is getting too dark to continue. He resolves to return soon and resume.

Because of several personal conflicts, Oakes isn't able to return with Valorie until March 15. Early that morning he arrives where his dog had alerted, determined to discover the basis for the disturbance and hopeful it will yield a clue. He begins the ritual as he always does, by giving Valorie her head when they reach the familiar spot. Once again the dog wails in a mournful, whimpering cadence that means, "There's a dead body here somewhere!" Valorie then unexpectedly bounds up the slope and races frantically under brush and over dead tree limbs, Oakes sprinting to keep her in sight. Finally the dog shifts direction and lopes toward the lone house at the end of the road by the apartment complex. Harry senses excitement. Valorie is definitely interested in something here. He hesitates, thinking, *Well I still have to do things right, but this could be our big break.* After carefully mulling over the situation, Harry walks up to the front door and knocks. A shirtless teenage boy pushes the door wide open. He stares at Oakes, then at Valorie who is panting and wagging her tail. "What do you want?"

Oakes extends his hand, but the teen refuses to shake it. "Well, I'm Harry Oakes, a private dog handler. I'm helping in the search for the missing girls and would it be okay, I mean can I have permission to let her explore the ground for scents?"

The shirtless one shrugs. "I don't even live here. I'll have to call my dad and ask him. If he says it's all right, then, okay. I'll be right back." He slams the door, leaving Harry standing for several minutes. The door opens again with the teenager, this time wearing a white tee shirt, smiling.

"My dad says it's okay, as long as you keep your dog away from the new concrete slab in the backyard. He's getting ready to install a hot tub on it. That slab was just poured and he doesn't want it messed up."

Harry thanks the boy for his cooperation and while the kid observes from the kitchen window, Harry takes Valorie around back and puts her to work. Valorie pays no attention to any surrounding ground but instead makes a beeline for the concrete slab. First she merely hovers over it, but soon she is pacing back and forth with increasing intensity. Finally, she throws her head back high in the air and unleashes her unique, blood curdling death alert. She lunges at the slab, scraping its hard surface with her front paws. Harry has to yank her chain to pull her back. Valorie erupts with a thirty-second non-stop bark blast. "Quiet, Girl! Quiet!" Harry commands. Harry is so shaken he pulls Valorie tightly and briskly walks her off the Weaver property and on down Beavercreek Road to a strip mall. He enters a store and asks to use their phone to call the police.

A female officer takes his call. Harry's heart is still pounding. "I'm telling you ma'am, there's something under the slab at Ward Weaver's house. It needs to be checked out." She records his telephone number and address before thanking him for the tip. That is the end of it! Nothing! When Oakes does not hear from the police, he writes a letter to Oregon City Chief of Police, Gordon Hurias, detailing

Valorie's March 15 reaction to Weaver's concrete slab. He sends copies to the Pond family and the FBI task force.[3]

■

On the same day that Harry Oakes and his dog are investigating Weaver, a blonde young man named Brian Taylor stands in the upstairs apartment above Lori Pond's unit, involved in an energetic exchange with two middle-aged males wearing FBI windbreakers. "Yes, on March 8, I was camping up at Bagby Hot Springs, out near Molalla."[4]

"Camping in March?"[5]

"Hmm, where are you from?"

"Chicago."

"Well I don't know about Chicago, but in Oregon it's not unusual to go camping in March."

The second agent asks, "You went camping on March 8. Does that mean that you left for your camping trip on March 7 and spent that night so you were at the Hot Springs on the morning of March 8, or…"

The young man interrupts testily. "No, I spent the night of March 7 here. I went camping about noon on Friday and stayed camping through Saturday night and came home on Sunday."

"Were you with anybody who can verify this?"

"No, I was alone. I go camping to be alone. How many different guys do I have to say this to?"

The interview comes to an end with nothing accomplished.

At this point, the Newell Creek complex is crawling with federal and county officers and their search dogs. They approach one apartment after another, but the procedures yield no information. Another young girl has vanished into thin air.

■

Meanwhile, Linda O'Neal is conducting her own investigation. Oliver Jamison is one of the people Linda O'Neal employs for technological work. They rarely interact face to face. Linda pays out hundreds a month in subscription fees to this disembodied voice for access to all of the top-notch criminal and civil databases available.

She purchases the technical capacity to find out any fact that is recorded somewhere and can measure that fact against others retrieved similarly. Unfortunately, Linda's personal computer skills are limited. Thank God for experts! Linda often pats herself on the back for the stroke of great luck that brought techno genius Ollie into her life by random chance. During their many years of working on cases together, she has always marveled at his uncanny knack to write the most astute queries. Not only does he know which database to search, but he can create a query that gets the information wanted and only the information wanted. Linda hates to admit it, but Oliver has evolved to a crucial level of importance in her professional life, because 80 percent of her investigations involve computer searches.

Ollie is a fifty-something, burly, retired army sergeant who is supporting a daughter born in Italy and saving what little money he has left over to afford a shabby inner city studio apartment. The dark walls are covered by bookshelves and file cabinets. Next to a scraggly futon are scattered piles of un-filed documents atop three folding card tables. Beside the tiny kitchen, Oliver has fashioned an elaborate workstation complete with gray cubicle dividers corralling his several computers and assorted accessories. The back wall of the cubicle is formed by an ancient big-screen television ingeniously rigged to display any of the various computer data. Linda's only visit reminded her of the control room of a space ship.

While the FBI task force continues to scrutinize Newell Creek and the surrounding area, "Commander Ollie," wearing a telephone headset with a lit cigarette dangling from his mouth, is ensconced in his pilot's chair tapping madly on one of his four keyboards. A shrill siren noise pulsates. It's his personally designed phone ringer. He presses a switch and becomes connected. "Oliver Jamison."

Linda is on the other end of the line and seems impatient. "Ollie, my good man. First of all, congrats on that great info you dug up on Espinoza. I just heard their whole case collapsed. He pled out to much reduced charges. They think I'm wonderful, but we both know who's really wonderful."

Oliver smiles and smashes his cigarette into an overloaded ashtray.

"Thanks, Linda. But I have a feeling you're calling because there's something else going on today."

"Very perceptive! I really need some of your genius. Will you check the records and see if there are any registered sex offenders living in the Newell Creek Apartments or in that general vicinity? Also, I need you to run a full background check on Ashley's birth father, Wesley Roettger. I don't have his date of birth, but he recently pled guilty to some sex offense in Clackamas County."

Jamison laughs. "Sex offense? I could have sworn you once told me you'd never ever troll that low for business. Are you sure? Sex stuff can be so slimy the pages will slip from your hands. And sex criminals? The lowest rung of the low-life ladder, to be sure."

"Roettger is Ashley Pond's biological father. I found out that he recently was convicted of some sort of molestation of Ashley.[6] The family waited a long time to tell us even this much, but we need to find out if Roettger might have something to do with her disappearance."

"No kidding! Are the cops looking at him as well?"

"Who knows? But listen, I also want you to check out another fellow, a nearby neighbor, Ward Weaver. I don't know his date of birth either, but he lives on Beavercreek Road in Oregon City across the street from the school bus stop where both Ashley and Miranda were headed when they vanished. Philip's daughter Maria told me Ashley had a beef with him last summer, but she's vague about exactly what went down."

"Okay Linda. Keep your fax on and as soon as I have something I'll send it."

An hour later, Linda is still sitting in her cluttered office pouring over a stack of case files, occasionally jotting notations in the margins. She can hear Philip from his side of the house deeply involved in a video editing scheme, the clicks and warped sound track chirping as he runs the tape forward and backward repeatedly. Then, silence, followed by Philip entering. "You have a visitor," he announces. "A lady. She is very anxious to talk to you."

Linda is intrigued and quickly examines her day planner. "I don't have a single appointment today. Did she say what she wants?"

"Something to do with Ashley."

"Really?"

Linda adjusts her hair and smoothes her skirt, then makes the short journey into the video studio's reception area where she encounters a striking redhead in her early thirties. She offers Linda a hearty grin and a firm handshake. "I'm Pamela. Remember I called about Rob, my husband, who is a psychic?" she says. "And I'm sorry to barge in on you like this, but you haven't returned any of my messages for several weeks now and you'd left me with the impression you believed me."

Linda waves a finger for the woman to follow her out the video entrance, around to the front door of the house and on through to her office where, after clearing a stack of files from a chair, she motions for the visitor to sit.

"I'm sorry, but I've been occupied for several weeks. Family emergency. I'm a bit behind on that stuff."

"Now that this second girl has disappeared, are you ready to do some investigating?"

Linda bristles. "Let me tell you something, young lady. I have been investigating. Ashley Pond is a member of my husband's family. I've been looking for her since the day she went missing."

Pamela's mouth drops open. "I had no idea! How weird this is-me picking your name from the private investigators' listings in the yellow pages. I'm telling you, there is something going on at this house in Molalla. Rob and I have been over there many times. It's positively spooky."

"Fair enough," Linda says pensively. "I believe you may have something here with this Molalla connection. But we need to get a few ground rules straight. I am willing to look at this Molalla connection in my own investigation, but I can't take money from you. Now, if down the line it turns out that there really is something to this connection and people ask me how I got on to it, do you want me to tell them that I first was alerted to Molalla by you and your husband? I could do that, but I can't work for psychics, because that's selling my credibility. And when it's all said and done, my credibility is all I have."

Pamela ponders then nods. "Sure, that's fine. Our main concern is that the girls get found, before, God forbid, another one disappears. Rob is convinced that there will be more. Like I told you before, Rob has strong visions of Ashley at this location asking for help, and after Miranda was gone, he had an equally strong pull from her.[7] Maybe it has more to do with the school bus stop that they both used or the fact that they were friends, but there is something going on in that creepy house in Molalla."

Linda agrees to visit the location in question herself. "Give me your phone number and I promise I'll call to tell you anything that I find. I promise."

■

Meanwhile, the FBI task force and K-9 units continue the methodic searching of every square foot of land in and around the Newell Creek Apartments. In the rear of Ward Weaver's place a large, disassembled hot-tub leans precariously against the house. A lanky teenaged boy clutches a garden hose[8] that sprays a stream of water onto a two-foot wide slab of freshly poured concrete.[9] He is so engrossed that he doesn't even notice the various dogs and cops wandering around.

The next few days pass slowly with no information surfacing for investigators, public or private.

Linda presses her own search. Linda and Philip are parked a hundred yards from a rural Molalla residence with an overgrown yard and so many derelict vehicles it seems abandoned except for one light reflecting dimly from the kitchen window. They've been in surveillance for an hour, hoping to discover some human movement among the stillness. As dusk approaches, they see a rusty Ford van with Virginia license plates chugging its way into the driveway.

Philip scrambles to attach a telephoto extension to the front of his camcorder.

The van slowly pulls up and parks. Within seconds the sole occupant emerges. At the same moment Philip captures the driver's image in his viewfinder. "I've got him; I've got him," he whispers jubilantly to Linda sitting beside him peering through binoculars. The man being videotaped is tall, thin and angular. A patchy gray beard and bald head stand out before he turns to head for the house.

"Get me a good close-up of his license plate."

"You got it." For several quiet minutes Philip continues to zoom his camera onto assorted objects. Next he exits the car and begins walking toward a distant fence.

Linda rolls down the window. "Where do you think you're going? Get back here before someone sees you."

He laughs. "It's almost dark, nobody's going to see me. Look at all those woods. I'm just going to slip over that fence and wander around, see what I can tape. I'll tell you one thing for sure, your psychic lady got it right. This house is very, very creepy."

At 9:15 PM the pair of video sleuths finally return home. As they cross through the living room, they are semi-acknowledged by their sons who are engrossed in a video game.

Once inside his studio, Philip hooks up the tape he shot at Molalla and soon is examining his playback. Linda notices a stack of pages dangling from the front of her fax machine. She puts on her reading glasses and snatches a fistful to peruse. While she saunters toward Philip's space, she becomes transfixed, absorbing paragraphs, slowly switching from page to page. Fully engrossed, Philip stares at some Molalla house footage showing the bald man with the scraggly beard. Linda startles him when she places a hand on his shoulder. "Philip," she exclaims, "I've just got the background checks on Roettger and Weaver. Ollie's note on the cover page says that while there were over five hundred registered sex offenders in Clackamas County, not one of them was registered as living in the Newell Creek Apartments."

"What about Roettger? What have you got on him?"

"Pretty much what we expected. They initially hit him over the head with a lot of counts. It looks like thirty-nine total counts of sodomy and child rape, but inexplicably it was all plea bargained down to just one count of 'attempted unlawful penetration of a minor'. But here's a really strange thing, the background check on Ward Weaver[10] says that right this minute he resides in San Quentin Prison on death row, awaiting execution for a double homicide committed in 1981."[11]

Philip shuts the video off and stares at Linda. "That's impossible, he's in Oregon City!"

Linda shakes her head and rattles one of the papers. "No, no. It says he had clubbed a stranded motorist to death." She runs her fingers along a paragraph. "It says he raped and strangled the guy's female companion before finally burying her in a grave and sealing it with concrete. This was all done in Weaver's own backyard. And he got the death penalty for it in 1984, yet incredibly, according to this, he's still alive. Unbelievable!"

Philip asks the obvious. "What the hell is going on, Linda?"

Linda reluctantly comes to the only conclusion she can. "There must be more than one Ward Weaver! I guess I need to get the date of birth on the Oregon City Weaver so we can find out if there is any connection between him and the one on death row." She shakes her head and shuffles the many pages. "You know, this is beginning to feel like that old movie, *The Hills Have Eyes.*"

"What about the stuff we taped tonight?"

"Did you get a clear shot of the license plate?"

For an answer Philip begins playing the videotape and initiates a freeze-frame depicting a close-up of the Virginia plate. She smiles and quickly kisses the back of his head before jotting the number down. "Tomorrow morning I'll have Oliver run that plate through DMV and the utility bills for that old house. Maybe we'll get the lead we need."

■

With no new information forthcoming on either Ashley Pond or Miranda Gaddis, frustration and fear build. On Saturday evening Linda, Philip and the two boys are in the living room watching *America's Most Wanted.* During a commercial break, Linda reminds the others about an important event scheduled early Sunday morning. "Maria called and said a massive private search for the missing girls has been organized.[12] Tomorrow morning, they plan to scour every inch of that whole canyon around Newell Creek," she says solemnly.

"They need more volunteers. I think we should all participate."

Her son, Jonathan, immediately protests. "Aw Mom, I'm going fishing with a friend tomorrow, I told you about it last week."

Philip's son, Damon, also complains. "I'm going bowling tomorrow."

Philip squeezes her hand. "I'll go for sure if you want to."

"I need to. I think a day of physical searching will do me some good. It's all so frustrating."

"Okay Love, but I've got to warn you, it is very rugged terrain with a lot of brush. You don't do well with sticker bushes and pine cones."

Linda's reply surprises him. "I don't care. I've got to look for these girls myself." At this moment, Linda feels like she's gotten nowhere and let Ashley and Miranda down. She is determined to do anything that will help find them or at least eliminate a place where they might be.

The commercial ends and the TV screen flashes a large graphic containing Ashley and Miranda's photos with a large caption underneath, "1-800-CRIME-TV." Then, for a few minutes, a full segment airs profiling the basic facts of the mystery before ending with a desperate plea for viewers to come forward with any tips that could be useful.[13]

Early the next morning, Linda, Philip and twenty other adult volunteers assemble in the back parking lot of the Newell Creek Apartments. They're joined by a platoon of uniformed, teenage Explorer Scouts, wearing backpacks and carrying walking sticks. A stocky thirty-year-old man approaches with a bullhorn. "Thank you all for your assistance this morning. This is the third search that I've organized.[14] Today, we will spread out and look over every square foot of both sides of the canyon. There are four sector leaders. They are the fellows wearing white armbands and whistles. If you come across anything, anything at all that seems suspicious, holler loudly and the nearest leader will take command. Any questions? Okay, let's proceed."

Clusters of citizen searchers slowly fan out from one another, walking one step at a time, eyes glued to the ground. Linda does her pacing between Maria and Suzie. She painstakingly explores her assigned area, but finds nothing. Turning to climb back up the steep slope, Linda trips over a protruding root and rolls into a patch of thick ivy. Philip rushes to her aid and pulls her up. "Are you okay, Sweetie?"

Upset at what she perceives as her own clumsiness, Linda scrapes some mud from her jeans and straightens her glasses. "I'm fine. I'm fine, really." A shrill blast from a coach's whistle rings out. The entire party converges on the sound, hiking up and over a steep embankment. They discover a skinny, dark haired fourteen-year-old scout on his knees, bending over a round white object and shouting excitedly.

Somebody asks, "What's he doing?"

Finally Linda and Philip have gotten close enough to recognize the round object. It is unmistakably a human skull. The feeling of accomplishment felt by the search party upon the discovery quickly dissolves when the Deputy State Medical Examiner[15] concludes that the bones are those of an adult who has likely been dead up to a year. The local press is puzzled by the fact that the FBI task force had supposedly traversed this same territory during several of their intensive sweeps. Why wasn't the skull spotted then?

The Medical Examiner tells newspaper reporters the remains could have been washed into the area by heavy rains after the initial FBI searches. An alternative theory suggests that despite the fact the FBI had searched Newell Creek Canyon six or seven separate times, they had not necessarily examined the spot where the skull was found, because there was no evidence that any human had been there in the months since Ashley disappeared. After all, he reminds them, the skull was discovered in a very steep, overgrown area near a stream that feeds Newell Creek. The bottom line: there is still no suspect and no crime scene.

CHAPTER SEVEN

Linda O'Neal Investigations

M ore weeks come and go. Despite over twenty-five hundred tips that have poured in from the ever increasing national publicity, none have proven fruitful. Linda begins to empathize with the FBI task force—many leads, but nothing to give her a viable suspect either.

Because private investigators get so involved in the murky behaviors that clash between perps and victims, they frequently are subpoenaed to put their observations up for public scrutiny. It's amazing how precise language must be when testifying "under oath." One misstatement of fact can sabotage an acquittal.

Linda O'Neal, at this moment, finds herself in just such a situation. Dressed in a black silk pantsuit and red scarf with pearls encircling her neck, she sits comfortably erect on the witness stand in a Multnomah County Courtroom. A young deputy District Attorney is cross-examining her. "Now Ms. O'Neal, can you tell the court again why you entered the scene on 24th Street that day in search of a car?"

Linda clears her throat and responds firmly and clearly. "No sir, I did not say that I went to the house on 24th Street looking for the defendant's car. I said that I went to the house on 24th Street to talk to the defendant's brother."

The DA interrupts brashly. "And why did you feel it necessary to talk with him?"

"I was simply trying to get a lead on the location of the defendant during the time in question. I figured it was worth a shot to check his story, you know. And it was while I was waiting for Mr. Terry Morgan to answer his door that I kind of looked around. I watched a squirrel chasing a blue jay. I noticed several barrels of trash that were spilling over. I looked at the garage. I remember thinking that it sure could use some new paint. I noticed through the open garage door that I had a clear line of sight to the interior of the garage. I could clearly see a brown, Pontiac Le Mans station wagon parked inside. I could even see the rear license plate. It was…" Linda closes her eyes momentarily and then recites the sequence confidently. "Now since I had been looking for the defendant in this case, I knew that was the defendant's car."

"Did you confirm the car's ownership with the resident?"

"Absolutely. When Mr. Morgan finally answered his door, I asked him about the car in the garage. And he readily told me it belonged to his brother, Peter. He said it had been there for several days, because it had broken down. I believe it had blown a head gasket and when they removed the cylinder head they discovered it was warped and needed to be shaved slightly. Anyway, after they took the head off the engine they took it to Allied Machine and left it there to be worked on. They were told it would take approximately three days. That head was dropped off on November 15. As I understand it, the crux of the case against Peter Morgan centers on supposedly airtight, eyewitness testimony that places him driving his Pontiac wagon to the convenience store. This armed robbery took place on November 17. It was physically impossible for that inoperable Pontiac to have been anywhere but where it was that day—in his brother's garage."

The flustered DA slams a file folder onto the table. "Your honor, I have nothing further to ask this witness."

The female judge thanks Linda for her testimony and nods. "You're free to go, Ma'am."

The moment she steps into the cavernous hallway outside the courtroom Linda turns on her cell phone, which rings instantly. She begins her journey from the courthouse to the underground parking lot at the same time she answers the call. "Linda O'Neal Investigations. Oh hi, Ollie. What's happening?"

His voice rises in excitement. "Linda, I've got some very bizarre results from that Virginia license plate. I really think you might be onto something. First of all, I ran a courthouse check and the house is owned by Barnaby Fairchild, a retired tax attorney. He currently resides in Palm Springs. He has three adult children, all in their forties. His middle son, Paul, has criminal history in several different states. He is a real roamer. Texas, Florida, New Jersey, Wisconsin, and most recently, he'd landed in Carson, Virginia. In fact, when I ran that tag, it came up with his last known address there in Virginia."

Linda reaches the lobby and purchases a pack of gum from the burka-clad blind Arab woman behind the concession stand, as she always does, before continuing toward the parking lot. "Carson, Virginia. Hmm. Something about that rings a bell." She stops and taps her forehead. "Yes, yes. I remember now, Carson, Virginia is where a pair of pre-teen girls mysteriously disappeared off their front porch last summer. One minute they were there, the next minute, poof! No witnesses, no crime scene."

Oliver responds. "That's right, you've got it! We learned a lot about that case from that child abduction hot sheet.[1] That Carson case stood out like a sore thumb, for obvious reasons."

"And now you can tie the Molalla guy to that area. Great work, Ollie."

"And I've also got that rap sheet you ordered on Ward Weaver III, the one that lives in Oregon City. And you were right on! The death row Ward Weaver is Ward Weaver Jr. His nickname is Pete and he's the father of the man who lives near Ashley and Miranda, Ward Weaver the third."

"What did you dig up on the Oregon City Weaver, anything suspicious?"

"Maybe. He was raised mostly in northern California and Portland.[2] Was in the Navy. Has a ton of kids. As far as criminal stuff, he was convicted in California on first-degree assault. Don't have the details yet, but he may have served some time on that. Several years later, he was also charged with assault of a girlfriend that he later married. Those charges were dropped."

Linda finally reaches her car, gets in and begins the slow drive to the exit before she continues the conversation. "Okay, it looks like we just may have a suspect or two in the making. Fax me everything you have and when I get home I'll digest it all."

When Linda arrives home, she finds the driveway empty and the house deserted. She turns on the TV just in time to catch Pinski Brown. "Folks, we have another update on the continuing story of the missing Oregon City girls, Ashley Pond and Miranda Gaddis. There is controversy over the recent discovery of a note purported to have been written by Ashley Pond.[3] This note was found Sunday morning near the town of Fort Pierce, Florida. It had been carefully inserted inside a waterproof bag that had been sealed in a cardboard box. The words 'Please Help' in huge red letters were scribbled on the outside of the box. When police opened the box and pulled out the note, they found the following message written in cursive pencil on a sheet of lined binder paper. 'My name is Ashley and I know my mom is crying, so please help me get away and home to my mom. I am thirteen years old and my friend Miranda is thirteen also and she is with me. Please help us get home fast. I love my mommy.'"

"Total bull," Linda mutters.

Brown goes on to say that the FBI and the Oregon City Police reacted with skepticism, but also reveals that the FBI crime laboratory specialists will conduct tests in their headquarters in Washington DC. Among the tests will probably be handwriting and fingerprint analysis.

Brown adds how two new websites have gone online to provide a place where people can call with tips and other communications or make donations to the victims' families. The site addresses scroll across the bottom of the screen. Brown then states, "It was announced today that the total amount in the reward fund for information leading to the return of the missing girls has now reached sixty thousand dollars. Because of the national publicity that this case has generated, FBI Task Force Director Charles Mathews announced today that the total number of tips and leads regarding the disappearance of the two girls has now surpassed three thousand. He said investigators are working around the clock to address the information provided in each one, but he added, 'It's going to take a lot of time to get through them all.' Despite this flurry of activity, the sad fact remains, as of tonight, there are still no suspects and no crime scene."

Linda turns the TV off and sits quietly for a few moments only to be interrupted by the shrill chirp of the nearby phone. She picks up. "Linda O'Neal Investigations. Can I help you?"[4]

A tiny voice on the other side of the line utters a soft greeting. "It's me, Suzie. Have you seen my mom today? She took off with Tony this afternoon and left me watching my brother and sister, but I have to go to play practice in an hour. And they aren't back yet and they haven't called."

"I'm sorry, Suzie, I've been in court most of the day and I haven't heard from anybody. I haven't checked my voice mail yet, but I haven't talked to your mom in over a week."

"I wish she'd just come home when she says she will. It's not fair."

"I'm sure she'll show up in time. You must be more trusting."

"That's easy for you to say. You don't have to live here."

Linda senses an opportunity. "Suzie, can I ask you a question about Ashley?"

"I...I...guess so. But I already told you as much as I could remember."

"Did Ashley ever confide in you about what happened between her and her biological dad?"

"I think she tried to. She didn't really come out and say 'Hey, this is what's going on.' I remember a couple of years ago she came to me and started crying. And I was like, 'Okay, what's wrong? Why are you crying?' She wanted to tell me, but she just goes, 'Nothing, nothing.' And I was like, 'Okay, you're not going to cry this hard just because of nothing.' But she wouldn't tell me anything. And then later we find out what her dad had been doing to her all the time, so I think she was trying to tell me about it, but she just couldn't get it out. I think she was too scared to come out and be like 'this is what's happening to me.'"

That last statement hits Linda hard, unleashing previously buried feelings dating back to her own childhood. Until this moment she had blocked her memories of certain incidents. Terror and sadness rush through her body like ice water. She remembers how she asked herself: why would anyone believe her word over an adult male's? After all, adults had all the power. Her mind revolves and her panicked heart races. She recalls the twelve-year-old Linda sitting on an adult man's lap, locked in an open mouth kiss. She never told on him; he said it was a secret. Suddenly, she remembers she's on the phone with Suzie. Holding back tears, Linda says, "Um, sweetie, were there any things she did tell you about?"

The girl pauses at the sudden change in Linda's voice, but isn't sure that she should ask. "Well, yeah…she eventually told me what her dad did to her. I remember we were upstairs. I asked her if she was okay about everything that happened…And then she just starts telling me about like when her dad had done all these awful things and also exactly the things he did to her."

Linda hugs herself and forces her voice to be even and calm. "What about her mom? Did Ashley tell her mom about what happened?"

"I'm not sure, but I don't think she did. Not right away anyway, cause of all the problems with her mom. But, me and her were really close then; I think I would have known before her mom. She told me that she was really upset, but that she was scared to tell anyone."

"I know these things are really hard to share. Thank you for talking to me about it." Linda pauses and her mind turns to someone else she'd been thinking about, "By the way, did Ashley ever tell you about anything Ward Weaver might have done to her?"

"She never really told me anything about him and I know that's funny, because she was over at his house so much, especially last year. I do remember her saying…no, I think it was her mom who told me that he was the one that took her on vacation with him or whatever. She even had keys to his house for a while. But anyway, something awful happened when they got back from that vacation and when she told her mom about it her mom just says like, 'Well don't go over there any more.' Like that would take care of it. And Ashley says, 'Well, duh!' She was really mad at her mom. She told me her mom 'just didn't get it.'"

"Okay honey, I'll let you go. Be brave, and if I hear from your mom or dad I'll tell them to get back right away. "

"Oh, wait! Linda, I hear a car. Yes, yes! They just drove up! Everything's fine now! Do you need to talk to them?"

"No, that's okay. And good luck, Suzie."

After Linda hangs up, she paces around the house, reviewing all she's found out and trying to put a perspective on so many details that are tumbling in her mind. She remembers Oliver's briefing and rushes to her fax machine. It has run completely out of paper. But a treasure-trove of documents lies in a wrinkled stack all full of many new avenues to pursue. She will now be able to create her own "Persons of Interest" list.

She turns to Paul Fairchild, the mysterious Molalla man with the Virginia license plates. He was from the same location where two girls had evaporated into thin air. Was it a coincidence?

And what about Ashley's father, Wesley Roettger? He had been charged with forty counts of child rape and sodomy. Yet he was allowed to plea bargain down to one count of attempted unlawful penetration of a minor and received no jail time. Why?

Linda decides that there are basically four avenues of investigation to seriously pursue. First, the Molalla man. Second, Ashley's birth dad and the reasons that he was allowed to plea bargain down to probation with no jail time. Third, Ward Weaver and the allegations that Ashley made against him. And fourth, the real story behind the supposedly helpful Internet sites that have popped up. Suddenly, a dark thought crosses her mind. Could the kidnapper be using an Internet site to keep track of what people knew and if the officials were getting close?

Linda is determined to discover what really happened to the Oregon City girls. And after watching the sadness of her extended family, Miranda's mother and the widening sphere of fearful parents in the community, she knows it better be soon. It's late at night and she's exhausted, but sleep is getting harder to come by—visions of another missing girl chase it away.

CHAPTER EIGHT

No Stone Unturned

April 7, 2002, is a cloudy, cool Saturday. Linda has given herself a little time off to clear her mind and think through what she's learned so far about the girls' disappearance. Early afternoon finds Linda fiddling with several hanging plants that dangle from the front porch of her home. She yanks a few weeds and squirts some water, then looks up to see a bright red BMW Z-3 roadster pull into the front driveway, its top down and her husband Philip at the wheel. She is shocked and shouts, "No, no, you didn't, you didn't!"

Philip turns the engine off and motions for Linda to come closer. "I told you I was going to do it, and I did it. Don't worry, I can handle the payments."

After he climbs out Linda steps back a bit and casts glances around the vehicle. "Good grief! Your image just got the million dollar makeover!" She turns her attention to her tired car parked nearby. "And I'm still stuck with that frumpy green machine."

Philip laughs. "If you be nice to me, I might let you drive mine once or twice a month."

Their attention is diverted when a Dodge minivan full of vacant child car seats pulls up next to the sports car. White lettering on the door reads, "Maria's Custom Child Care." Philip's daughter, Maria, sticks her head out the driver's window and tosses a comment to her dad and Linda. "So you really went and bought it, huh, Dad?" She gets out of her car and slips into the driver's seat of the Beamer. "Can I borrow it tonight, Daddyo?"

Philip opens the door and gently assists her exit. "Nobody is getting their mitts on this car until I have her broken in."

The front door to the house swings open, releasing Linda and Philip's energetic kids who swoop over to the red BMW grunting remarks of approval. Philip beams with pride. "You guys were the only ones that really knew I was getting her for sure."

The boys laugh. Linda runs her hand along the smooth surface of the fenders. "I hardly ever see you as it is, but hell! You'll never want to be home now that you've got this baby."

"That baby's already got a name," Philip smiles proudly. "Marilyn."

"Huh?"

"Marilyn. I'm naming her Marilyn, and she's always going to be my special girl, uh, well, next to my beautiful wife, that is."

Linda and Philip's sons donate a few more comments about how much they love the new car before dashing back into the house to resume a *PlayStation* contest. Suddenly, Maria's expression changes and she pulls a folded letter from her purse and hands it to her stepmother. "Linda, I almost forgot in the excitement over the car why I came over. I think you and Dad should take a look at this. It's a letter that Lori got from a dog handler, Harry Oakes. He also sent a copy of this letter to the cops. It's about Ashley."

After studying it for a few moments Linda licks her bottom lip. "Harry Oakes, Harry Oakes, you know I've heard that name somewhere before."

Philip approaches and reads parts of the letter over Linda's shoulder. "Ward Weaver," he says. "Oakes's search dog is supposed to have sniffed something suspicious under a concrete slab in Weaver's backyard. Do you think it's true?"

Maria scowls. "Don't you think the police ought to investigate?"

Linda ponders before folding the letter up. She attempts to hand it back to Maria who shakes her head. "No, no, you keep it; Lori thinks maybe he's a crackpot, but I thought you'd want to check it out anyway. Do you suppose the police have checked the slab by now? I mean, Oakes was there March 15. That's three weeks ago."

Linda gently grasps Maria's left hand. "Let's see what, if anything, this all means. The FBI has had dozens of dogs going over that ground after Ashley and Miranda's disappearances. For all we know, Lori's instincts may be right on the money."

"You're right Linda. But Lori told me this guy was in touch with her several times before he even came out with the dog."

"Maybe so, but give me a few days to run some checks on him before we make any noise about concrete slabs, okay?"

Maria pulls her hand free and embraces her dad briefly. "You guys are just great."

Philip smiles. "Linda has been working her buns off and I think she's making some progress. Just hang on, okay?"

"Sure. Oh, I've got to tell you about another funny thing that happened. I don't know if it will help, but let me tell you about Irene."

Linda is curious. "Irene?"

"Yeah, she's Tony's sister's best friend. You know, the sister who lives next door to us. Well anyway, Irene has always been a sort of psychic. She can tell the future, read palms, tarot cards…and Tony's sister says she's very gifted."

Linda's eyes narrow. "I'm not a fan of psychics, but we'll take clues even from otherworldly sources."

"Well, Irene tried to see if she could get any vibes about where Ashley might be, and you can't believe what happened. She went out to the school bus stop, spent over half an hour meditating while burning some special candles and she says she got a powerful vision. She is sure she can pinpoint a location."

Philip shakes his head. "Look Maria, this whole case is crazy enough without going in that direction."

"Okay but at least let me tell you what she said."

Linda nods, "Fair enough. What's her theory?"

"Fourteen miles. She said the answer is exactly fourteen miles from the bus stop. So all we've got to do is get in the car, drive to Newell Creek Apartments and drive fourteen miles. We watch the odometer, and when it shows fourteen miles, we stop and see what we can find."

Linda laughs. "I was with you for a minute, but fourteen miles in which direction, Maria? East? West? South? Which side of the Willamette? I don't think this can possibly help the situation. Maybe we ought to politely ignore this Irene and her candles." Linda pauses. "But...well, maybe I'll check her theory." She sighs, "That shows you how frustrated I am."

"Well, I better get going, Suzie's watching her brother for me and I promised I'd be back by four. Oh Dad, one more thing before I take off. Could you help me organize a video of Ashley with whatever video clips we can round up? You know we took a lot of home videos when we used to go camping on the boat. And Lori never had a video camera of her own, but I remember you used to loan her that old VHS a lot of times, so she has some stuff, and I think you probably do too, don't you?"

Philip nods, his face serious. "I'd be honored to help you put together something. When can you have the footage all rounded up?"

"I'll do it as quick as I can, but give me a week."

"Call me when you're ready and we'll burn the midnight oil in the editing room together."

Maria gets into her van and begins backing out when Linda approaches the open driver's window to interject a final comment. "Don't worry, Maria. I will look into this Harry Oakes and his dog as soon as possible."

Maria waves and drives off.

■

Two days later, April 9, Linda is cruising by the Newell Creek school bus stop in her car, checking out where Ashley and Miranda were headed preceding their disappearances. Linda drives very slowly. She presses a button that zeroes the vehicle's trip odometer, then accelerates rapidly and directs the sedan southward along Beavercreek Road into late afternoon traffic.

Meanwhile, Philip is in his studio office carefully attaching spine labels to a stack of VHS videotapes. Linda's office phone rings and he quickly picks up. "Linda O'Neal Investigations."

Oliver Jamison is on the line. "Can I speak to Linda, please? It's very important."

"I'm sorry, Ollie, she went to Molalla. But you should be able to get her on her cell phone."

Oliver becomes alarmed. "Molalla? Hell! I've got some crucial information for her about the Virginia guy. If she calls in, have her call me."

At that same moment, having traveled several miles to the outskirts of Molalla, Linda pulls into a long driveway. She parks as close to the front of the house as possible and then stares at the trip odometer in disbelief. It shows almost the exact mileage that Irene, the psychic, had trumpeted: fourteen point one miles. A shudder creeps into her shoulders. "I'll be damned."

After hesitating for a few moments, Linda lays her cell phone on the passenger seat and picks up a clipboard and a handful of freshly minted real estate business cards with her name on them. Getting out of the car, she cranes her neck in search of the Ford with the Virginia plate, but doesn't spot it. She glances around at the thick, surrounding woods before she looks up to notice foreboding clouds which seem to become darker the longer she stares at them. As the rain starts, she takes a deep breath and begins a determined journey toward the long front porch. Inside her car, her cell phone rings several times, but Linda cannot hear it. She continues at a deliberate pace while visually sweeping all directions, eager to discover something, anything that might prove useful. A tattered curtain in a narrow side window triggers her focus when she notices some errant movement. Linda stares for a few moments and is convinced she sees the outline of a very slender female with long, gray hair peering out.

Linda steps up onto the porch, losing her footing as her heel slides sideways on very slick moss which seems to cover the entire surface. She wonders how the occupants can possibly get in and out of the place. Struggling to the massive oak door anyway, she knocks without hesitation. No one comes. She knocks a second time and soon sees the same, thin elderly woman, this time staring from behind a different window. A short while later, the door opens slightly, a long fingered hand gripping the edge. Linda's nose is instantly assaulted by an overwhelming combination of disgusting odors, the most dominant of which she identifies as cat litter boxes. A pungent stream reels through the eight-inch crack but is cut off abruptly when a middle aged male slides through the same crack onto the porch and tightly shuts the big door behind him. He clings to the tarnished brass knob to keep from sliding further and gruffly barks, "What do you want?"

Linda studies this strange sight and wonders if he could truly be the Virginia man. His lanky body is clothed in threadbare gray slacks with a plaid wool shirt, collapsed at the elbows. His incredibly long arms dangle ape-like at his side and he refuses to provide Linda with direct eye contact. Finally she makes her inquiry. "Are you by chance Mr. Fairchild, uh, Mr. Paul Fairchild?"

The man speaks in barely a whisper as he continues to stare at the floor. "Nope."

"Well, my name is O'Neal, sir, and I work for a developer who's very interested in your property here."

The man does not respond.

"We are prepared to come up with a very good offer. Here's my card."

The man refuses to accept the card and grunts.

"Anyway, would you mind if I walked around a bit, maybe take some notes?"

Carefully, the man turns the big brass handle and pushes the door open. "Not interested. Get off this land and don't come back," he mutters before slipping back into the house and slamming the door loudly behind him.

Linda is positive she can feel several pairs of eyes scrutinizing her every move as she carefully makes her way off the porch. She gets back into her car and backs it up to turn around. She keeps one eye on the rearview mirror as her sedan slowly crawls along the gravel driveway. Within seconds she makes out a pair of figures. She smacks the dashboard with her right palm. "Damn!" Linda assumes they are jotting down her license number.

She has no time to contemplate this problem. She needs to get on with her investigation. When Philip helped her with the video surveillance they had found a perfect angle from the Baptist church just a few blocks away. Its rear section was dominated by acres of baseball fields. A dilapidated fence behind the backstop served as the official boundary separating church property from Fairchild's woods. She smiles slyly before parking behind a backstop. Now she has a clear view of the ancient house. Linda pulls her binoculars from the glove compartment, scrunches down in the front seat and begins surveillance. It's time to see what she has stirred up.

Within an hour full nightfall has arrived. Bright headlights appear from the church entrance, the focus of the beams illuminating the green car. A Chevrolet Impala pulls right behind her car. Its lone male occupant, Oliver Jamison, rarely ever ventures into the real world. Leaving the Chevy's engine running and lights on high beam, he stumbles out, grabs his cane, hobbles over to Linda's car and gasps. It is empty. His heart pounds and he strains to see any sign of his boss and friend. A curious rustling noise twenty feet into the thick woods captures his attention. He retrieves his flashlight and approaches the fence, shining it back and forth. He can make out a movement. He stares a bit then hears a shout.

"Who's there? Who's there?" Linda O'Neal emerges a moment later. She carries her folding port-a-potty, its gleaming white seat reflecting brightly from the Impala headlights. She strains for a view of the intruder and recognizes a bulky human form with a brush-like gray goatee. "Ollie, is that you?" A few more steps and his identity is confirmed. "It *is* you. For Pete's sake, shut those headlights off. There's no use letting the world know we're here."

Ollie obediently ambles back to the Impala and cuts the lights as Linda approaches the car, still clutching the port-a-potty. She opens the trunk and unceremoniously deposits it atop a pile of file sacks. She shakes her head and approaches Jamison, who is leaning on his cane and sweating profusely. "What are you up to? How did you find me, or more to the point, why?"

"I just got some hot info on Paul Fairchild, and I know how you are when you get your teeth into something. You haven't confronted him yet, have you?"

She shakes her head. "Well I came out here to, but apparently he wasn't home so I figured I'd rock their boat a little bit."

"I hope you didn't sink it."

"What's up, Ollie?"

"Paul Fairchild is a dead end. He absolutely could not have had anything to do with the Oregon City girls. I tried to get you on your cell, but…I was worried so I figured I'd better fire up my car and find you."

Linda sighs, "Another dead end. There seems to be one after another. And I was beginning to feel I've undervalued psychic visions since this place is fourteen miles from the bus stop!"

"Huh?"

"Never mind."

Oliver pulls some papers from his inside jacket pocket and shines his flashlight onto them. Linda pores over the text while Oliver reads on: "On January 9, Paul Fairchild was sitting in a jail cell in Escanaba, Michigan ten days into a thirty day misdemeanor sentence for drunk-driving. He was released January 22 and take a look here…" He shuffles to another page and points to a specific paragraph. "When he was released, he packed up his stuff and decided to come back to Oregon. Here's a list of his debit card gas purchases. January 30, he was in Wisconsin. By February 23 he was lingering around the St. Paul area. See? Two weeks at a motel. But most importantly, on March 8, the day Miranda went missing, Fairchild was in Wyoming and most likely didn't even arrive in Molalla until at least a few days later."

Linda is exasperated. "Well, we've got to move on to the next suspect. And I mean right away, before another girl disappears."

During the long drive home, Linda's head pounds with frustration. She berates herself for having been duped into such a complete red herring episode, which has so deftly siphoned valuable time and energy away from her finding a real solution. She mumbles, "I'm really no closer to finding what happened to Ashley and Miranda than the hapless FBI task force." But she resolves not to give up and keep investigating until she finds the person who has stolen the girls.

By the time Linda directs her car into the front driveway, she has calmed down and with spirits renewing, goes to her cluttered desk and begins to re-examine the piles of documents. Somewhere there is an answer. Somebody took those girls. But who? Where is the evidence? Philip brings her a sandwich and drink a few hours later while she sits, staring at her computer screen, scrolling through pages and pages of documents. The hour moves toward midnight. Philip quietly enters the room and squeezes her tired shoulders with a firm grip. "Hey Sweetie, don't you think you ought to give it up for today? It's bed time."

"Okay." Wearily she rises, but before following him, she grabs a file folder. It is stuffed with court records about Ashley's biological father. Once in bed, while her husband is engrossed in watching that evening's TV episode of *Politically Incorrect*, Linda props herself in front of several pillows and carefully studies photocopies detailing the step-by-step legal entanglements that had entwined the life of Ashley Pond's biological father. She grimaces as she absorbs one sordid detail after another. She continues her perusal, anxious to discover exactly how so many atrocious allegations against the man could have evaporated. She is so repulsed by what she finds that she shouts a comment that startles Philip. "Hey, take it easy," he whispers.

"What kind of 'sexual history' can an eleven-year-old have?" Linda exclaims.

Finally, her husband convinces her to turn out the light so they can go to sleep. A restless Linda tosses all night.

■

The next day Linda decides she needs a new direction since Roettger's case seems steeped in what she believes is misplaced exoneration. Perhaps, she thinks, her intern Allison's analytical abilities will provide fresh insights. After equipping her intern with the complete case documents, she instructs Ally to study them intensely. "In four hours we'll meet for lunch, and I'm going to pick your brain. See if you can identify the faults in the case for me."

At the lunch meeting, Linda says, "Allison, as you know, ninety percent of my work is for defense attorneys. Our mission is to dig up every available fact, then dissect them—turn them over seeking the inconsistencies. If we are good, we'll get a handle on how to proceed. It's a critical part of a detective's job description, and it takes enormous patience because most of the time it turns out to be a dead end. So here's what I have in mind. Right now you're up to speed on everything anyone could know about the case. Show me what you've got, and I'll try to knock it down. Let's see how you do?"

Allison looks for enlightenment. "So District Attorney Linda O'Neal, I'm working through a cumbersome case that perhaps you may be able to give me some direction on."

Linda polishes the spotted spoon with a napkin and replies. "Sure. How can I help you?"

"Let's go over our leads one by one."

For an hour they go back and forth. Finally, they discuss Ashley's allegations against her biological father. He was allowed to plead out when it was brought up by the man's attorney that the girl had made similar false allegations against other men.

Linda frowns and wrings her hands. "Ashley was asked about this person," she hesitates. "She did not deny having made allegations of attempted rape against him. And it was at that moment when they realized the Roettger case was dead meat. In retrospect, they were lucky to get him to plead out to anything. If her dad's lawyer would have pushed a bit harder, chances are there wouldn't have been any conviction at all. At least now they've got her father registered as a sex offender and he can't have contact with any kids, even his own children. So in a way it's a moral victory."

Momentary outrage grips young Allison and she blurts, "Moral victory? Ashley has been gone four months, and Miranda for two. And there are no solid clues that seem to lead anywhere. God knows what happened or who was responsible. This whole thing is a nightmare! For all we know, it could be Roettger and the courts just let him go. Moral victory…legal injustice!" The girl fumes. A few moments of awkward silence ensue, and then she retreats. "I'm sorry, really." She pauses. "After all who am I? Just your humble intern. But it pisses me off. Now before I eat, please, can you at least tell me who the man was who was so influential?"

"Sure. A neighbor, the father of one of Ashley's friends."

Allison cringes as she anticipates what's coming next.

"Ward Weaver. It seems Ashley told wicked tales about him to several people and when it finally got back to him, he was furious and did everything he could to put the stories to rest."

"Nevertheless, he admitted to the police that she had made the allegations?"

"Of course. And he was very credible. She, unfortunately, began to appear more and more unreliable. Weaver claimed that she had even recanted her original complaints about her father, and he said he was prepared to testify in court to that effect."

"Did they investigate those allegations? To verify if they had any validity?"

"They have very specific policies they must follow when third hand abuse is uncovered. They did what they were supposed to do. They called the Department of Human Services and reported the allegations to them."[2]

"Did they follow up?"

Linda shrugs. "Allison, I think you just might make an investigator after all. Your questions were incisive and underscored weaknesses. And I guess that's the whole point of everything today. Now it's our turn. What weaknesses do you see in her father's lawyer's position, if you were going to attack that one?"

"Ward Weaver."

Linda smiles. "Exactly what I've been thinking."

CHAPTER NINE

The Search Continues

On the afternoon of Saturday, April 13, Philip greets his daughter Maria, with a stack of home videos under her arm. He has agreed to create a program of edited video clips juxtaposed with still photos of Ashley. How the final production will be used is still unresolved, but there was a strong desire by all family members to have this project completed.

Linda joins them in the editing room so she can see what Ashley looks and sounds like on videotape. She turns to Maria, "Why didn't Lori come along to see this?"

Maria smiles sheepishly. "Lori doesn't go anywhere much lately. She won't even answer her phone most of the time. She screens every call. She doesn't even go over to Mom's house any more. Her and Dave just sit around, like they're waiting to be called. She keeps thinking that maybe Ashley is gonna show up and maybe all this will just go away. But I got her photo albums and she also dug up what few videotapes they had."

Linda listens for a bit, but soon her mind is focusing on the unsettled issues in the missing girls' case. She pulls the Harry Oakes letter from a file while gently opening the conversation. "Maria, I looked into this Harry Oakes dog handler situation, and frankly, he is not very well received by the sheriff's department. It's hard to know what to think about his concrete slab warning. It's my guess that the FBI is not likely to act on his tip, mainly because their dogs have already scoured Weaver's yard multiple times with negative results, but I'm going to try to look into it."

Maria stares at her. "You aren't going to let the FBI stop you."

"I'm going to follow my own instincts, but you have to understand the rules and procedures that take precedence in situations like this. Every citizen has constitutional rights to privacy. It isn't that easy to go to somebody's house and dig up their yard or whatever. Search warrants are required and judges don't issue them willy-nilly, like they do on TV crime shows. There has to be reasonable probable cause, and unfortunately, Oakes' letter obviously hasn't convinced any of the powers that be of anything."

"But Linda, don't you think Weaver could be involved?"

"Sometimes I do, other times, I'm not as sure. Monday I'm going to talk to the Department of Human Services people and see if I can unwind some facts that will shed a bit more light on all of this."

Maria offers, "I had a long talk with my little sister, the other night and she told me Weaver was mixed up in Ashley's life a lot more than people realize, Linda, especially last summer. Lori doesn't admit it, but I think Ashley practically lived there and became like one of his kids or something."

Linda quirks an eyebrow. "Can you give me an example?"

"Sure. Like, she told me about something from last July, a very hot Saturday, and she was over at my Mom's picking up my kids to take them to the big amusement park in Sellwood. They had a special. All rides were only fifty cents. Anyway, Ashley was at Mom's visiting, and she asked if she could go along. My sister said 'Fine.' So anyway, they were there for about an hour or less, and guess who shows up?"

Linda nods. "Weaver."

"Exactly! When he and his daughter came to Mom's to pick up Ashley and found she'd gone with her aunt, he flipped out and in no time, there they were. And for the rest of the afternoon they stuck like glue. Once he got there, she was like a different person. He bossed her around, wouldn't even allow her to ride the bumper cars. She wanted to stick around longer, but he said they had to leave, and off they went, him, his daughter and Ashley. She didn't even say goodbye, just said 'I gotta go now, see ya later.'"

During all of this Philip has been playing some video clips on his monitor. He interrupts when the images of Ashley and Suzie suddenly appear. They are in bathing suits lying on their tummies at the front end of a cabin cruiser docked on the river. "Where was this shot taken, Maria?"

"On the boat. I think it was two summers ago. Suzie was barely fourteen then."

For several minutes they all just watch the video screen as Philip repeatedly puts a tape in before pressing "play" on the VCR. The last one he displays turns out to be the most recent, having been recorded six weeks before Ashley disappeared. The tape is actually a video of her uncle's community college graduation party, but in a brief segment near the very end, Ashley and her sister ascend the stage, mikes in hand and sing their hearts out to the karaoke soundtrack. As the young girl skips confidently back and forth, Linda feels she is seeing the real Ashley, happy, carefree and absorbed in her passion for Karaoke. The Ashley in the video seems momentarily to have forgotten the pain that infiltrated her first dozen years. While not even a teenager yet, her brief childhood had encompassed more sorrow than it ever should have. Linda stares at the spirited youngster on the TV screen. A true connection is established which prompts her realization that Ashley is a testament to the resilience of the human spirit. She verbalizes her thoughts, "Ashley was such a vibrant girl. I'm still hoping that she had the confidence to run away rather than...I don't want to believe that she was kidnapped. Or worse."

Maria interrupts. "That reminds me of another time, also last summer. You'll probably want to put this in your 'not credible' file too, but Ashley's dad's sister[1] called our mom to complain that she[2] tried to go see Ashley at Weaver's house and he told her to 'Get lost.' He absolutely would not let her see Ashley even for five minutes."

Linda nods her head. "And Lori allowed this?"

Maria shakes her head. "I think she had too many problems of her own to pay attention to what was going on with Ashley. That's just my opinion, though." Maria sighs heavily.

"Maria, we're not giving up—not now, not ever."

Maria flashes her a grateful look.

∎

A few days later, Linda pays a visit to the Regional Office of the Oregon State Department of Human Services and is directed to Veronica Woodruff, a dark-haired woman in her fifties.

"Ma'am," Linda says quietly, "I know that on August 31 of last year, the Assistant District Attorney notified your office of allegations made by a minor, Ashley Pond, of attempted rape that occurred a few weeks earlier. I also discovered from their office that Ward Weaver allegedly committed this assault. And what I need to know is, did your office conduct an investigation? And if so, what was the determination?" Linda leans toward the woman, giving her a business card. "Please, I'm just trying to help the family find out what happened to her, and there may be some clues here, can you help us?"

Sinclair swiftly hands Linda back her business card before folding her arms and scowling. "That issue involves sealed records and no information about it can legally be disclosed, especially to a private entity. You have absolutely no standing with us, Ms. O'Neal." The woman glances at her wristwatch. "Now, if there is nothing else…"

"If there is nothing else? Nothing else? Lady, that poor little girl is missing and could very well be dead. Nothing else indeed! Good day!" Linda abruptly turns and walks away, adding more frustration to her ongoing search.

As more days pass, Linda reluctantly must give attention to her bulging collection of neglected cases and postponed chores commissioned by her attorney clients. They hire her on behalf of indicted defendants desperate for any creative angle that could reduce criminal charges or provide an outright acquittal if there is a trial. She must scrutinize databases, interrogate witnesses, write reports and hold conferences. Yet in the little spare time she has, she cannot get her mind off Ashley and Miranda.

In spite of her intense desire to hatch a significant breakthrough, she feels somewhat stalled. The police and the FBI are also stymied. The news media, too, seems to temporarily forget the story. But Linda and the families of the missing girls cannot forget.

On May 1, Linda's parents depart on a vacation on a cruise ship to Maui, Hawaii. Her father had reasoned that although his wife had been diagnosed with moderate-stage Alzheimer's, she was still in plenty good enough shape to be traveling and doing the things they'd always wanted to do. After all, there will be lots of stimulation onboard. She won't have to cook or clean and she can't get lost. It's a boat. Their days will be spent eating, basking in the sun and enjoying the ocean view. Their evenings consumed with attending musicals, gambling in the onboard casino and dining. Once the ship docks in La Haina, Maui, they'll be delivered to a posh hotel for a five night stay then flown back to Portland with a bag of souvenirs and wonderful memories.

On May 8, Linda gets a telephone call from her mother. "Oh hello Linda," she says. "We're having a wonderful time."

"Where are you?"

"Where? Well, we're at...we're at the coast, the Oregon coast and it's beautiful, so very beautiful."

Linda frowns, "The Oregon coast? How long have you been there?"

"Oh, just a day. We'll be driving home tomorrow. We heard of this very good restaurant to have lunch at, but your father couldn't find it this afternoon. I don't know what is the matter with him."

"Driving? Mother, is Dad there?"

"He's in the other room watching baseball on TV."

"Let me talk to him, okay?"

When her father gets on the phone, he seems irritated. "Hi Linda. What's going on?"

"Dad, Mom just told me you're at the Oregon coast. I thought you went to Hawaii."

"No," he insists, "she wouldn't say that. She knows where she is. You must have misunderstood. We had a lovely cruise and we just got to the hotel yesterday. We don't fly home until the fifteenth. Are you still going to pick us up at the airport?"

"Of course. Well look Dad, keep an eye on her, will you?" Linda says, trying not to convey the worry she feels.

"For Pete's sake, how far could she go? It's an island."

Linda realizes how different it must be for him. He's in denial and she knows this conversation is not the time to change that. She bids her father good-bye and hangs up the phone. A short while later she sits at her desk staring at the huge pile of case files in front of her. She can hear Philip clanking around his studio flipping switches and rewinding videotapes. Her phone rings. "Linda O'Neal Investigations. Can I help you? Oh, hi, Ollie. What have you got? "

"Some stuff on the Quintantilla case you're working on."

They go over business for a few minutes. Finally, Linda asks the inevitable question about the girls.

"God! I almost forgot to mention. I finally got that damn 9-1-1 tape from Clackamas County. In fact, I just finished transcribing it."

"You mean the call Lori made to report Ashley missing? What took so long?"

"They stalled me for weeks, but I finally got my hands on it."

"Anything illuminating?"

"Probably not, but then I didn't pore over the phrases with a 'Linda O'Neal Fine Tooth Comb.' It's only five pages. I'll fax it with the other stuff and you can make up your own mind."

"I'm really frustrated. Why can't we find out what happened to the girls?"

"You haven't given up, have you?"

"No, but...I don't know. So many possibilities, and yet nothing you can definitively point to as conclusive, you know what I mean?"

"Mostly dead ends, and the poor FBI people, I heard they've spent several million bucks so far and they aren't any closer than we are."

Linda ponders his words and then asks, "What about Ward Weaver? Remember, you were going to search out stuff on his family. Anything worthwhile come up yet?"

"As a matter of fact, there is one thing I stumbled onto about a Weaver family connection."

"Really?"

"I've run some public records databases for any links to Newell Creek, Ward Weaver and family relations, and I've come across a reference to a lady who was married to Ward Weaver from 1996 to 2000."

Linda feels a tingle. "His wife?"

"Jayne Patan. And she's still involved with his family. I have a hunch she knew Ashley Pond and Miranda Gaddis."

"Got an address or phone number?"

"Phone's unlisted, but I do have her address. Why don't I fax it over with the other stuff and you can figure out what to do with it."

"Sure. Thanks a lot Ollie, but being his wife, she may be very protective of him."

"Ex-wife, Linda, ex-wife. Maybe she doesn't like him any more. Husbands and wives usually don't when they split."

"Right on! Okay. I'll check into her and let you know what I find."

An hour later, Linda, Philip and their sons are seated at the kitchen table having supper while watching the local evening news. An animated sports reporter is discussing that day's NBA playoff highlights. Between bites, Linda examines the pages that Oliver has faxed over. Philip sprinkles Parmesan cheese onto his spaghetti and then taps Linda's arm and comments, "Can't that stuff wait till after dinner?"

She sighs, "It's the tape when Lori called to report Ashley missing."

Philip's demeanor quickly changes. "Anything there?" he asks anxiously.

She scrunches her forehead and ponders. "Well, when emotions are at a fever pitch, sometimes feelings and ideas spill out."

Philip nods. "By the way, Maria called while you were dealing with your faxes. She says there's going to be a public dance recital at the middle school, and Ashley's dance team—y'know, The Fallen Angels—well they're having their final performance of the year Friday night. There's going to be a few other dance teams performing too. A lot of group emotions up for display. Anyway, she's begged me to bring my big camera to videotape their numbers. I was thinking, I know you're horrifically busy of late, but if you can squeeze it in, you might want to come along. I'm taking Marilyn and we can put the top down. Maybe get a bite on the trip home or something! What do you say?"

Linda smiles. "While you're taping, maybe I can roam around and do some sleuthing. Heck! I might be able to waylay some of Ashley's buddies and sift out some tidbits. Y'know, I've wanted to interview a few of them anyway, but could never get any access. This could work. Okay. It's a date. What time do you have to be there?"

He shakes his head, "Once you're on something you never let up, do you?" He smiles at her, "Thank God. I'll meet you here at five and we'll go over. "

On the TV news, the sports guy has vanished and reporter Pinski Brown stands in front of the Newell Creek Apartments. When she mentions Ashley Pond, Linda shushes the family and quickly turns up the volume.

"Two girls from Oregon City, the same age, the same school, the same dance class, and living in the same apartment complex. Two thirteen-year-old friends, Ashley Pond and Miranda Gaddis vanished two months apart on their way to school. Previous cases are under scrutiny for similarities, but again, the absence of evidence makes comparisons difficult." Brown begins to talk about the possibility of the girls being abducted. The FBI had issued warnings to area police earlier that week to be sensitive of young girls missing so that a third abduction could be averted. Having now passed the second month, the FBI also warned of a possible cyclical problem. Linda and Philip look at each other, glumly nodding, then turn back to the TV and listen as Brown goes over Ashley and Miranda's disappearances and the growing certainty that they were abducted by the same person.

Linda grimaces. Brown is staring intently into the camera lens. "Now it's important to note, the FBI has told us they do not have specific information that a third girl is in line to be the next abduction victim."

A young woman appears, with a caption beneath her face, "Beth Anne Steele, FBI." She speaks with a bold, matter-of-fact cadence. "This is strictly a precautionary move. If there were a definite threat to public safety we would certainly warn parents in the area."

Next there is a close-up of a large billboard depicting the smiling faces of Ashley and Miranda underscored by wide lettering "MISSING! UP TO $50,000 REWARD OFFERED. YOUR TIP COULD HELP BRING THE GIRLS HOME!"

Having finished their meals, the boys quietly excuse themselves before hastily exiting to the living room where their *PlayStation* is on hold. Meanwhile on the TV, Brown has shifted her voiceover to a description of a recent interview she had with Lori Pond regarding the fateful morning Ashley disappeared. Lori is shown seated on a couch next to Brown, her hair tied back, and very pregnant. Brown asks her, "Do you remember the last conversation that you had with your daughter, Ashley?"

Pond speaks solemnly. "Well, the very last time I talked to Ashley, I wasn't even really talking to her. I was lying on the couch and I remember she was just leaving to go to school. She looked at me and she said, 'Goodbye, Mom. I love you.' And that was the last thing she said to me. I watched her walk out the door and then she ran off to the bus stop and I never saw her again."

As Brown reminds viewers that none of the thousands of tips that have poured in have yielded a significant answer to what happened to the girls, a dejected Linda turns the TV off. Philip embraces her and whispers, "Linda, you're doing everything you can." He pauses and can't help asking, "Do you really believe a third kidnapping is imminent?"

Before responding Linda picks up the manila folder and pulls out some papers. "Something doesn't make sense. Take a look at this, honey." She runs her finger along some text. "Oliver faxed me this transcript today of what Lori said when she made her 9-1-1 call on January 9. Listen." She reads, "'Dispatcher: last seen wearing blue jeans. Pond: Yeah, and she wears white Skecher shoes, like the sneakers, you know, and ma'am, I have no idea what shirt she'd be wearing. I didn't get up with her this morning.'" Philip shrugs, but Linda senses she is on a roll and continues. "But listen to this. Now later Lori said, 'We looked at what ones are missing,' now she means sweatshirts here. 'There's—yeah, I think she's wearing her blue sweatshirt. Let me ask her sister real quick. She might remember.' Then she asks her daughter,

'Do you remember what shirt Ashley was wearing this morning?' And the girl answers, 'I didn't see her this morning.'"

Linda drops a page and frantically scans another one. "Wait, wait. Here it is. Here it is. Listen to this. This is Lori talking. 'So you didn't see her at all, huh?' And then Lori says to the dispatcher, 'Yeah, cause I remember her getting up this morning and thinking she was late and she wasn't and then I had fallen back to sleep.' So, nobody in that house actually saw Ashley that morning. Lori has no idea what time her daughter left. She might have left at seven o'clock, or five o'clock, she might not have been there at all. Maybe she never even came home the night before. Don't you see? Neither Lori nor Ashley's sister say they saw Ashley that morning.

"Since January the search for Ashley has been based on the premise that she left her apartment about 8 AM on the day she disappeared. That information has been repeated in police and family statements to the media. Think about it. In all her statements, including the excerpt we just watched on the evening news, Lori has maintained that she physically saw Ashley the morning of January 9. Yet the 9-1-1 transcript doesn't support that. So this business about Ashley getting up at seven o'clock doesn't make any sense, because her sister says she didn't even see Ashley that morning.

"We already know from our earlier interviews that the younger girls leave the house about 7:15 to catch the school bus for elementary. The school district has to stagger the buses. First the elementary kids, then after they get dropped off, the drivers return for the middle school kids, then finally the high school. Her sisters were in grade school, so they left to catch their bus at 7:15, which is at least an hour sooner than Ashley, who didn't catch her bus until around 8:20 every day!"

Philip is dazzled, but he remains confused. He grabs her by the shoulders. "Calm down. Calm down. Just what exactly are you driving at, Linda? What does this all mean?"

"Lori did not see or talk to Ashley that morning. Nobody else in the house did either, so the entire premise that the cops have been working from, since the very moment they began their investigation, is false. The time-line for her disappearance is not what it was believed to be. In fact they've all been laboring under at least two misconceptions since the 9-1-1 call that Lori made, which obviously they never examined. The first misconception was procedural, and I made it too. The 9-1-1 dispatcher assumed that since a teenaged girl was missing, based on the typical profiles, it was a simple case of running away from home. That misconception cost at least a week of crucial investigative effort. The second misconception was that Ashley disappeared precisely at 8 AM on the morning of January 9, when it was just as likely that she could have disappeared as early as after school on January 8."

"Hold on a minute," Philip says firmly. "You may be going off on a tangent here. Why do you feel so strongly about all this?"

Linda frowns, "Because the most crucial aspect of a disappearance centers on that first hour. So much trickles down, once it is firmly established. In Ashley's case there were nothing but assumptions— assumptions that were accepted as facts. So what I am saying is that this definitely impacts the truth surrounding her disappearance. It doesn't necessarily prove what happened to her, but it does cast doubt on some fundamental issues that have been at the foundation of everything surmised about it. What if she disappeared the night of January 8, but nobody missed her for twenty-four hours instead of twelve? That could change the whole emphasis of the search!"

CHAPTER TEN

Final Billboard

The following Wednesday morning, dozens of people have gathered to witness a press conference on the outskirts of Portland beside a massive highway billboard, covered by a thick canvas tarp. Police officers and FBI officials stand on a portable stage underneath the structure, a stack of clustered microphones anchored in front of them. Several manned television news cameras are pointed in their direction. Linda and Philip arrive and merge into a quiet crowd anxious to witness the event. Within minutes, a dramatic unveiling of the tarp initiates the proceedings as it drifts to the ground revealing a gigantic sign, with bold red text describing cash rewards and an appeal for tips on the disappearances of Ashley Pond and Miranda Gaddis.

Charles Mathews, FBI Special Agent for Oregon, a tall, distinguished fellow in his late fifties, approaches the podium and in somber tones, begins an amplified speech. "Today we are posting the twelfth and final billboard for the Portland area which seeks the public's assistance in finding Ashley and Miranda. Similar signs have been previously set up at a variety of locations throughout our metropolitan area. This one is the last. I'd like to take a moment to express sincere thanks to the Portland Company, AK Media, and their Director of Public Affairs. These folks care so much that they have financed each of the twelve signs themselves and were also instrumental in creating the unique design." The audience claps, interrupting him for a moment.

Mathews continues. "As you all know, it has been over four

months since Ashley vanished and more than two months since Miranda's disappearance. Their plight has captured national attention and has been featured repeatedly on many network TV shows, including *America's Most Wanted*. I've just been informed that *People Magazine* has been doing interviews on the missing girls. That would be incredible media exposure and maybe it'll trigger the big break we're seeking. And yet, in my gut I don't think we'll find our answers from Chicago or Los Angeles or Miami or the hundreds of other cities that became aware of this perplexing mystery, following the national media exposure. I think the solution lies somewhere around here, right under our noses. I really do. Therefore, right now our primary focus is still local. We are using today's occasion to once again heighten awareness of this unusual case in the hope that out there is a person who knows something, anything, that can resolve this tragedy."

Linda observes the presentation intently and is touched by Mathews' melancholy demeanor. She identifies with the frustration that permeates his comments, but finds it ironic that in spite of many months and millions of dollars spent pursuing every possible avenue of investigation, the FBI—the most prestigious and high powered law enforcement agency in the world—is standing before the public admitting they are stuck. "Amazing," she says to herself.

Mathews continues. "Let me offer a brief review of the known facts, which are sparse and so far have not yielded many substantial clues. We know that Ashley Pond disappeared between 8:00 and 8:15 AM the morning of January 9. But that's about all we really know. There have been no witnesses who claim to have seen her once she left her apartment to head for the school bus stop, which means we have no crime scene."

Linda taps Philip and shakes her head. "See?" she comments, "Even the FBI may be clinging to a big misconception."

Mathews gestures, raising his arm. "Now we know that Miranda Gaddis went missing between 7:30 and 8:15 AM on the morning of March 8. She, too, disappeared on her way to the school bus stop, and just as with Ashley, to this date no witnesses have come forward who saw her. And again, we have no crime scene. Normally, if we think we know who committed a crime, even if we can't prove it, we classify a case as having a subject. But unfortunately, even though it has become one of the highest profile missing person cases in the history of the FBI, it still is classified as having no subject, meaning no suspect. And with no suspect, we are nowhere. So once again I implore every citizen who is listening to me at this moment to please help us. We need your help if we are ever to discover what happened to those precious little girls."

■

Two days later, with a big camcorder resting on his right shoulder, Philip stands in the Gardiner Middle School hallway next to the double door entrance to the gymnasium. He peers through the doors' tiny windows and observes intense activity. Hundreds of people are perched side by side on the steep bleachers that extend from the gym's walls. They are excitedly watching a troupe of costumed, rouge-faced teenage girls rhythmically prancing about, waving their arms in precise unison and kicking their legs to the music. He glances at his watch and begins to fret just before a hand slapping his left shoulder surprises him. When he turns he laughs. It is Linda and Maria. "I didn't think you'd make it," he says.

Linda, dressed in her courtroom clothes, smiles. "I'm sorry, but I didn't get done till they recessed. It was grueling. So I called Maria and she agreed to give me a lift so I could ride home with my honey," she chuckles.

Maria interrupts. "Did we miss the Angels' performance?"

Philip takes another peek through the window before answering. "No, these other girls just got things going. The Angels are still getting lined up." He points. "Down the hall, Room 213. I taped them coming into the building and as soon as they get set I'll resume."

"You're a peach, Dad. Well listen, I'm going to go find Mom and my sister. See you later." Maria slips through the double doors and is absorbed into the audience.

A commotion down the hall triggers Philip and Linda to turn their heads in time to witness a long chain of girl dancers emerging from Room 213. One by one, they trot along the hallway, chatting nervously while adjusting shoes, belts and hair bands. Within a few minutes there are more than twenty of them, each cherubic face dominated by bright red lipstick. Linda seizes the opportunity. "I'm going to mingle a bit," she says.

Philip turns his camcorder on and begins taping the waiting dancers. "It'll be a few minutes before they enter the gym," he says. "I've got to concentrate. I'll meet you out here when they're finished."

Linda slowly walks along the hall, ignored by the giddy dancers. She notices a very short, dark haired teen who stands away from the others and seems subdued. Linda looks at her for a long moment. "Can I ask you something?" she says.

"I have to hurry; we're getting ready to do our routine."

"I know, but it will just take a minute. We can do it before you have to go on. How about it?"

The girl smiles nervously. "O-Okay."

"How well did you know Ashley and Miranda?"

"Pretty well. I mean, I never went over to their houses or anything like that, but I talked to 'em a lot, mostly during dance practice."

Linda glances back and notices Philip slipping through the double doors to line himself up with a good angle for the Angels' grand entrance, which is only a moment away. Recognizing time is getting short, she resumes. "What's your name, Honey?"

"Mary, Mary Madison."[1]

The African-American supervisor for the dance team bursts from Room 213 and with a firm voice declares, "All right girls. Let's prepare. We've only got a couple of minutes and remember, go left then right once we get to the center floor. Left then right. Settle down. Settle down! Oh darn! I forgot the tape!" She runs back into Room 213.

Linda smiles and gently touches Mary's arm. "Did you ever hang with Ashley or Miranda any place besides dance practices?"

"Well, not Miranda so much, but I used to see Ashley, sometimes over at another friend's house."

"Who? What's her name? The friend?"

Mary points to a brown-haired girl about eight places up the line engaged in a giggly conversation with another dancer. "Her. Mal. Mallori. Mallori Weaver."

Linda takes a deep breath and resumes. "You mean Ward Weaver's daughter?"

"Yeah."

"You say you 'used to.' What happened?"

"Well, I got to feeling kind of strange whenever I went over there. At first, there were a bunch of girls hangin' out there—a lot of 'em. It was a cool place to go. And for a while Ashley was there almost all the time. I think she even sort of lived with 'em or something, but then it got kind of weird."

"What made you feel strange?"

"I dunno exactly. But Mal's dad hung around us all the time, and it was creepy. So I just kind of quit going there."

"Creepy. Creepy? Please, dear, I need to know what you mean by that."

"Well you know he would, like, just would hang out with us girls. I mean a place full of twelve-year-olds! Give me a break! At my house, when there are even just two of us girls together, my dad can't stand to be in the same room. So he just leaves, but Mal's dad was different. I think that's weird and it gave me the creeps. But I gotta tell ya, a lot of the other girls really liked him and thought he was really a cool guy."

Linda strains to learn all she can in the brief encounter with the friendly child. "You were friends with Mallori, right?"

"Sure. I've known Mal since fifth grade. She's okay."

"What about Mal's mom? Did you ever meet her?"

"I don't think so. Her real mom didn't come around much, but I did meet her other mom, and she was very nice."

"Her other mom?"

"Yeah, Jayne. She used to bring over treats for all the girls that hung out at Mal's. Mostly jelly donuts. Everybody liked Jayne."

"Did Jayne know Ashley?"

"Sure. I think so, anyway."

Suddenly, the door to Room 213 swings open and once again the dance coach rushes out, this time holding a cassette tape between her teeth and carrying a plastic bag stuffed with cardboard wands decorated with colorful paper streamers. She rapidly advances along the line of dancers and thrusts one of the wands into the hands of every third girl before she removes the cassette from her mouth and snaps her fingers loudly. "Okay, I'm going in first to get this tape cued up. After the other dancers finish their exit, when you guys hear the beginning chords, flip the doors open and take your positions and fly in just like we rehearsed. The audience will be clapping so loud you'll have trouble hearing the tape, but I know you'll be okay. Good luck, girls. Let's do this one for Miranda and Ashley." She disappears through the double doors.

Holding her decoration high and awaiting the cue to begin the grand entrance, Mary briefly glances at Linda. "I'm sorry ma'am, but I can't talk to you any more now. I've got to go."

Linda nods. "Just, one more thing."

The teenager shakes her head firmly. "I'm sorry. The show is about to begin, but listen, if you really want to find out about all this kind of stuff, you've got to talk to Victoria Sampson. She was over there a lot more than anybody else. She can tell you a lot of stuff, a lot of stuff about what was going on at Mal's house and what happened to Ashley over there. Talk to Victoria. But I have to go."

At that moment the double doors burst open and The Fallen Angels glide through. The crowd cheers uproariously. Linda leans against the wall, watching the spectacle and admiring the tremendous display of young people's energy. After their first number, Miranda's sister steps apart from the team and performs a solo dance that Miranda choreographed as a special way of remembering her friend Ashley. Miranda's mother, Michelle, sobs uncontrollably as she remembers her daughter's sorrow and determination to design a tribute worthy of her lost friend. It had now become a danced prayer for them both. At the end of the routine, the girls place roses on the two white empty chairs where their classmates would have sat. Thinking of Ashley and Miranda, tears spring to Linda's eyes. She realizes that for these classmates, life must go on.

■

Another week comes and goes. Linda spends most of the time untangling her increasing backlog of regular investigations, in order not to become too overwhelmed with the new ones flowing into her "To-Do" basket. As a successful private eye, she routinely gets as many as a dozen new criminal cases a week, each one requiring hours of painstaking attention. There are police reports to scrutinize, witnesses to contact, subpoenas to issue, and most importantly, detailed reports to write. Although she is able to delegate some of the less complicated cases to Allison, Linda finalizes the reports for the rest of the cases they handle herself. Fifty percent of her chores are accomplished over the telephone. The other half require the so-called gumshoe approach, necessitating driving, walking, ringing doorbells, quizzing those who answer and attaching her business card to the door handles of those who don't, hoping they will call. One of the people whose empty house she knocks at is Jayne Patan, Ward Weaver's ex-wife. Evenings she continues to work on the Oregon girls case and most often literally falls asleep in front of her computer to be awakened by her concerned husband, pleading for her to come to bed.

On Memorial Day, realizing the building tension about Ashley and Miranda is affecting her immediate family, Linda schedules a backyard barbecue with Philip and the boys. When she begins the preparations, she realizes she's out of hamburger rolls. No problem, a market is two blocks away. As she goes through the "10 Items or Less" checkout, she is shocked to see Ashley and Miranda staring at her from the cover of *People Magazine*. Under their photos a huge red headline asks, "WHO TOOK THESE GIRLS?" She grabs a copy and tosses it on the belt. As soon as she exits the store, still pushing her cart toward her car, she lifts the magazine from the sack and flips through the pages, anxious to grasp the slant the authors had taken for their portrayal of the mystery. At that precise moment her cell phone rings. Linda fumbles to retrieve it from her purse and answers. "Linda O'Neal Investigations, can I help you?"

A husky female voice falters nervously. "Uh, are you the private investigator?"

"Yes I am. My name is Linda. What can I do for you?"

"Well, uh, you, you left a card on my door. I was gone for the weekend and I just got home and your business card was on my door. I guess I'm calling to…to find out what's going on. I mean, what's this about? Why did you leave your card on my door?"

Linda puts the magazine back into the grocery cart and shifts her concentration to the cell phone. "Thank you for calling me so quickly. But I left my card on about ten doors Friday. Please, tell me who you are and I'll explain."[2]

"My name is Jayne Patan."[3]

"Well Jayne, I left that card at your house, because when I stopped by, you weren't home and I wanted to talk to you about a case I'm working on. I always leave my card when witnesses aren't home."

"Witness? What do you mean? I'm not a witness. What kind of case are you talking about?"

"I'm sorry. I'll back up a bit. First of all, I am a member of Ashley Pond's extended family and I am working on their behalf trying to help them find out where she is."

"But that's been taken over by the FBI."

"Have they talked to you?"

"Oh yes, several times. But why do they need you?"

"No, you don't understand. I'm not working with the FBI. I'm a private investigator. I'm running an independent investigation, totally separate from whatever they are doing. That's why I left you my card. I've come to understand, through some of my sources, that you may have some information that can shed some light on the girl's disappearance."

"I've already given all the information I had to the FBI. I'm sorry, but I don't think I can help you, and I'm not sharing the reward with anyone. Goodbye."

Linda panics. "No, no, wait! Please! I have no interest in the reward. Can I just ask you some simple questions that might help in finding Ashley, that's all, and then I'll let you go."

A confused Jayne Patan hesitates for a few moments. "Well, I guess it'll be okay."

"Thank you so much. Okay, now I understand that you are Ward

Weaver's ex-wife. Is that true?"

"You want to know stuff about Ward? Well, yes, I am, well, one of his ex-wives. I was his second wife. But we broke up back in '98."

"Do you still have contact with his children?"

"I do. I love them all very much."

"Did you know Ashley Pond and Miranda Gaddis?"

"I knew of Ashley, mostly from Mallori, and I had met Miranda. You see last September I started picking up Mallori to come home with me for weekend visits, but by that time Ashley was on the outs with the Weaver clan. They were all angry at her."

"Why was that?"

"Let's just say that Ashley had accused Ward of doing something to her after they all went on a vacation together to California."

"Who went on the vacation?"

"All of them. There was Ward, and Mallori, Gerri, Gerri's daughter and Ashley. Well, they went in a rented car and they were gone for at least a week. From what Mallori told me, everything was hunky-dory for a while, but eventually, it all went sour, and that's when Ashley claimed that Ward did the rape."

"Did you believe that?"

"Well, I do believe that Ashley and Ward had a sexual relationship, because Mallori did tell me that while Ashley was living with them, she was sleeping in Ward's bed. But as to whether rape was involved there, uh, I don't know. From what I hear, rape is a crime more of violence than it is about sex. But, on the other hand, I can assure you, Ward could be violent too and that's all I want to say about that."

Linda yanks her notebook from her purse and consults some scribbling before she asks, "Maybe you can set me straight about another issue. I thought that Ward had a live-in girlfriend during this period when Ashley was hanging out with the family. Is that the Gerri you are talking about?"

"Oh yes, Gerri Glass.[4] She's the main reason Ward and I split up. She moved into the house with Ward and Mallori back in 2000. But Gerri is not a bad person. I essentially got along pretty well with her."

"If Ward eventually ended up sleeping with little Ashley, wouldn't that have sort of put a strain on Gerri?"

"Oh yeah, probably so, but in that house it was always what Ward wanted that counted, not what anybody else wanted. You might say he was the king of his castle. I remember something Mallori told me that blows my mind. She said that at one point, probably about the time Ashley began sleeping in Ward's bed with him, that Ward moved Gerri's cosmetics out of the bathroom to make room for Ashley's stuff. Yeah, I'm sure Gerri was pretty stressed by then, but it was hard for me to work up a lot of sympathy, because after all, Gerri did the same thing to me back in 1998.[5] I finally just left. And Gerri eventually left too, because of Ashley. "

"When did that happen?"

"She moved out on Christmas day, last Christmas, 2001."

"Wait a minute. That doesn't gel, because you just told me Ashley was on the outs with Weaver in September. Why would Gerri have waited until almost January to leave over Ashley, especially when Ashley was out of the picture?"

"Because Ashley and Ward buried the hatchet sometime around Thanksgiving and Mallori wasn't very happy about it."

"Did you ever see Ashley over at Weaver's house then?"

"No, not personally, but something must have happened because I did hear Ward scold Mallori and tell her not to be so hard on Ashley because it wasn't nice. And just a few weeks before, they were all ragging on the poor girl something terrible. Anyway, Gerri moved out on Christmas Day. Christmas Day! Nobody moves on Christmas unless they're mad about something."

"Jayne, hold on a minute." Linda has reached her car. She tosses her groceries into the back seat before getting into the driver's seat. She consults her notes again. "Jayne, are you still there?"

"Uh-huh."

"Great. Listen, I won't keep you much longer, but please let me ask you about one more subject. You can really help me here. Do you have any knowledge about a concrete slab in the back of Weaver's house that supposedly was poured sometime in March?"

"Oh yes, it was definitely in mid-March, and I already told the FBI all I know about it."

"Can you tell me what you know about it?"

"Well, just that we all thought it was funny, him putting a slab down in the rain and all. The first time it came up was a few days before Miranda disappeared. He showed me a hot tub there in the back yard. It was all in pieces and he said it was going to be placed over a hole that his second son was digging near the house. Two dark blue, little short barrels were sitting nearby. Then I was back there a week later, this was after Miranda was missing. The hole was completely buried and covered by concrete and the barrels were gone. And when I asked him about it, Ward was like, 'Yeah I had to throw the barrels into the hole to make sure the foundation for my hot tub doesn't sink.' But I didn't buy it. I'm not a rocket scientist or anything, but I know when you dig a big hole in the ground you don't have to put something in to support the foundation. The slab was going to make a foundation for the hot tub. Now like I said, this was right after the second girl disappeared and the police had already been around talking with him. So I asked him if he didn't think it was going to look kind of fishy, him pouring that slab right after those girls went missing. But he just laughed and said, 'Let 'em come and look. They're not going to find anything.' Now I told a few of my friends and relatives about this slab and they jumped right on me about it. 'You better tell the FBI,' they said. 'This is important.'"

"Well is that what you did?"

"Absolutely. I called the task force tip line and got a very quick response from the FBI, because a lady agent came right out to the company where I work, and I think we must have talked for about an hour, but not in great detail. But to tell you the truth, she didn't really seem much interested in the slab, though. She just asked about my relationship with Ward prior to our marriage, during our marriage and then after our marriage. Just kind of basic background stuff more than any real thinking he was guilty of anything. This was around the first of April."

"Did you tell the FBI anything else that could help me?"

"I don't know if it'll help you, but I told them about Bagby Hot

Springs, over by Molalla, which would have been a perfect place to dispose of any bodies, if he really was the killer. We used to go camping there a lot when we were married and Ward knew every nook and cranny of that place. There are dozens of spots that you'd never find where he could have easily buried them."

"To your knowledge did the FBI follow-up on your tip and conduct any searches at Bagby Hot Springs?"

"The Oregon City Police picked me up one day and we drove all the way out there and I showed them a few spots I knew.[6] And later somebody must have gone back and searched all around with their dogs, because I came home from work one night and who should call me, but Mr. Ward Weaver himself. He was hot. He says, 'You talked to the FBI and told them about Bagby Hot Springs.' And I said, 'No I didn't.' And he says, 'Well whoever did is going to pay!' And I believed him. Weaver is a really aggressive person and when things don't go right his way, he has to find another way to take things out." Patan takes a deep breath and sighs sadly. "Listen, I've already talked more than I was going to and I really don't have any more to say on any of this. So I'm going to hang up now, if that's okay."

"Certainly. You've been very generous to me, and I really do thank you for finding my card and calling me back. But Jayne, if you really think Ward is that violent, then he very well may have been involved in these crimes. I'm not saying he is for sure, because I can't prove it and obviously neither can the FBI, but remember, if somehow Ward was responsible for what happened to those two girls, who's to say it couldn't happen to a third girl? That's how serial killings happen sometimes. The perpetrator gets away cleanly, gains confidence, actually feels omnipotent then strikes again. You think about that. In the end, the only way to stop the violence is for the truth to come out. The truth is always the antidote. So please, if you discover more things that might shed some light on all of this, don't hesitate to get hold of me. Day or night. You can always call me. Good luck Jayne, and thanks again for your help."

CHAPTER ELEVEN

Friends and Foes

On June 7TH, Linda's car is parked under a tall canopy of fir trees that encircle the south parking lot of Portland's Washington Park, a sprawling thousand acres of woods, trails, meadows and world-famous rose gardens. The noon sun radiates a hazy glow through a thin cover of gray clouds. While she takes occasional sips of her latté, Linda sits at a nearby picnic table waiting for her friend Ginger, from the sheriff's department, wistfully watching the antics of a few small children as they giggle and romp about playfully.

Then she feels a hand on her left shoulder. Startled, she jerks back and when she sees a familiar face, she laughs. "Ginger! You sneaked up on me!"

Ginger, Linda's old friend, stands beside the picnic bench dressed in a jogging suit, her long blonde hair held in place by a blue headband. She glances at her slender wristwatch. "I told you 12:15, and it's 12:15, on the nose."

"Your sense of punctuality has always been your greatest asset." Linda stares at Ginger's attire and smiles. "Your second, I might add, is that you always look, well, just amazing. I don't know how you do it. Are you still into the kick boxing?"

"Nope. After my accident, well it wasn't really an accident, but I got hammered really hard and tore some cartilage in my left shoulder, so I had to give up boxing. And I miss those boys a lot. But for the last month I've been training—now don't laugh—but I'm going to do marathons. Now that the shoulder is better, I've been training every day. I'm up to six miles without stopping, and I can't tell you how much more energy I have now. Running is so good for the human body."

"So I see."

"How about it, Linda? You want to get with the program too? We can train together. It'll do you good."

"Oh, I don't think I'm quite ready for marathon running at this point in my life."

"But you're only two years older than me."

Linda shakes her head and chuckles. "Ginger, you have always been, well, something else, a total original. I, on the other hand, find more adventure than I desire in my work. Physically, I don't want to climb any mountains. At least, not right now. So, what was it you wanted to talk to me about? Did those agencies finally rescind that stupid gag order?"

"No, they didn't, but since they don't seem to have found the break they need and are still searching every miscellaneous nook and cranny, I doubt that I will be in any danger here." She laughs and the two of them giggle.

"You know, last week, after that *People Magazine* spread came out, they were inundated with 'well meaning' leads, but so far nothing momentous." Ginger takes a long sip from her water bottle and studies Linda's strained face. "So Linda, how's your husband's family getting along? I know what an ordeal this must be for them."

"The family? Well…different members have different notions about who did what, but they all agree that not knowing is the hardest part to deal with, and they are pressuring me to dig up something substantive. I certainly have put together my 'persons of interest' list, but I have no idea how it might compare to the task force list."

Ginger sits down next to Linda and her expression tightens. "Well I think you'll be interested to know that after several months of flying blind, they're finally administering some polygraphs."

Linda straightens up and takes a deep breath. "And?"

"The tests seem to have become their basic barometer for where to go. Some subjects have refused to get involved. Others have taken the test more than once and failed. Some results have underscored marked deceptions. Some have been inconclusive. But remember, these cases are both so unique compared to just about any that have ever confronted those hot shots, because of two primary issues."

Linda's eyes narrow. "Let me guess. 'No crime scene and no witnesses.'"

Ginger nods.

Linda pulls her notebook from her overstuffed purse and flips through some pages. "How about if I run a few names by you and you give me an indication of polygraph results?"

"Okay. Go for it."

"Dave Roberts?"

"Passed, with flying colors."

"Wesley Roettger?"

"Refused the test."

"Ward Weaver?"

"Flunked, across the board."[1]

Linda looks at her friend and nods, "So did they shake him down a bit?"

"They were concerned enough to put a tail on him when they turned him loose. Thought maybe he'd run, but he just went home and went to bed."

"Doesn't that strike you as a bit too cool? Have I missed somebody, here?"

"Well, they're seriously looking at two white males, Jake Pace[2] and Tom Watkins. Both early twenties; they live together in the Newell Creek Apartments. Both took the polygraph. Both flunked, big time. One of them had a run-in last year with a twelve-year-old girl. The biggest thing they're looking at with regard to Pace is he has no alibi. Claims he was camping, all by himself when Miranda disappeared."[3]

"Okay, I'll start looking in that direction myself. I'm still interested in Weaver. I'm having trouble rounding up some of his relatives, like his first wife."

Ginger smiles slyly. "Look in one of those houses directly behind Rose's Ice Cream store on Foster Road."

"Can you give me anything else?"

"Maybe. While you're out and about I suggest you drop by and see if you can have a word with Ashley Pond's sixth grade reading teacher. She has some information that will absolutely knock your socks off, if true, but that's all I can tell you."

"Now then, what can I do for you here Ginger?" Linda asks with sincerity.

"Anything you can give me to get things off dead center. Detective Valenzuela-Garcia is thinking along the same lines that you are Linda, but there is a layer in the task force that seems impervious to the idea."

Linda catches her breath and looks around for eavesdroppers. "Look hard at Weaver's family. The apple doesn't fall far from the tree."

Later that afternoon Linda is behind the wheel of her trusty sedan, headed toward the ice cream store behind which Kathryn Diaz was said to be residing. Perhaps Diaz would be willing to answer a few pertinent questions. As she weaves in and out of afternoon traffic, Linda contemplates what she ideally would like to glean from the interview. Her cell phone rings. Keeping one hand on the wheel, with her free hand she grabs it, punches the green button and says, "Linda O'Neal Investigations. Can I help you?"

"You left a message on my voice mail last week. I'm returning your call.[4] I'm Ron Shumaker."[5]

For an instant Linda's mind slips out of gear. She wonders which of her three-dozen active cases this name is connected to. Finally she replies, "Shumaker?"[6]

"I'm calling from Kern County in Central California. On the voicemail you mentioned you're seeking some background info surrounding a fellow I prosecuted way back in 1984 on a kidnapping and murder charge. Ward Weaver Junior."

"Thank you sir, for returning my call. Well, I have been investigating a possible suspect in the disappearances of two girls up here a few months ago. Perhaps you've heard of the Ashley Pond/Miranda Gaddis case."

"I think it's safe to say there probably isn't an aware person in the whole country who doesn't know about them. It's been plastered all over the news down here. Are you saying you think there's a Weaver connection somewhere?"

"Possibly." Linda doesn't want to say too much until she has hard evidence to back up the direction she's taking. "I'm looking for background stuff on Ward Weaver III's family, and I understand that you are a walking encyclopedia on the subject. Is that right?"

Shumaker laughs modestly. "Well I don't know about that, but let's just say it's become a macabre fascination of mine."

"Have you been contacted yet by any FBI folks about this subject?"

"It would be inappropriate for me to comment on that; however, I am free to discuss any aspects of the case that are a matter of public record, and I can assure you, the public record on Weaver Junior is hundreds and hundreds of pages thick. Remember, it was a capital case. We nailed him. He's on Death Row as we speak."

A large delivery truck unexpectedly swerves in front of Linda's car and she reacts by dropping the phone and slamming on her brakes.

Shumaker is confused. "Hello? Hello? Are you still there?"

Once she has averted the collision and has the car realigned, she grabs the phone again. "I'm sorry," she says breathlessly. "I almost had an accident. But it's okay now. Could you maybe give me a thumbnail description of just how you nailed the guy?"

"Sure. In fact it's kind of ironic, but you might say that in a way his mother created a monster, set him loose on the world and then gave him to us."

"His mother?"

"Let me back up a bit because, as you may know, this became a very convoluted tale. In 1981 Ward Weaver Junior, a thirty-five-year-old long haul truck driver, was convicted and sentenced to forty-two years in prison."

"What did he do to get that long a sentence?"

"Plenty. He had picked up two young runaways and arranged for a friend to shoot one of them, an eighteen-year-old male. Then Weaver repeatedly raped the other one, a fifteen-year-old girl, before letting her go. It was during his time serving the prison sentence for that attack that he confided to a cell mate that he had killed another couple earlier. He had beaten eighteen-year-old Robert Radford to death with a pipe. This kid was hit so many times you couldn't distinguish one blow from another. He literally pulverized the skull. I remember getting physically ill the first time I examined the crime scene photos."

Linda gulps. "Oh my God!"

"Then he kidnapped, raped and strangled Radford's twenty-three-year-old fiancée. Her name was Barbara Levoy. Well, his cell mate snitched him off to the authorities in exchange for some reduction in his own sentence. And when police showed up to the prison to question Weaver about all of this, he had only one request, and a strange one it was."

Linda is intrigued. "What did he want, immunity or something?"

"No. He wanted to talk to his mommy. That was it. He said he needed to confer with his mother before he'd talk to them. And so they phoned her, put him on the line, and he must've chatted for half an hour. It was weird. But anyway, once the conversation was over, he laid it all out. That was 1982. The trial ended in early '84, and he's been on Death Row ever since."

Linda is disgusted. "That's the standard sob story I get fed from every other perpetrator. When all else fails, blame Momma."

"Oh no, Ms. O'Neal, no, no, no. This story is far from the usual. It's a real doozy. I've been a prosecutor for thirtysome years, and I've never encountered maternal influence that had the repercussions of Weaver's mother. It's almost impossible to believe, but believe me, it's factual."

"What the hell did she do to him?"

"What didn't she do? First of all, you have to understand, she was a man hater. Once, she chased her son and some neighborhood boys around the yard hoisting a butcher knife high in the air and screaming her intention to cut off all their penises."

Linda shakes her head. "She sounds like a psycho to me."

"Exactly my thoughts. For example, biting was her chief method of discipline. She bit Ward Junior so hard when he was a little boy that she frequently drew blood. When I interviewed his ex-wife, your Ward Weaver's mother, she had showed up to testify in court to explain why Weaver Junior may have gone berserk and strangled Barbara Levoy. It seems, while he was trying to gag her after the brutal rape incident, she fought back furiously and began biting. She practically bit the end of his thumb off. His ex told me, 'More than anything, he hates being bitten.' She said that once when they were wrestling around playfully, she bit him on the hand. He reacted with an emotional explosion and got so out of control he began squeezing her throat to the point where she almost lost consciousness."

Linda sees the store she was looking for and slips her car into the right turn lane. "Was she okay?"

"Yeah, he finally came to his senses and snapped back to reality. But on another occasion, she also bit his hand and that time he again grabbed her by the neck and she said 'He looked dazed and glassy eyed.'"

"Well, Weaver was interviewed at length by a court appointed psychiatrist, who eventually testified that Weaver Junior revealed that during the early years of his marriage he assaulted his wife numerous times and got away with it. He finally got so despondent about his behavior he joined the Army and volunteered for combat duty. He wanted to get killed. Here's the important thing. During all of these instances when he was assaulting his poor wife, Ward Junior and his ex had moved in with Weaver's coldhearted mother and her husband. So our psychiatrist was convinced Weaver Junior's assaults on his wife were what he termed 'transference-actualizations' centered on the love-hate dynamics at the core of his relationship with his mother. Suffice it to say, Ward Weaver Junior was as close to a 'created psychotic killer' as I've ever prosecuted. And whether you are inclined to agree or disagree, the consensus of the experts we consulted was that most of the deep disturbances sprang from his ties to his mother. And in retrospect, it seems obvious to me that his mother's influence has traveled down through the generations, because Ward Weaver III, your Ward Weaver, was convicted here in California and served prison time for an assault on a female. His son, Ward Weaver the fourth was convicted on an assault in Idaho. He shot somebody."

Linda slows her car and glances out the passenger side window where she examines three one-story houses on a side street, tucked unobtrusively behind the large store. She notices some children playing on the front porch of one. On another porch, freshly washed bedding is hanging from a makeshift clothesline. She slows her car to a crawl, and then turns her attention back to her phone call. "Now I've heard that a concrete slab was a crucial element in the murder case. Can you tell me anything about it?"

Shumaker takes a deep breath and slowly lets it out. "According to court records, Weaver Junior buried Levoy's body in three separate places before finally moving her remains to a hole his son helped him dig. This hole was behind his rented house in Oroville, California where he lived at the time with his second wife and their young children. He asked his son to help him finish filling in the hole where he had buried Levoy's body. When we interviewed the son about it, he unquestionably remembered having packed the dirt. Later his father sealed the grave with concrete and built a wooden deck above it. On the afternoon of July 26, 1982, a pair of detectives showed up at the two-story house and wanted to speak to the youngster about a ditch he had helped his dad dig. They brought in a backhoe and after tearing up the deck, cracked the concrete into two chunks. From his bedroom window in the upstairs of the house, Weaver's son watched as they lifted one of the pieces up and there was the victim, Barbara Levoy, all scrunched up and deteriorated. Later, he said it was a sight that has never left the back of his mind. It gave him nightmares for years, as you can well imagine it probably would have. The poor kid was only eleven years old when it happened."

Linda reaches a dead end on the street behind the store and is forced to turn into a nearby empty driveway, stopping for a few minutes to resume her conversation with the Kern County man. "Have you ever had personal contact with Weaver Junior's son?" she asks.

"Can you hold a moment? I have another call." Shumaker puts the phone on hold, returning twenty seconds later. "I'm sorry, Ms. O'Neal, but I have to go. Something has come up that demands my immediate attention. Listen. Let's discuss this again, another time. But I've got to end our conversation for now."

"I understand, believe me, I understand. Thank you so much for talking with me. Goodbye."

Linda next devotes full attention to the three houses she had earlier passed by and tries to determine which one was most likely to be occupied by Kathryn Diaz. She soon dismisses the one with the small children frolicking when a blonde woman appears, refereeing a skirmish between two little boys. She glances at the next house, the one with the sheets and blankets flapping from a porch-mounted clothesline in the afternoon breeze. Then, the third, but it seems somehow vacant with the blinds down and grass overgrown.

She decides on the wet blankets, parks her car a half a block away and soon knocks loudly on the front door. Within thirty seconds, a tall dark haired woman opens the door and holds up her left arm to shade the afternoon sun spilling over from the porch roof. The women stand silently for several moments awkwardly staring at each other. Linda notices the woman wears no make-up, but has a pleasant face. Finally she breaks the ice. "Excuse me," she says politely, "but would you happen to be Kathryn Diaz?" Before responding the woman walks out onto the porch and runs her fingers around the edges of the sheets and blankets, looking suspiciously over her shoulder.

Linda sees an opening and touches a blanket. "It's a beautiful weave and color; was it handmade?"

The woman smiles slightly. "Oh yes, indeed," she says. "And that blue is as bright as the day I finished the cloth, and it's been washed many times."

"You're very talented."

The woman blushes and casts her eyes down.

"Are you, by any chance, Kathryn Diaz?" Linda gently asks.

"I might be. Who wants to know?"

Linda hands the woman a business card. "I'm an investigator, ma'am, and I'm trying to find Kathryn so I can ask her a few questions about some information her children might have. You *are* Kathryn Diaz, aren't you? Please help me. Do you have a son?"

The woman hands Linda back the business card and nervously glances at the front driveway. "Yes I do, is he in some sort of trouble?"

"Oh no, not at all. But does he live here with you? If not, where can I get a hold of him?"

"He mostly lives with Emily. They have a son. I see them a lot. Maybe I could give him a message."

"Yes, that would be great. Thanks. Now do you also have another child, a daughter named Mallori?"

Diaz smiles. "She's my baby, my only girl."

"Does she live here with you?"

"She comes and goes, but she mostly lives at her dad's."

"And who would that be?"

"Ward Weaver." She points. "He lives about seven miles away, in Oregon City."

"She comes and goes? So do you see her more or less on a regular basis?"

"I see her, but not like any regular days. She stays here sometimes. Sometimes I go over to Ward's and see her. Why do you want to know about Mallori?"

"I'm interested in an incident involving other kids that supposedly happened in front of her house on a Thursday night a few months ago. It would have been the first week in March. I want to find out what she remembers about it."

"Thursday night? Thursday night the first part of March? No, she couldn't've seen anything. She was here with me that night.[7] I do remember that night because it was a school night and Mallori never stays overnight on a school night. But on that Thursday, her dad just dumped her off here. And Mallori was very annoyed, because she had something or other going on the next day at school and didn't want to take a chance on not making it. She wanted to get back home."

"So did you take her to school the next morning, then?"

"No, she was making such a drama out of possibly being late that when my husband got home, I said, 'I think it would be better if we brought her back to her dad's. So we put her in the truck and drove her back over to Ward's. We dropped her off and said 'good night.' On the way home we went to the store first. And when we finally drove up, there was Mallori sitting on the porch again."

"So the next morning, did you drive her in to school?"

"No. My husband goes in to work early and we only have the one vehicle. So I didn't have any way to get her to school that morning and she was very angry because it meant she had to miss a big dance thing that afternoon. She wouldn't shut up about it. I blame her dad because we took her there so she'd be on time. He wouldn't have it. He can be damn stubborn sometimes."

A Ford pickup screeches to a stop in the gravel driveway, a blond thirty-ish male at the wheel. Linda has only enough time to notice his huge hobnailed boots and his denim work shirt, because before she can make many assumptions about him, he leaps from the truck, stomps up to the porch and challenges Kathryn Diaz angrily. "What the hell is going on here? Who's this?"[8]

"It's okay, sir," Linda says, forcing a smile. "I'm a private investigator just asking her a few questions on a case I'm working on."

The man ignores Linda completely and slips through the front door, briefly disappearing into the kitchen.

Linda watches her closely as Diaz's demeanor tightens and she slowly backs toward the door. "I'm sorry," she says quietly, "You have to go."

Linda sets the business card onto a nearby windowsill. "Kathryn, just let me ask you one more thing. Can you remember if Ward brought Mallori over to you on any other school nights to spend the night with you?"

Before Diaz can reply, her mate reappears on the front porch. He glares at Linda and shouts at Diaz. "Now, I've got to get back to work. Get your sorry ass into that kitchen and fix me some goddamn food!"

Linda's mouth drops open as she watches Diaz turn and follow the obnoxious man into the house. He slams the door loudly behind them. Shaking her head, Linda quickly retreats to her car.

Two hours later, Linda is sitting in her home-office, frantically typing one of several overdue investigation reports. She can hear her sons' laughter frequently echoing from the living room where they are glued to the TV. A *Saturday Night Live* re-run has garnered their attention. Her fingers continue to pound on the keyboard, carefully isolating helpful phrases and sentences as she painstakingly recreates the essence of an interview she conducted a few days earlier with an eyewitness to a horrific school arson. Then she hears the familiar slam of Philip's video studio door indicating he has finally arrived home from a long afternoon of corporate seminar taping. Within minutes he enters her office and plants a kiss on her forehead.

"You look stressed," he says while affectionately massaging the back of her neck.

She looks up and smiles warmly. "Don't stop," she grunts, "Don't stop. A little to the right. Don't stop."

Philip continues the massage for awhile and then finally asks, "Did you find Weaver's ex-wife?"

Linda's eyes light up and she sighs. "Yes, I found her all right and I had the strangest interview. I fell into my standard 'Ah, shucks' routine, you know, dancing around the issue a bit before I hone in, and pretty soon I got her talking about her kids. I acted like her daughter, Mallori, could be a witness to something out in front of Ward's house. I threw out March 7 as some way to tie the conversation into that fateful first week of March. But keep in mind, I didn't want to mention anything about Miranda and the fact that she vanished the very next day. I just wanted to talk in general about the kids and look for an opening. Anyway, she bit on the March 7 date—vivid, specific recollections. I was blown away. She told me that Mallori couldn't possibly have witnessed anything at the house that night because she was at her house, and she said the reason she could remember it so specifically was because it was so strange that Ward brought her over to the house in the first place. It was a school night and Mallori never spent school nights with Kathryn Diaz. The times when she would sleep at her mom's would always be on weekends or maybe some holidays. I guess Mallori threw a fit, because she wanted to go to school the next day because of something that was happening after school with the dance team. So Kathryn acquiesced and took Mallori back to the Weaver house. She thought that would be the end of it. But before she and her husband even got back home, Mallori had already been deposited back onto Kathryn's front porch and was standing there waiting when they drove up. The damnedest thing! Now Philip, that's weird. I don't know exactly what to make of it yet, but damn! It's weird."

"Linda, half the stuff you wade into as a regular course of duty would be considered weird by eight out of ten normal people. But this time you and I want so badly to find out what happened to Ashley… you have to get a little distance to evaluate what you're finding out."

Linda sighs. "You're right, but I'm telling you there's something going on with this Ward Weaver thing. I can feel combustion. It's in my deepest place." She slaps her lower abdomen. "This whole Weaver angle is starting to gel, at least for me it is. So the big question that I'm still chewing on is, what about the task force? Why didn't they sweat Weaver after he flunked the polygraph if they really see Weaver as a serious contender here? It's bizarre!"

"Well, maybe the task force isn't looking hard at Weaver, because maybe he just might be exactly what he purports to be, a hard working, lovable if eccentric, single father who cares enough about his young daughter to invest tremendous time and energy into her upbringing. And from the looks of things, he's been doing a decent job of it. His daughter gets good grades, she's in extracurricular activities and so forth. She has oodles of friends. It's about impossible to link the guy with molestation and kidnappings. Why would a father hurt his daughter's friends? It's crazy, at least on the surface. But I do understand the need, you know, to take a jaded view of the man, and be inclined not to grant him the benefit of the doubt. Otherwise a guilty culprit may slip through. But Linda, a guy in his position has earned a few benefits of the doubt, that's all I'm saying."

"Maybe, but this Ward Weaver situation is rife with red flags. I'm just saying that if you or I were involved in so many suspicious coincidences surrounding a crime of this magnitude, the cops would be snapping at our heels a lot more aggressively than they seem to with Weaver. And if they don't or won't, I will."

■

Linda decides to act on some of Ginger's tips by contacting the grade school teacher who'd been close to Ashley, Donna Clark. After several aborted attempts she finally gets the elusive Clark on the phone.[9] "This is Donna, how can I help you?"[10] Her voice has a slight edge.

"Hello, Ms. Clark. My name is Linda O'Neal. It's sure nice to finally talk to you. You're a hard person to get a hold of." She hears a chuckle. "You see, I'm a private investigator. I'm working on the Ashley Pond disappearance trying to help unravel this complicated case. And I understand that you may have some information about Ashley that, quite frankly, is startling. Is that right?"

Clark sighs, "I…I don't know where to begin. I am so glad you got through, because nobody seems to give a hoot about that poor girl."

Linda pulls out her pad and pen and asks, "Did you call the authorities about Ashley?"

"Oh yeah," she says bitterly, "on several occasions, and it hasn't made one bit of difference, has it?"

"Well, perhaps we can change that. Why don't you tell me about when you first suspected something was wrong concerning Ashley."

"How much do you know about Ashley's life?"

Linda is momentarily startled and tries to formulate a response. "Well, my husband is her step-grandfather. I didn't know her that well, but during my investigation I've learned plenty. She had a rather difficult childhood."

Clark gives voice to her own feelings, "That's putting it mildly."

Her comment hangs in the air a few moments. Then, Linda continues. "But the aspect that most mystifies me about her is the dynamic between Ashley and Ward Weaver. Can you shed any light in that direction?"

"I sure can." Clark pauses as though considering carefully what she will say next.

Linda bridges the awkwardness, "Did you ever really see him with her?"

"I did, and it made me sick."

Linda coaxes her to continue. "Please tell me what happened."

"I witnessed an incident in May, 2001."

"Something involving Ashley?"

"Yes. One morning, just before classes began, I was looking out the window next to my desk. You get a view from there of the front driveway and you can see the cars pull up and let out kids with their books and backpacks. It's a morning ritual, and many times I enjoy just watching that boundless kid energy. Well, one morning, I noticed a strange vehicle, an old pickup truck, but one that I'd never seen before. It pulled up right in front of the school's main entrance with a man at the wheel. Ashley was cuddled close beside him. I had no idea who he was. Ashley and I were really close during those months, yet she had never mentioned anything about him. So I quietly just kept watching and before I knew it, Ashley moved over closer to this fellow, so close she was practically climbing into his lap. I couldn't believe my eyes. And then it got even more…graphic, I guess you would say. I watched the two of them exchange a long, lingering kiss, on the lips. Then finally, she jumped out of the truck and trotted into the building like she was on cloud nine. Only twelve years old, and exchanging passionate affection with a man old enough to be her father!" Clark suspends her comments and takes a few deep breaths.

Clark's words resonate with Linda, sending a shudder rushing frantically down her spine. She asks Clark, "So, um, what did you do about it?"

"What could I do? Of course I was concerned, but my jurisdiction over the personal lives of students is very limited. When she came into my classroom, I immediately questioned her about the man in the truck. But she seemed so relaxed and she casually described the man as a close family friend and even kind of a substitute father figure with whom she shared a warm, close relationship. I asked her to tell me his name and she said, ever so nonchalantly, 'Ward Weaver.' Later, I did discuss what I had seen with my principal, but she decided that the threshold had not yet been breached that would justify any official intervention. In any event, she suggested I keep a special eye on Ashley and come forward if anything else happened."

"Did anything else get your attention again?"

"Yes, after summer vacation a few months later. Even though she was going on to middle school, I still kept in close touch with her. Anyway, this was September 4, just before school was going to begin for the new term. She was very excited about being a seventh grader. So, on that day we got together and I took her shopping to get some new school clothes. While we were driving around, we had a long talk. Ashley told me that she was afraid of Weaver. When I pushed for an explanation, she told me that a few weeks earlier, Weaver had attempted to rape her. 'Donna, he didn't rape me, but he tried to rape me, and I know the difference,'" Clark says, trying to imitate the fearful tone she was remembering in Ashley's voice.

Linda recalls the Clackamas County prosecution, in which Weaver quashed some allegations by Ashley against him during the last days of August 2001, just a few days before the incident. She clears her throat. "Did you report it?"

"Absolutely. The day after Labor Day I phoned in a complaint to the child welfare agency. I gave them many details to pursue. And I told them this, and this is why I know that the sexual abuse must have been ongoing and it chilled me to the bone. This twelve-year-old child said, 'Usually when I am over there, Ward only lies on top of me. This time he tried to rape me.' The caseworker I was talking to said that she would take all of my information down and be sure to give it to Ashley's caseworker and that it would be carefully followed up. I thought that they would act on it."

Linda writes a few comments. "So what did they find out?"

"I have no idea, because I never heard from them. They never called me at all to follow up, not once. Then I called one more time, January 12, right after the poor child disappeared. I called Detective Garcia of the Oregon City Police[11] who at that time was leading the investigation on Ashley. I told her about the abuse allegations from the previous summer that Ashley had made to me about Weaver and that I had reported it to the child welfare people in September."

Linda is astonished. "And what did she say?"

Clark relives the frustration of her experience. "There was just this silence on the other end of the phone," she says softly. "And then Garcia said, 'I have the complete file in front of me from Ashley's caseworker and there is no record of your ever having filed any report at all.'"[12]

"That's impossible!" Linda exclaims. "You made several reports. What happened to them!"

"I wish I knew," Clark says dejectedly.

"You're not the only one," Linda replies, the frustration in her voice undeniable.

CHAPTER TWELVE

Strange Insights

On a warm afternoon during the second week of June, Linda O'Neal sits quietly in her parked green sedan. The fragrance of blooming lilacs wafts gently through her open window. She taps her knuckles on the steering wheel in time with a song playing on the radio.

A mud-splattered school bus two-thirds full of teenagers rumbles in front of Linda's car, casting a long shadow as it lurches to a stop, brakes screeching. The wafting lilacs give way to diesel stench. The bus door slaps open allowing an exodus of spirited students, clutching bulky backpacks.

Linda scrambles to find a news clipping that she quickly examines before turning to scrutinize the exiting students. Recognizing one, she leaves the car and boldly approaches. "Excuse me," she says to a pert-faced brunette dressed in a plaid tank top and jeans. "Are you Victoria Sampson?"[1]

Most of the students keep moving. One teen stops, looks at Linda for a moment and offers her reply. "Yeah."

"Aren't you friends with Mallori Weaver?"

A couple of the other girls stop when they hear "Weaver," and with increasing curiosity, linger to witness the exchange. Victoria smiles. "Yeah. In fact I'm practically there 24/7."

"Do you know Mal's dad very well?"

"Yeah, Ward is a real cool guy. He buys us pizza and—"

Linda zeroes in. "Us. You mean several of you hang out at the Weaver house at the same time?"

"Sure. It's like a big party there a lot of the time. He rents movies for us. Like last week we saw the coolest…"

Linda prods. "Was Ashley Pond one of the crowd that hung out there?"

"For awhile, but it got pretty bad and she didn't come around any more, because Ashley's mouth got her in trouble with Ward. She said some lies about him that weren't very nice."

Linda pauses for a moment and decides to keep at it. "How about Miranda Gaddis? Was she there too?"

Victoria scrunches her eyebrows forward and shakes her head. "Not much. Her sister was there a lot more. I remember Mal's birthday sleepover. Miranda told one of my friends that Mal's dad had tried to molest Ashley and she shouldn't spend the night cause the same thing could happen to her."

"When was that party?"

"Well, I think it was a week or so after Valentine's Day. In February."

Linda begins to write on her note pad. "Regarding Mal's dad," she says. "Does Ward get mad a lot?"

"Yeah, he yells a lot, but mostly at his oldest son. He's nicer to the girls. He's never yelled at me for anything. Like I said, he's mostly a real cool guy. We all like him a lot."

Victoria's friends intrude. "Come on, we're late."

The teen waves to Linda. "Bye." She rushes away with the others.

■

Starting the engine, Linda's mind drifts to her extended family. As she drives away, she is thinking of her relationship with her stepson. The role of stepmother has evolved radically since Cinderella was first sent to clean the fireplace while the birth children attended the ball. Stepmothers can be maligned and hated or praised and worshiped. This adult role model can influence the development of a young child with long lasting effects. For any woman who seeks to take on the responsibilities of raising her husband's children the role is challenging.

Linda O'Neal knows this from first-hand experience. In 1995, she married Philip Tennyson and took on the responsibility of raising his then seven-year-old son. Now, the boy is a spirited teenager.

Driving through rush hour Portland traffic, she ponders her stepson's request for a new curfew. Suddenly, her cell phone chimes and she answers to find Ashley's stepmother returning her call. Claire Stevens had been Wesley Roettger's common-law wife and was the birth mother of his other children.[2] Linda knew that Stevens's relationship with Ashley had spanned many years and continued even after Ashley's birth father was charged with molesting Ashley. Excited to finally interview Claire, Linda quickly begins with, "So you've known Lori ever since she found out that Wesley was the father of Ashley?"

"They had just introduced Ashley to Wesley."

"How did they figure that out, that Wesley was the father?"

"Uh, process of elimination?"

"Did you know him at the time that Ashley was introduced to him?"

"No. It was a few months after."

"You met him after he was introduced to Ashley. How did Ashley act around him?"

"She acted very happy around us most of the time, but sometimes she would come over and stay and tell us, you know, some things that were kind of bothersome."

"Did you meet Lori Pond through Wesley?"

"Uh-huh. I didn't know her before. In fact, I didn't know any of them before I got involved with Wesley."

"Just a minute." Linda lays her note pad on the dash, pulls a pen from her purse and with the cell phone cradled on her shoulder she frantically attempts to scribble some brief remarks while still keeping the car in a straight line. She resumes the interview. "Are your kids Wesley's?"

"Yeah, but he doesn't get to see them."

"So you don't see him at all?

"I did see him for a short while, as far as like getting money from him and collecting child support and stuff. But it became such a hassle that I cut him off."

"Well, were you shocked about this whole thing about him being charged with molesting Ashley?"

Claire heaves a heavy sigh. "He changed my attitude about men and people in general. I mean, to live with a person for three years and have them doing this! How could I not know? That bothers me. Yes, shocked."

Linda writes a few words, notices the cars in front slowing for a red light and as she brakes, she asks, "Did Ashley talk to you much about her home life?"

"She did for awhile, but I could never make it out because she would say things that kind of didn't make sense to me. She'd talk about her mom yelling and arguing with her. And there was that time in March of last year when somebody at Newell Creek Apartments called the police to report that Ashley had been locked out of the apartment and was walking around the parking lot, crying her eyes out."[3]

"Was she accidentally locked out?"

"No, I think that was one of Lori's weird attempts at discipline. She wanted Ashley to know that it's a rough world outside the safe apartment walls, and by God, if she couldn't follow the rules, she could just stay out. Hell! It happened again in May, and a neighbor called the cops. Those Oregon City cops knew that whole family very well, because they must have gone to Lori's a dozen or more times last year for one thing or another. There were reports and rumors of drunken Friday night parties and loud fights between Lori and different jerks who would hang around her place. Oh, Ashley told me many heartbreaking stories about some of that stuff. One time, I heard that all the girls, plus a cousin, got hauled off to a foster home after Lori had left all the kids overnight with a twelve-year-old babysitter. The rumor was DHS almost yanked those kids for good over that."

"Did she confide in you about Ward Weaver or did you ever see Ward Weaver at the house when you went over to Lori's?"

"No. I just went over there and Ashley would be up at his house. He was never at Lori's."

"Did you know Weaver's girlfriend, Gerri Glass?"

"No, I never met her personally, but I did talk to her on the telephone one day when I was over at Lori's. Gerri wanted to talk to Lori about Ashley, but Lori couldn't deal with it and handed the phone to me. And Gerri gave me an earful. She was so upset. She was crying. I guess Ashley was staying up there a lot and Ward was singling Ashley out from the rest of the family. Mallori and Ashley were bickering. Ward and Gerri were fighting, because Gerri wanted Ashley to go home, but Ward wouldn't hear of it. And she told me when she tried to push it, he'd get physically abusive. And then she said that she was sleeping in the garage or something, and Ashley was sleeping with him, and I was like 'Whooooaah!' I told her it was inappropriate behavior and she needed to put a stop to it. But she was scared, too scared to send Ashley home. And later I talked to Ashley for two solid hours about it. But she insisted he was just being a good father figure in her life. There wasn't any sex stuff going on at all. She promised."

"How did her mother react when this woman was calling her house telling her Ward Weaver was possibly bedding her daughter?"

"That's what I don't know because she just handed me the phone and told me to deal with it. I was a little upset with Lori. You know, I don't always agree with things that Lori does and we definitely parent different. I'm a very strict parent. And she is so lax."

A passing car honks at Linda, its male driver gesturing that she should not be on the phone and driving at the same time. Heeding his concern, she pulls her car into a nearby parking lot in front of an all night convenience store. Then she resumes. "What did Ashley say?"

"She was very defensive of him. She trusted him. Everybody that she relied on, especially men, they just all took advantage of her. I was so angry at the way this poor child's life was."

"Can you remember Ashley being ostracized?"

"Yes! After she accused Weaver some of her schoolmates were shunning her. She was especially being shunned by Ward Weaver and even some of her neighbors! That stuff was seriously out of line. That's the kind of stuff that makes people go and kill themselves."

Linda's cell phone battery dies at this exact instant. "Damn!" Disgusted, she hopes she can pick up the conversation where they left off.

The stepmother slant would soon twist Linda's attention in another unanticipated direction. Linda continues home. As she walks into her office, her phone is ringing.

"Hello?" she says, picking it up.

It's Jayne Patan, one of Ward Weaver's ex-wives and stepmother to his kids. Patan tells Linda she has made repeated attempts to provide what she believes is revealing information to the FBI on the missing girls' case, especially regarding Ward Weaver's possible connections. The official investigators have seemingly ignored her suspicions. Fed up that the FBI did not view her as a credible source of information, Patan has desperately turned to Linda, hopeful that what she has to say will make a difference.

"I've thought a lot about what you told me," Jayne says softly, "and I want to help you get the truth out."

Linda sympathizes with her. "You've been through a lot. I can tell. But here's what I need to know to get something going. Do you remember a sleepover party at Ward's house? It was Mallori's birthday, I think."

Patan is silent for a moment, then she says, "Yeah, it was about the last week in February. Let's see, her birthday is February 17, so somewhere around then. It was a Saturday. And there were six or eight little girls there, including Miranda Gaddis and her sister. They stayed all night. I was there for a couple hours. Ward's other ex-wife was there too. I remember that we had to go get some ice cream, because Ward lost the key to his freezer. Anyway everybody had a few drinks."

"Even some of the kids?"

"I'm sure a few of 'em did. It wouldn't be the first time. Ward always keeps his house well-stocked."

"Did anything happen that night to upset Ward?"

"Oh, I could see he was mad all right, but he was holding it together until the kids finally settled in for the night. Ward is funny that way. When something doesn't go to his liking, Ward always looks for some way to increase his odds. When I finally left about 11:00 PM, he even followed me out to my car ranting and raving about Miranda. He was pissed off about something she supposedly told another girl. He was so angry then."

"Did you and Ward have any kids together?"

Patan laughs shyly. "No, we never did have any together, thank God, but he had plenty of 'em—four, from his first marriage. I raised them as if they were my own, in fact I still see 'em regularly and I still call 'em 'my kids.'"

"Tell me about them."

"Well Francis, the oldest is nineteen now. The next is seventeen. Then, the youngest is fifteen. And finally, there is one girl, the baby, Mallori who's just thirteen. Those kids have been through so much. I feel so bad for them and I love each of them dearly."

"Has your ex-husband ever hurt you or those kids?"

"Oh, yeah," she mutters sadly. "One hot night in July of 1995[4], Ward and I had been arguing. I'd finally had enough of the arguing and was drifting off to sleep on the living room floor, wrapped up in a blanket.[5] And then whack! I thought something had fell off the TV and hit me. I never dreamed it could be something else. But it was the second whack of the twelve-inch cast iron skillet that really woke me up."

Linda is incredulous. "He smacked your head with a frying pan?"

"Absolutely, and more than once. I threw my hands up over my head to protect myself and he just kept on hitting me. And it was not like little taps, it was full-blown blows to the head. He kept hitting me. I was crying and screaming for him to stop. I thought I was going to die. When he finally quit hitting me, Ward said, 'You're lucky. I was looking for a butcher knife when I picked up this pan.'"

Linda tries to absorb the gruesome story and finally asks another question. "Did you take off from the house at that point?"

"I sure did. I went straight to the cops.[6] They locked him up and I went to live with my sister in California."

"Hold on a minute," Linda says. "Didn't you say this happened in 1995? I thought you married Weaver in '96. You don't mean to tell me that after he almost killed you, you turned around and married the guy."

"Oh Linda, you don't know the hold he has on people and the things he can do to manipulate you. When Ward got out of jail, he found out that I was in California and somehow got my sister's phone number. Then he called me up, told me to drop the assault charges, come back to Portland and become his wife. I told him he must be on drugs or something to think I would even consider getting back with him after what he'd done. Then he made me an offer I couldn't refuse. He said I had exactly one week to come back, drop the charges and marry him, or he would kill my grandmother. He told me, 'You know that I know where she lives.'"

Linda is aghast. "What an evil man!"

Jayne Patan continues. "Ward's violence problems go so far back. Tammy Weaver, his younger sister, was probably the first one to get it bad.[7] To this day she hates his guts. She once told me some stuff that I found hard to believe then, but not hard at all, now. Did you know that the main reason Ward joined the Navy had to do with what he did to his baby sister. The story goes that the judge gave him a choice, jail or the service. Naturally, he chose the service. A lot of good it all did, because they kicked him out of the Navy for staying AWOL all the time over in the Philippines. Ward spent years in prison for an assault before I even met him."

Linda says, prodding, "Yes, I believe it happened back in 1986 in California, but I haven't been able to dig up specific details."

Jayne confides, "Well, Ward tells that story making it about a bad babysitter who was hurting his kids and he was only protecting them." She laughs. "But the truth is a lot different. Kathryn Diaz knows the real story. Ward smashed a teenaged girl upside the head with a twelve-pound block of concrete,[8] and she wasn't his babysitter, and in fact she hadn't done a thing to him. You asked me before if I thought Ward had it in him to kidnap the girls. I don't think there is anything that he wouldn't do to get his own way in any situation."

■

The next day Linda is at home, taking a break from the investigation to let her mind roam on what she's found out as she putters around her potted pansies on the back deck. Taking a few minutes to relax, she sits in the chaise lounge reading *The Oregonian* and for no good reason turns to the classifieds where she makes an interesting discovery. There is going to be a yard sale at Ward Weaver's address. *"Is he really inviting the general public to come on in and tromp around?"* she wonders. *"You know I may just have to go see if they have any good spatulas that would go with my collection."*

Allison walks out of Linda's office and stoops over to smell the pansies. "They look really nice, Linda."

Linda smiles.

Allison says, "I just got off the phone with the Fairfield, California records clerk. And she found that assault you were curious about, but this will blow your mind. There is no record of Weaver smacking the teenaged girl with the concrete block."

"Damn. You'd think it would have been retrievable."

"Listen though, there was an assault conviction in 1986, and the victim's name was Erin Stone, definitely not a teenager.[9] She told me it was the second time today that someone had requested that bit of information. It struck her as very odd."

"Did she tell you who the other party was?"

"An Oregon City policewoman, a Detective Garcia."

"I'm glad she is looking into Weaver's past. This isn't a race between the police and us. There are good people working on the official investigation; we're just adding a new perspective." Linda looks at her intern for a long moment before she asks, "How would you like to go to a yard sale with me on Saturday?"

Knowing Linda's mind, Allison says, "It must have something to do with the case."

"You bet! It's at Ward Weaver's house."

Saturday morning the sun is shining and the birds are singing. Linda pulls her car into the driveway of Weaver's house and parks directly in front of a well-organized display of used merchandise. The advertised yard sale has been arranged around several card tables covered with various household items, clothes, children's toys, stacks of car parts, tires and scuffed up sports equipment. Several halter-topped barely teenage girls circulate among the merchandise, arranging items and attaching price stickers. To Linda the scene resembles one of those carwash movies.

Mr. Weaver supervises and is in charge of car parts and the muffin-pan cash register. This is Linda's first view of Weaver in person. He seems larger than she had imagined and is doing a fine job of entertaining his bevy of teenage co-stars. When he finally takes notice of Linda and Allison, he smiles and offers a greeting. "See anything that you absolutely can't do without, ladies?"

This is Linda's first opportunity to have a one-on-one with the man that keeps showing up in the center of her Ashley Pond investigation. She gingerly steps toward the burly man and picks up a blue dinner plate. "Do you have a whole set of these?"

Weaver shakes his head. "I'm sorry, most of that set got broken." He laughs. "That's what you get when you have lots of kids."

Allison goes over to a table of clothes and shoes and starts rummaging through them. A woman with a couple of small children is looking over the same merchandise.

Linda continues, "I don't see any large appliances out here."

"No, I had a stove for sale, but some guy bought it first thing. I do have a hot tub I'm thinking of getting rid of. Hell! I may still put it up, but I'd probably sell the tub if the right offer came my way." He laughs again.

She's actually got Weaver engaged. How to keep the conversation going? If Weaver wants to peddle the hot tub, why not show some interest? She says enthusiastically, "It's so lucky that you've got one to sell, because my husband and I have been looking at new ones to put on our new deck. But they want five or six thousand for anything decent."

"I'd let mine go for a thousand, including a brand new cover."

"Would you show it to me?"

"Oh, I don't know. I-I'm not quite ready to sell it just yet. In fact, to be honest, I've never set it up. So it seems premature to just get rid of it."

"Come on, you said a minute ago you'd like to sell it. At least let me take a look at it. I've been shopping for a hot tub for two months now. If I see it I'll know right away if it would work for me. What do you say?"

"What the hell! Okay." Weaver leads Linda around the side of the house to the back. Her footsteps traverse the cement slab that Jayne Patan had told her about. The hot tub assembly is stacked sideways, leaning against the back of the house. Several sections of wood skirting are stacked neatly nearby. Examining, she struggles to say something that will keep him interested but not rope her into buying a tub she doesn't need. "You know, maybe you really ought to set it up. I can't tell if my husband would like it when it's in pieces."

His temper flares for a moment. "Lady, isn't that what I tried to tell you before you had me drag you all the way back here? What a waste of time."

One of the teenagers approaches Weaver, "Ward, Francis is here and he wants to know where you want him to put those boxes of video games he's selling."

Weaver calms and turns to Linda. "Thanks anyway for looking." Weaver and the girl disappear around the corner leaving Linda alone near the slab. She lingers and stares at the concrete. She walks beside it slowly, wondering.

Linda is still deep in thought when she reaches the front of the house. She is distracted by a young man who looks a little like Ward who is unloading boxes from the trunk of an older car with the help of a blonde teenaged girl. She concludes he must be Weaver's oldest son. But who is the girl? Linda speculates. His sister? No, not his sister, girlfriend, maybe. An insistent Allison joins Linda.

"What kind of shoes was Ashley wearing when she went missing?"

"Skechers I think, why?"

"A woman just bought a pair of Skechers at the yard sale. If we hurry we might be able to catch up to her. She's on foot. They crossed the street and headed for the ice cream store."

Hurriedly, Linda and Allison get in the car and back out the driveway. The two sleuths hurry to the parking lot at the next intersection but the woman and her new Skechers have disappeared.

■

During the rest of the weekend Linda plans her next move. She goes over her notes and finds the ones on Kathryn Diaz which, as she reads them over, still leave questions open.

Linda's first meeting with Kathryn had been cut so short by the rude intrusion of her uptight husband. Perhaps she should try again. As mother to four of Weaver's children, having lived through so many chaotic events with him, Diaz could be a gold mine of information if Linda could somehow find a way to get her to talk. She thinks about how to get to Kathryn and decides on the direct approach. Linda picks up the phone. When Kathryn answers, Linda asks, "Can I buy you a cup of coffee and finish our chat from the other day?"

Kathryn laughs and says that she would much rather have a drink with her. She agrees to meet Linda at a bar in her neighborhood at two o'clock the next day.

On that afternoon, Linda arrives at 1:45 PM to get a table before her subject shows up, but Kathryn is already there. Without saying a word, she takes Linda by the arm and walks her out the back door. Once in the alley, Kathryn whispers, "We have to go to the store to get something to drink and then we will go to laundromat."

Linda asks, "What's all the cloak and dagger stuff for?"

Kathryn replies with another whisper, "My husband does not want me to talk to you and I am afraid that he might recognize your car." She continues. "He won't set foot in the laundry unless he thinks I am up to something, so we will leave your car here. That way if he sees your car at the bar he'll go in, not find either one of us, and think he was wrong."

"Does he allow you to talk to people in general? I mean is it just me that he doesn't like?" Linda inquires as Kathryn leads her stealthily away.

Kathryn does not say another word until Linda pays for the six-pack of malt liquor purchased from the convenience store two doors down from the nearby laundromat. Then the pair enters the run-down laundromat and Kathryn points to a table surrounded by a few chairs. Linda wipes some lint off one of the chairs and sits down while Kathryn takes a cart and unloads clothes out of a dryer.

Soon Kathryn returns to the table and says, "Help me fold clothes while we talk." She moves the clothes from the cart and piles them into a heap. Afterward, Kathryn opens two of the malt liquor bottles, gives one to Linda and then sits down taking a large swig. "So, what did you want to talk about?"

Not wanting to appear rude, Linda takes a sip from the bottle and begins sorting socks from the pile on the table. "Do you remember a sleepover at Ward's house for Mallori's birthday?"

"Oh yeah, quite a party, that one."[10] Kathryn squeezes the reply between the two gulps that finish off her bottle. "Why do you want to know 'bout that?"

Linda searches in vain for the second red sock to match the one in her hand. "Oh, I was just wondering if you knew the girls at the sleepover." Linda pulls another bottle out of the six-pack and pries the top off before handing it to Diaz.

Kathryn hands over the red sock that Linda had been searching for, takes the drink, raising it in thanks. "Sure, I knew most of them. I am over at Ward's a lot."

Linda continues sorting socks and then looks up. "Your husband doesn't mind you going to your ex-husband's house?"

"As I said, he doesn't want me talking to anybody unless there is something in it for him."

Linda leans toward Kathryn, "Did anything happen at that party for Mallori that was out of the ordinary? You know, anybody get in a fight or anything like that?"

"No, no fights that I remember. Ward was pissed off at one of the girls there about something, but then Ward was always angry about something or other." Kathryn folds a pair of jeans and a T-shirt and by accident knocks some socks on the floor.

Linda scoops them up and lays them gently on the table before she begins folding more clothes. A short silence ensues while she decides what else she needs Kathryn to flesh out. She decides to ask about the relationship itself. "How did you and Ward get together in the first place?"

Kathryn lights a cigarette and inhales deeply. "I was a cocktail waitress in the Phillipines. Ward was a sailor. He seemed like a nice boy and pestered the crap out of me every time I was on a shift. Before long he asked me to marry him." She takes another long drag on the cigarette. "I said yes."

Linda quits folding clothes and starts taking notes. "Where did you live when you got married?"

Kathryn folds another T-shirt before answering. "We lived at Ward's mother's house.[11] They didn't get along so well, so after a while we went to California."

"Did Ward ever visit his father when you were in California?"

"Yes, he went to see his father in jail about the time of his father's trial. That was very strange to me because Ward had always said he'd not seen his father since he was three years old." Kathryn quits folding clothes for a moment as a couple of teenage boys carouse through the large room, knocking over garbage cans and riding the wheeled laundry carts. Their shenanigans disrupt the laundry chores of several women who respond by shaking fists and scolding. When the boys eventually leave, Kathryn continues. "A funny thing about Ward going to see his father—he was never the same after that. When I asked him about the visit, all he would say was he caught up on a lot of lost time."

"'He was never the same, how do you mean?'"

Kathryn stares at the floor for a moment. She shakes her head slowly. "I will tell you one thing about Ward Weaver that will help you figure him out, Linda. He was violent, very violent, but never so violent as he was after that prison visit. I can't explain why exactly, but I can show you the marks." As a tear moves down her cheek, Kathryn slowly pulls her shirt over one shoulder revealing ancient cigarette burn scars lining the indentation made by her shoulder blade. "I can't tell you how many times for no reason at all he would just flip out and slam me and the kids around. I finally couldn't take it no more. I left him in 1993. I even had to get a restraining order. I got away and if I hadn't, I might be dead by now."[12]

"But you still have a relationship with him."

"Only for the sake of the kids. The boys mostly hate him anyway. But Mal and he are very, very close."

Linda jots a few words onto her note pad before asking, "How long were you in California with him?"

"We moved to Canby, Oregon, soon after he got out of prison. It was 1988. Mallori was born about a year after we came here."

Linda reacts with mock surprise. "Why was he in prison?"

Kathryn grimaces. "I told you he was violent. Violence took him down big time. We were living in Fairfield. We had two little boys and I was pregnant. Anyway, Ward and me, we were fighting all the time then." She closes her eyes to firm up a recollection. "It was June, 1986.[13] Ward had drunk six beers, six screwdrivers and four shots of whiskey." She counts on her fingers then resumes. "Then he snorted a gram of meth and smoked a quarter ounce of pot. All this before he went to the bowling alley."

Linda nods. "Sounds like he was pretty wired."

"You got that right! So Ward spent some time in there and it was late at night, around 11:30. Now, maybe, he knew he was way too messed up to get home on his own, maybe not, but for some reason he called our landlord and their daughter came to pick him up in the minivan.

"The teenage daughter, very sweet girl. Our boys got along real well with her. She had just gotten her license and I think she felt proud to be sent out, you know, like she was being treated like a real adult. Her sister was a year younger, but she went along, and I think for good reason. They both knew how wild Ward could be when he was that screwed up. When they got to the bowling alley it was midnight. Ward tried to buy them a beer, but they told him no. Then he told them to wait in the parking lot while he smoked some more weed. After that, he got in the back and told the girls to drive to a bar. But then he had to urinate real bad, so he made them pull over into a parking lot. He got out to relieve himself, but instead of doing it, he picked up a concrete block that was sitting there and carried it back to the minivan and hit the younger sister in the head with it. Then he grabbed the older one and tried to choke her. He tried to hold onto her, but he was so wobbly from all the drugs and booze, they were able to get away from him. They ran a quarter mile up the street to the bus station and called the cops. By the time the cops got there he was long gone."

Linda is scribbling notes furiously. She looks up. "Is that incident the one that put him in prison?"

Kathryn smiles wistfully. "Well, that was certainly part of it. See, the very next day, Ward evidently broke into some woman's house and she woke up when he put his hand over her mouth. She starts fighting him off and he starts choking her.[14] Somehow, she managed to get away from him and call the cops. This time they got him." Kathryn reaches for another beer, which Linda hands her.

"How much time did he get when they convicted him?"

"That's another funny thing. Ward was already on probation from the time he beat me up." Kathryn's eyes tear as she begins recounting the attack. "He grabbed me by my hair! He kept hitting my head against the side of the dresser. Then he slammed it into the side of the headboard, and kept banging, banging, banging back and forth, over and over! I was almost unconscious. Then he started smacking my face with his fist. He's a crazy man! I don't know how many times he hit me, but I remember falling to the floor. I must have passed out. So anyway, the judge put him on three years probation for that, and he was still on that probation when all this other stuff happened." Kathryn shakes her head. "He tried to get off with more probation, but the judge wasn't in any mood for that. He was mad as hell and gave Ward three years, but Ward found a way to get out early anyway. In January of '88, we all moved to Canby and then started our gift shop. But that's another story, it didn't even last one year—just more bullshit that never turned out good. Then the state took all our kids away. They said we weren't fit to be raising children."

Linda begins to feel sympathy for the tortured figure beside her in the bustling laundromat. She studies Kathryn's face and recognizes the telltale signs that prompt her next question. "Kathryn were drugs a part of all these problems?"

"By then, Ward was heavy in to dealing meth,"[15] she said grimacing.[16] "But anyway, somebody turned Ward into the cops, not for meth, but for thumping too hard on the boys.[17] Now here's where

Ward shines the most. He can snap his fingers and change personalities sometimes like you or me would change clothes. Somehow, he did some wheeling and dealing and in no time we got the kids back, just like that." Linda then puts a hand on Kathryn's shoulder, leans closer and with a gentle smile asks, "So, with all of this stuff that went on, when did you finally leave this jerk?"

"Ward's rules kept getting stricter and stricter. And the punishments for breaking those rules kept getting worse. I thought sooner or later he was going to end up killing me or my sons, especially Francis."

"What kind of rules?"

"First, I could never even leave the house unchaperoned. Then it got to the point where I couldn't even leave the house at all. I'd have to give him a list of things I needed from the store and he'd get them if he thought I needed them. The last straw came when I couldn't never have anybody over to the house, man or woman! If he came home and found anybody at his house it was a beating for me for sure. And then he'd make damn sure that they knew that I was going to get a beating courtesy of them. That was to make sure the person didn't come back again." She pauses a moment to reflect. "In the fall of 1992, I got another restraining order to keep him away and the divorce was final in '93. But hell! We have four kids together. I will always be tangled up in his life."

At this moment a stout Hispanic woman angrily slams an empty dryer door, shouts in Spanish and approaches Linda and Kathryn sitting directly in front of the stack of laundry they had neatly folded during their long conversation. Linda is startled. "Why is she yelling at us?"

Kathryn translates the Spanish outburst into English.

"She's mad about you messing around with her dried clothes."

"Her clothes? I thought these were your clothes!"

Kathryn smiles slyly. "Nope, I just needed to keep clothes in front of us, in case my husband came in. I'd get too nervous otherwise."

CHAPTER THIRTEEN

Barbecues and Revelations

Sunday, June 23, a barbecue is unfolding at Linda and Philip's home to celebrate Father's Day. Four of the Tennyson/O'Neal children are in attendance as well as several friends and associates.

On the spacious backyard deck a propane barbecue grill sends delicious puffs of hamburger-flavored smoke upward. Linda's husband Philip hovers nearby, covered chest to knees by an apron adorned with huge red letters, "Kiss the Cook!" He tends smoldering meat patties, squeezing out drips of sauce onto each from a yellow plastic bottle.

Carrying a bowl of potato salad, Linda O'Neal enters through the sliding door with Allison following close behind dangling a grocery bag overflowing with burger buns. Linda dispatches her assistant to deposit the buns at the grill as she puts the potato salad on a nearby table already stacked with other dishes.

At the left end of the deck a group of adults mill about chatting. Looking up, Linda notices Oliver Jamison among the guests and gently pulls him aside. "I'm so glad you could make it. Can I talk to you?" she asks softly as she points to the backyard.

Oliver follows her until they are alone behind a wide fir tree. Linda resumes. "Ollie, you know I rely on your opinion. I've got a very important question to ask you. I really need a solid answer."

"And you know I'm here for you," he says. "What do you want to know?"

"On the morning that Ashley disappeared, did Dave Roberts personally see her when he was getting ready for work?"

Oliver shakes his head. "Nope. He didn't. Because he left for work about the same time her sister was leaving to catch her bus." He pauses to reflect. "That was about quarter after seven."

"So how can you be sure that Ashley was even there that morning if he didn't see her?"

"Well I guess they just assumed she was there. Had no reason to think she wasn't. I mean she was usually there, and she always liked to sleep in as long as possible. According to the reports I've studied, sometimes she'd still be sleeping at eight o'clock and her bus comes at eight-fifteen. She was late many times. So that particular morning, Roberts didn't think anything about whether she was there or not, but he's pretty sure she was there."

"Okay, thanks. By the way, I've got your check."

Ollie grins. "That gives me an extra reason to be glad to be here!"

Linda smiles, "There's also another reason for this gathering beyond Philip's special day."

"Why am I not surprised?"

Linda laughs, "After everybody has something to eat, I'm going to gather them all up and give a briefing."

For two more hours the party continues as participants meander about, eating their burgers and entertaining each other. Linda and Philip sit together. "I think it's about time for the hearing," she says.

Philip grins and jumps up. He bangs a spoon against the side of a glass, capturing the crowd's attention before loudly proclaiming, "Linda's grand jury will assemble on the left side of the deck in five minutes. Bring your chairs and face this way. All are required to attend." There is a serious look on his face.

In anticipation of her coming graphic presentation, Linda escorts the few children in attendance inside the house to watch a Disney video.

Linda stands in front of the barbecue, opens her briefcase and pulls out a thick file of documents. She proclaims, "We have reached a point in our investigation of Ashley's disappearance, that, if we were the prosecutor, we would be going to the grand jury to gain authority to proceed. Since I'm working on behalf of this family, I need you, family and friends alike, to act as my grand jury. I want you to weigh the case as I present it to you and then, if you believe my case is strong enough, I need you to instruct me, 'charge me,' is the term they use in court."

Family and friends, many feeling agonized by the long—so far fruitless—search are anxiously fixed on Linda and her firm words. She continues. "There are a few loose ends that I need to tighten up before I can fully reveal my conclusions. One of those loose ends has to do with the morning that Ashley disappeared, the morning of January 9. The FBI task force is acting under the assumption that Ashley disappeared on her way to school. The whole case has been officially and unofficially investigated with that premise at the forefront. Unfortunately, I feel that story conflicts with the 9-1-1 tape when Lori called police to tell them Ashley was missing. There have been some inconsistencies that have come to light between that story and the story that Lori told the police later on. So before I can continue, I first need to get at the unvarnished truth."

Linda clenches her jaw and then, "First, I need to find out some things that only Lori can fully explain. Now, I know that she's been consistently repeating the story that on the morning in question she woke up when Ashley got up.[1] Ashley thought she was late for the school bus, but it was seven o'clock and she wasn't late yet, and Lori told her she wasn't late and she went back to bed. Lori went back to sleep. She doesn't really know exactly when Ashley left. Have I got it correct?"

Philip's daughter, Maria, is briefly astonished but quickly responds.

"Yes, because that's how it happened. It's as simple as that."

Linda takes a few steps toward Maria then bends over and lowers her voice. "I have a couple of questions here that are bothering me because of that 9-1-1 call. Now Lori said she remembered Ashley getting up and telling her that she thought that she was late. But then Lori asks her other daughter if she'd seen Ashley that morning, and on the tape the little girl says that she hadn't seen Ashley. Now this whole issue is bothering me because something just doesn't add up. If Ashley had gotten up at seven o'clock, somebody in that house should have made contact with her. Lori had one daughter up and getting ready for school and her boyfriend Dave up and getting ready to go to work."

Linda shakes her head. "Now somebody should have seen Ashley, yet nobody saw her. So I guess what I'm asking about is how accurate a recollection did Lori really give. For example, can she be sure that the incident she is remembering in fact happened on the morning Ashley disappeared? Can she be sure, since most mornings were pretty identical, it didn't maybe happen another morning and she accidentally blended the two memories together somehow? You know a mind is a crazy instrument sometimes. We can get our minds to dredge up exactly what we want to remember sometimes to the exclusion of other details. I just need to know, did Lori really talk to Ashley the morning of January 9, or was this perhaps some foggy recollection that she had later when she was trying so hard to remember the specifics, all the little details of what happened?"

Maria stands up and calls out. "I don't understand. What difference does it make? I mean, Ashley got up. She got ready. She went to the school bus, and before she got there, she disappeared."

"I'm asking you to consider another possibility. Please. This is not an attack on Lori, but we must dig for absolute truth! If we're going to find out what really happened to Ashley...If things get left out—if chunks of vital information are somehow censored from our consideration, no matter how well intentioned they may have been, or how insignificant they may seem, it makes the whole investigation almost pointless since it was based on mistruths. With that in mind, I have concluded that it is possible that, if Lori didn't positively see

Ashley the morning she disappeared, then she could have been gone for eighteen hours or twenty hours when Lori made her call to 9-1-1. It's possible that she could have slipped out of the house or been abducted the night before, after Lori and her boyfriend thought she'd gone to bed." Linda looks at Maria, "Did she ever slip out?"

Maria smiles nervously. "Sure she did, a few times but…"

"Don't you see? If you've eliminated that first ten or twelve hours that she was missing, then you've eliminated the possibility of the truth of what happened ever surfacing"

By now, the others are listening intently, all heads are turned toward Maria and Linda.

Maria is adamant. "Lori didn't mix up her memories. What's this all got to do with anything, anyway?"

Linda resumes. "You've got to understand everyone's roles here. Lori's the tragic mother of the victim. With the exception of Ginger, Ollie and Allison, the rest of you have known Ashley most of her life. You all love Ashley. You all miss her tremendously. But I have been commissioned to direct our journey, no matter where it takes us to find the truth. And when one seeks the truth, sometimes, one has to crawl through some disgusting trails and look in very uncomfortable places. But sometimes, my detective work taught me well, that the truth often is found."

Linda returns to her spot in front of the barbecue and her voice takes on a steel edge. "Now I'm going to ask you to join me in seeking the answers we need if we're to find out what happened to Ashley. You will be the grand jury. So, everybody, listen carefully to the facts as I present them. Then you must collectively decide if I should take my findings to the FBI. Every fact that I present to you has been confirmed by a second, and at times, a third witness."

Ginger calls out, "I just talked to the FBI yesterday afternoon, and they told me there's still no suspects."

Linda lifts up her manila folder. "The FBI maybe didn't get this one right. I think I did. Hear me out and then decide. Now, first of all, let's examine Ashley's position at the time of her disappearance as most described her. What I see as a pivotal plank in this case is the fact that Ashley spent so much of her time in the spring of 2001 at the Weaver house."

Oliver Jamison stands near the back with some others. "Why do you think that?" he asks.

"Because obviously at that time in her life she must have felt very comfortable there. She felt that she had finally found the family life that she'd always coveted but rarely experienced."

Maria shakes her head. "Lori had lots of positive stuff in her own family. Ashley didn't have to go over there looking for it."

"Nevertheless, in Ward Weaver, she finally had found what she at first felt was a decent, caring father figure who could fill those voids. Ashley gravitated to Weaver and his household because it felt good."

Linda trains her eyes on Maria who is becoming increasingly uncomfortable. "It's not criticism of your sister," she says. "But Weaver could offer Ashley elements for her life that, at the time, Lori couldn't compete with. When Ashley was over there, this father gave her the type of attention that most girls, especially those from dysfunctional backgrounds, only fantasize about. But for Ashley it was genuine. He was always happy to see her. He took her places. He doted on her. He talked to her. He listened to her. He gave her advice. Ward Weaver, for a while, became the only best friend Ashley had. She naturally gravitated toward him. Who wouldn't? Everything was peach perfect for quite a while. Now, naturally things must have deteriorated for Ashley and, of course, they did. Some of us, to this end, have spent months talking to many witnesses in order to piece together a solution to the puzzle.

"Whether you accept my conclusions about Weaver and he becomes a suspect or not, knowing his connections to Ashley is essential for a full understanding of this case. Perhaps, at first, Weaver's friendship with Ashley was harmless. Being especially nice to a fatherless female child when you cross paths with one is admirable. Getting your special attention means a lot to them, and when you give of yourselves to them, you feel great. A good deed feeling." She takes a breath. "But Ashley and Weaver each developed a strong emotional bond with the other."

A few in her audience scoff. One man says, "I can't listen to this crap much longer."

But Linda is not going to be deterred. She feels that the theory she's formulated and is now revealing gets at the truth, no matter how hard it is for them all to hear. "Ward Weaver spent many months courting Ashley, some would probably call it 'grooming Ashley'. She was riding high for a while and enjoying whatever was going on. This was happening to the dismay and displeasure of Weaver's own daughter. Mallori eventually was forced into a rivalry with Ashley for her own daddy's affection. And eventually the same thing happened with Weaver's adult housemate, Gerri Glass.[2] Ashley soon became her rival for Weaver's favor. It's most bizarre, but that's what happened."[3]

Allison raises a hand.

"Yes?"

"What about Ashley's birth father?"

"Wes Roettger got convicted of one count of child molestation. Thirty-nine counts evaporated. As Ashley's closest friend and confidant at the time, Weaver probably heard every gory detail about her father's violations, directly from her lips.

"Weaver had been the one to drive Ashley and Lori to the prosecutor's office a few times during the early fact-finding phase of the case against Roettger! He even took them once to an appointment to talk to the medical experts. So my point: Ward Weaver had become overly involved and immersed in young Ashley's life. It was a red flag waving that, at the time, nobody seemed to notice."

Maria tosses a question to Linda. "You make everything sound like it was so hunky-dory. Well, when did things change between them?"

"I think it was after she went on the Weaver family vacation to California in the summer of 2001. Ward slyly arranged to take Ashley along on a week long car trip and nobody thought a thing about it."

A defensive Maria shouts a reaction. "We had a family meeting and we all agreed she could go, because Gerri and her daughter and Mallori were all going along. Everybody agreed it was okay."

Most of the audience members briefly look at the floor, some of them uncomfortable, feeling they had been named conspirators in approving an event that Linda was revealing as having ended with dire consequences.

Linda resumes. "I believe the vacation trip is the turning point. Because up to that time I do not think Ward had approached Ashley for sexual intercourse. That's not to say he hadn't exercised many other avenues of inappropriate exchanges of affection. He was seen kissing her passionately one day when he dropped her off at grade school. I've talked to witnesses that even described him sleeping in the same bed with Ashley.

"What happened I think was a, well, I call it a Lolita-like obsession. He flipped for Ashley like a lovesick teenaged boy. He was content in the early months to just possess her heart and soul in every way possible except sexually.

"After that trip, everything was set for him to spring his plan for sexual conquest. He must have been practically salivating, constantly seeking out the perfect occasion. I can't say exactly when and where it happened, but in one moment everything changed between them. Because when he made his move he got the surprise of his life. She didn't want him and wasn't going to cooperate with his little set-up. "

Allison interjects. "So you think Weaver raped Ashley after the vacation trip, then?"

"No, not rape in the traditional sense. Normally when we think of rape, we think of a brutal male who violently accosts an unsuspecting female and forces himself on her sexually. These crimes are mostly crimes of violence. Now don't get me wrong, Weaver had a much documented history of criminal violence, especially against young female victims. In California, as I've found out, he once smashed a sixteen-year-old in the face with a concrete block and served prison time for assaulting another woman the same day. But he actually backed off when Ashley forcefully declined his advance. He was most definitely humiliated and I can bet this total rejection in the face of several months of grooming must have enraged him.

"When Ashley told her teacher about Ward's actions, she was careful in her own characterization. She told me Ashley said, 'He didn't rape me, he tried to rape me, and I know the difference.'

"So in my opinion, we have Ward Weaver who didn't force himself on Ashley all those months they were together. He didn't have to. She idolized him. Ashley expressed much love back to Weaver for a long time. Now part of that was just her naive reaction, the typical reactions of any troubled, fatherless child in her age group."

Oliver waves his hand for Linda's attention.

"Yes?"

"So why wouldn't Weaver rape Ashley if he wanted to have sex and she didn't?"

"There are three possible reasons why a two-hundred-pound man only attempted to rape a one-hundred-twelve-pound girl and did not succeed. The first possibility, she outran him. But that doesn't make a lot of sense here, because she came and stayed at his home after the incident. So she probably didn't take flight. The second reason, he was interrupted. Maybe somebody came in or came by and he had to back off. Maybe. And the third possible reason, he all of a sudden became impotent. Maybe the drastic shock of being unexpectedly spurned pulled his carnal plug, and if that's true, what an irony! Remember, he wanted her to be willingly involved. He could have killed her and he certainly could have forcefully raped her, but he held off, at least then."

Maria approaches Linda and says, "Ashley is a very strong-willed kid. I'm sure she had the power to say no to any sex with Weaver."

"I agree, Maria. But from Weaver's demented viewpoint, think what it must have done to his ego. I mean, as a man so used to always having full control of underlings, always calling every shot. He was temporarily pulverized. He was defeated so abruptly. A mere child beat him at his own game. And when she told on him, he was forced to face some uncomfortable realities. In my opinion, anger began to percolate, because very soon he became the mastermind behind a series of nasty retaliatory actions. His revenge tactics border on the diabolical."

Someone asks, "What the hell did the son of a bitch do?"

"First, he hit where he could do the most damage with the least effort. It was easy for him to contact Ashley's father's attorney and sabotage the criminal case. He simply informed them he had 'evidence' that proved Ashley had made sex abuse accusations against several other men, including him. She was obviously a very disturbed child and possessed no credibility. When the attorney confronted the district attorney with Weaver's revelations, thirty-nine counts were dropped and Roettger, who had spent nine months in custody awaiting trial, was immediately released. And it all came down that way, I believe, because of Weaver's anger taken out against Ashley."

Ginger slams her fist onto a coffee table. "That asshole! And he didn't stop there, did he?"

"He was just getting warmed up. I'm telling you, Weaver is a guy you don't want for an enemy. Next, using his daughter Mallori as a proxy, he cleverly orchestrated a shunning of Ashley by most of her schoolmates and other friends in her circle. The most important thing in the world for a seventh-grader is to be popular with her peers and Weaver was powerful enough to manipulate them against her because his house was a Mecca for seventh-grade girls. She was taunted, bullied, totally ostracized. It took a huge toll on this weary kid. Ashley had just not been equipped by her chaotic life experiences for this level of intense conflict, but she nevertheless maintained her allegations against Weaver. She told her few remaining friends and teachers that Weaver had attempted to rape her. She also stayed completely away from Weaver for a few months. Those were the loneliest and most depressing months of her life. Eventually, the pressure by her peers took its toll. She cracked and soon was recanting her previous allegations. Not so surprisingly, once Weaver became convinced that Ashley had learned her lesson, he instituted a new courtship, this time more covert, discreet. And this time she was easy prey. She'd slip out at night to secretly rendezvous with Weaver, usually in his car. They'd spend hours some nights driving around, parking and talking. He was starting from scratch, rebuilding the relationship, rekindling the trust—the love."

Maria is shocked. "When are you saying this all happened, this getting back with Weaver?"

"I believe Ashley secretly returned to Weaver's fold by early December. How triumphantly he must have welcomed her back into his life! Now this was so intense that it triggered his girlfriend to move out by Christmas Day. She flat couldn't put up with it for one more day and she split, leaving Weaver living alone with daughter, Mallori. He was seeing Ashley secretly as much as possible, with her sworn to secrecy about the whole affair. It was perfect for him."

Maria becomes bitterly angry and shouts a denial. "No, it's not true!" she cries. "She was not sneaking out then. She was with us at our house over Christmas."

"He wanted to experience a conquest. He wanted Ashley to come to him willingly. It certainly raised the degree of difficulty for his challenge, but his ultimate reward likewise would be amplified, if he succeeded.

"So after a few weeks of intensive grooming and courting, he set up a situation where he tried a second time for a full consummation of their relationship, but just like she had after their California trip, stubborn, brave little Ashley wouldn't cooperate. She was very, very strong to reject him, because the easier path would have been to simply submit to get it over with. But this time Weaver was prepared to react with anger. Remember, the first time she rejected his advances he was shocked. He couldn't believe that this would happen. This time his anger turned to rage. And I believe that he killed Ashley as a result of his anger. The man has a long history of experiencing black-out rages. I think that Ashley's rejecting his advances for a second time triggered what can only be characterized as a homicidal rage."

Ginger makes a sobering statement. "As much as we've all hoped against hope we'd find Ashley, I have to admit what you say happened to her makes sense. But all of what you said so far doesn't even touch on what happened to Miranda Gaddis. I mean, I can understand Weaver's love/hate thing for Ashley. It makes a lot of sense now that I think back on it all. But how is Miranda involved? If you think Ward killed Ashley, do you think he also killed Miranda? And if he killed Ashley out of love/hate passion, did he also have that same feeling about Miranda? Or are you saying that the two cases aren't connected—that whoever killed Ashley didn't abduct Miranda?"

"An excellent question. Let's take a brief glimpse into Miranda's background. We now know that Miranda was a firsthand molestation survivor, and you can all imagine what that sort of conditioning can do to a young girl's frame of reference. Most people don't know this secret, but her mother's live-in boyfriend, a scumbag, criminally attacked Miranda. He not only molested Miranda several times, but he also got to her sisters. There was a trial and the guy's in prison right now for what he did.[4] Because of what happened, the state removed all of the children from Miranda's mother's custody for about a year.

"I'm told Miranda flourished in her foster home. She didn't even want to come back. Miranda certainly was no stranger to deviant sexual behavior in adult men. Those experiences pushed her into a role she felt responsible to assume. I think she recognized Weaver was a pervert and wanted to unmask him.

"Getting back to your question. Yes, I believe that Miranda has been murdered by the same man who murdered Ashley. And that man is Ward Weaver. But I believe his motives for each killing were different. I believe that Weaver murdered Miranda to keep himself from being exposed. One witness of the sleepover that took place at the Weaver house February 23, said Miranda was in attendance with seven or eight other little girls. And as importantly, Weaver's two ex-wives were also there. Miranda was overheard telling one of the other little girls that Ashley had been molested in that house by Ward Weaver and if she didn't want the same thing to happen to her, she shouldn't spend the night in that house. She was becoming a protector of the younger girls. Well, evidently Mallori overheard this conversation and tattled to her father. She recreated Miranda's cautionary warning word-for-word. This really got to him. I think he spent the rest of the evening seething over Miranda.

"Now that in itself wouldn't mean so much. I could see how anybody hearing they were accused of molesting a child would be upset. It's just about the ugliest charge that can be made against a person short of outright murder. But here's a strange twist. The night before Miranda disappeared, that would be the night of March 7,

Weaver delivered his daughter Mallori over to his ex-wife's house, her mother. He told her she was going to spend the night there. But Mallori didn't want to spend the night there because it would possibly prevent her from going to school the next morning. She was involved in a dance performance the next day, and they don't let you attend an afterschool function if you are absent that day. So when Weaver dropped her at her mother's house, she threw a fit to the point where her mom and her mom's husband took her back to Oregon City and dropped her off." Linda's voice hardens.

"Yet by the time they made it back home, there was Mallori waiting for them on the front porch. Ward Weaver had brought her back a second time, absolutely refusing under any conditions to allow her presence in his house that specific night. Now the next morning Miranda disappeared.

"What possessed Weaver to put that much effort into getting rid of his daughter for that particular night, a school night, a night when typically she never stays somewhere else? Was his reason that he could be alone with no witnesses on the morning when Miranda disappeared? Miranda's daily morning ritual was that at about 8:10 she walked up toward the school bus stop near the front of Weaver's house by herself. It would have been easy for Weaver to watch through his front window until he saw her on the sidewalk. He opens the front door, maybe glances about to see if anybody is around and calls out, 'Miranda. Can you come in the house for just a second? Mallori is having a fit about which shoes to wear today and I think she needs a mature opinion. Can you help us out, dear?'"

Finally Oliver asks, "Well, if he killed her, what did he do with her body?"

"We don't know for certain. However, about the time that Miranda disappeared, actually the week before Miranda disappeared, Ward Weaver and his sons started work on an excavation project in his backyard. They spent a couple of days digging a huge hole. A few days later they filled in the hole and covered it with concrete to create a large, smooth slab. This concrete project was characterized by Weaver as a necessary first step to the larger project of installing a hot tub. They dug the big hole before Miranda disappeared, and covered the hole over with the cement a couple of days after Miranda disappeared. I believe that Ashley's or both bodies are buried in Weaver's yard under that concrete slab."

Allison calls out the question they all are silently posing. "Can you prove it, Linda?"

"That is the question that you, my grand jury must answer. I have given you the elements of these crimes. I have demonstrated that Weaver had the motive and the opportunity to commit these murders. You have to look suspiciously at any of your neighbors who dug a grave-sized hole in his yard right around the time that one of these young girls disappeared.

"But here's something even more eerie! Let's take a brief look at Ward Weaver's father, Ward Weaver Junior, also known as Pete Weaver. This man sits on California's death row this very minute, having been found guilty of killing a twenty-three-year-old girl and burying her remains in his own backyard under a concrete slab after having moved the body several times. That's the absolute gospel truth, a concrete slab in his yard. Now that's not evidence, but I ask you to consider the bizarre concrete slab theme and how it might be woven into the fabric of this mystery.

"I would like you to consider Harry Oakes and his search dog, Valorie. Some of you already know this story, but for those of you who hadn't heard, this will blow your mind. On March 15, one week after Miranda disappeared, and after the concrete slab was poured in Weaver's backyard, Harry and Valorie were following a scent trail that the dog had previously alerted on March 10 in the bottom of Newell Creek Canyon right below the Weaver house. Lori had given Harry an article of Ashley's clothing for scent and Harry was looking for Ashley while the other dog teams were looking for Miranda.

"On March 15 he went back to follow that trail. The trail led him onto the Weaver property. He asked for permission to search the property with his dog, gained the permission to search outside with the proviso that he stay away from the freshly poured concrete slab. And wouldn't you know it! The only spot in that whole yard that intrigued Valorie was that damn slab. The dog was so excited that Harry had to drag her off the property.

"Harry went directly to a telephone, called the Oregon City Police, and told them what he'd found. When he hadn't heard back from the police by March 17, he wrote a letter to the Chief of Police of Oregon City, and to the FBI investigators. He even sent a copy of it to Ashley's mother."

Linda pulls a document from a nearby folder and holds it up. "Here is a copy of Oakes' letter pleading with the authorities to check into the concrete slab, because his dog's cadaver instinct had been soundly triggered there.

"Now in my opinion, considering the timing, the removal of the only potential witness the morning that Miranda went missing is enough to get a search warrant. In my investigation, that slab has risen to such a position of prominence that I think it has become the center-piece of this mystery."

Linda takes a deep breath and makes eye contact with every member of her transfixed audience before resuming. "Now I ask you, ladies and gentlemen of the Ashley Pond family and friends, my grand jury, do I have a case strong enough to take to the authorities to seek an indictment?"

Several people on the deck respond at once, creating mounting murmurs. Linda steps forward and shouts a statement that quiets the crowd. "Hang on a minute. Hold it! Please! Now we need to vote on this. Give me a show of hands. How many of you are in favor of turning our evidence over to the FBI to light a fire under their investigation and get Ward Weaver behind bars where he belongs?" She implores. "How many? Come on, let's see those hands." Soon, hands go up with two holdouts, Ginger and Allison. Linda approaches them and says, "I see that there is a small contingent of undecided. What questions do you need answered before you can join the rest of the group?"

Ginger shakes her head. "I've heard direct comments from people who've had personal contact with Weaver over Ashley and I can tell you that being on his bad side is not a good place to be."

Suzie has been silent during the whole session. Suddenly she interrupts. "So what happens to all of us who are raising this stink about the slab, if when they look under it, they find nothing? Do you have any idea how mad that will make Ward Weaver?"

Linda's expression hardens. "In fact, it shouldn't make Mr. Weaver mad at all. Having his slab dug up with no dead bodies turning up is exculpatory. That would most likely exclude him from any further scrutiny. So he shouldn't be upset at all. On the contrary, he should be delighted to get the cloud removed."

Allison asks, "Are you sure that there are no other viable suspects besides Weaver for this crime?"

"My investigation has shown that Mr. Weaver had motive, opportunity and a strong likelihood that he buried the bodies on his property. No other person of interest has ever satisfied all of those elements, potential motive perhaps, but not the others. So I ask again for a show of hands. Shall I take these findings to the FBI?"

The rest focus their attention on Ginger and Allison who ponder for a few moments before they both slowly raise their hands. This triggers the unanimous vote in favor of Linda's indictment.

"All right, I'll make the appointment to meet with special agent Rob Morgan tomorrow morning." She smiles. "He's the lead investigator for the FBI task force."

■

Two hours later, Linda is behind the wheel of Philip's bright red BMW roadster, doing errands. She is fantasizing about the meeting she will be having the next morning with the FBI. She wonders if her revelations will finally lead to the arrest of Ward Weaver, yet she is perplexed about why the obvious clues of the complicated case haven't led the task force officers to the Weaver conclusion on their own. As she turns onto her street, seeing her house up ahead she notices an unfamiliar vehicle, an older Ford pickup prominently parked in the main driveway. As she gets closer she downshifts the car and spots her son Jonathan standing in front of his jalopy, its hood raised and the engine idling roughly. She parks and then discovers her son is not alone. Some guy is standing next to him with his head leaning into the engine compartment and his right hand gripping a carburetor cable. "What's going on?" she calls to her son, walking towards him.

He grins proudly. "Oh, hi Mom. I finally got it to start. This man helped me figure it out. The choke was stuck." He laughs.

For a brief moment, Linda glances at the stranger, a stocky fellow of about forty or so she surmises. When he finally pulls his head up from the engine compartment, Linda absorbs the full-faced image of the man slamming down the hood. Unmistakably, she realizes it is Ward Weaver. He gently pats the boy's arm. "Just keep that cable tight, and she should be fine," he shouts over the noisy engine. "These three-sixties are a solid block."

The boy thanks him for his help, shuts the engine off and trots into the house. Meanwhile, Linda has turned her attention to Weaver. He grins broadly and wipes the grease from his hand on the side of his jeans. "Howdy, Ma'am!"

She stands erect, arms folded. "Hello, Mr. Weaver. Is there some compelling reason that brings you to my doorstep today?"

He chuckles lightly. "Mighty fine boy you got there. I hear you also have a daughter. Kids are so naïve, aren't they?"

Linda looks deeply into Weaver's piercing, blue eyes. "I don't believe that my family is any of your concern, Mr. Weaver."

Weaver nods. "You know it's kind of funny that you brought that up, Ms. O'Neal, because I dropped by to tell you the same thing about my family. Any time you need any information about me, feel free to drop by." Before Linda can respond, Weaver turns his back on her and saunters defiantly to his pickup. Within seconds he is behind the wheel driving away. Linda follows the truck with steely eyes as it disappears down the street. Then she becomes relieved to see her trusty green car pass the pickup from the opposite direction. Her husband Philip is behind the wheel and soon pulls the green machine into the front driveway and parks. Linda rushes to the sedan calling out for her husband and leans against the back door heavily panting. Quickly getting out, Philip embraces her. "Your heart is racing like hell," he says. "Are you okay?"

Linda straightens her hair and forces a smile. "I'm fine. Ward

Weaver was just here helping my son fix his car."

Philip looks at her aghast.

"Don't worry, I'm going to meet the FBI guy in the morning to tell him my theories and lay out the evidence I've collected."

"Good," he says, his face grim.

She nods. "Philip, I need to get some stuff out of the trunk. You go ahead. I'll join you in a few minutes."

When Philip disappears into the house, Linda immediately opens the trunk and yanks out a Ziploc bag containing her snub nose revolver and speed load clips. She closes the trunk and lays the gun bag on the lid. Next, she thrusts her right hand through the plastic until her fingers come into contact with the grip and trigger. With careful precision Linda flips the revolver's cylinder open, fills the chambers with fresh ammunition, then carefully inserts the gun into her purse where she pushes it out of sight to the bottom. With a deep sigh she begins slowly walking to the house.

CHAPTER FOURTEEN

Meeting the FBI

The FBI command center for the Oregon City Girls has been carved out of several large rooms above a fire station in downtown Oregon City. On the Monday morning of June 25, it is stuffed with desks, telephones, computers and dozens of people scurrying about. Several dry erase boards cling to the walls with incomprehensible lists scribbled on every available surface. Linda O'Neal, clutching an oversized expanding file, enters and is approached by a uniformed officer. "Can I help you?" he asks abruptly.

Linda nods. "Hello. I have an eleven o'clock appointment to speak with Agent Morgan. Where can I find him?"

The officer stares at Linda suspiciously and then points to a chair near a back wall. "Go wait over there and I'll check for you. Do you have a card?"

Linda fishes out a business card from her purse and hands it over. The officer departs, leaving Linda's attention to be swept into the colliding actions that seem to shake the floors. Phones are continuously ringing, land lines and cell phones simultaneously. Dozens of fingers are smacking keyboards with an almost rhythmic pulsation providing harmonic counterpoint to the static and squelch noise repeatedly blasting from a two-way radio base station. Five minutes pass with no contact. Another five minutes. Ten minutes. Linda by now is squirming and repeatedly glancing at her watch. She looks up in time to view the uniformed officer returning, still holding the card. "Follow me," he says. He leads the female private eye down a makeshift corridor to a small cubicle where a graying middle-aged man in a blue suit is seated. He stands as she enters. "I'm Rob Morgan," he announces as he shakes her hand. He invites Linda to have a seat. "What have you got?" he finally asks.

Linda opens her file container and immediately begins to tell Morgan about her qualifications. "My name is Linda O'Neal and I'm a licensed private investigator working out of Tigard, Oregon. During my career I've worked on numerous capital cases in the State of Oregon, and before I went out on my own I was the primary staff investigator for Des Connall, a prominent Portland area defense attorney."

Morgan smiles. "I know him. He was Multnomah County District Attorney for several years."

"Yes, and after he retired he set up a lucrative private practice. I learned most of my skills working under Des. He is absolutely the most brilliant attorney I have ever known. But my experience goes way beyond my years with him, because before that job I put in ten years working for the Washington County Sheriff's Department, so I do have an extensive law enforcement background."

Morgan's facial expression remains nonchalant. "When we talked on the phone the other day you claimed you had some information about the Pond/Gaddis case."

"Yes."

"May I ask why you have taken it upon yourself to investigate the matter?"

"Well, you see sir, I'm a peripheral member of Ashley Pond's family. Some of the family got me involved many months ago, in part I think because the official investigations seemed to be stalled. They figured I might be able to help. And I've spent hundreds of hours on this, many times chasing down dead ends. But finally, everything is coming together and I feel I know what happened to the girls and who's responsible."

Morgan scowls. "With all due respect, Ms. O'Neal, the complete details of our investigation have never been revealed, so there's no way for any outsider to have determined how 'stalled' our approach is. Anyway, so what did you bring me?"

As she pulls documents out for him to peruse, she says with deep conviction, "I'm sure you've heard of Ward Weaver."

Morgan immediately folds his arms and cuts her off. "I would be very surprised if Weaver had anything to do with the disappearances."[1] The phone rings and he spends a few moments involved in what seems to be a crucial call. Telling the party on the other end of the line that he'll be right back, he puts the phone down and abruptly tells Linda O'Neal, "Look, we have over one hundred highly trained federal agents working eighteen-hour days on this case. We cannot discuss with anybody what leads we have. But I assure you, we are on top of this case and we certainly do not use private investigator information on a high profile case. So with all due respect, thanks for coming in."

A nearby assistant snaps his finger and gestures toward the door. Linda turns back to Morgan protesting vehemently. "But Mr. Morgan, don't you understand? Weaver had groomed Ashley, and he was suspicious of Miranda because…" Morgan once again motions for her to exit, then resumes his telephone call.

Slowly, Linda is escorted down the corridor and out the front door. Standing on the firehouse steps, she is too stunned to react.

■

Finally, back at the house, Linda O'Neal sits in her home office, still consumed with dismay over the FBI's dismissal of her months of painstaking work. They had treated her with as much disdain as she had originally treated Pamela, the psychic's wife. Morgan had obviously felt Linda was a total nonentity whose conclusions about the case couldn't possibly be relevant. What bothered her most was the fact that the red flags that hijacked her attention had not done the same for him. In Linda's opinion, the task force deployed too much of its energy toward qualifying sources of information. They somehow seemed unable to differentiate the priority of information once it surfaced.

"I can't believe this!" she slams down a book on the desk. "It's crazy! What the hell can I do now to make them pay attention?"

Philip, who has come out of his studio, overhears Linda's rants and approaches her. "Are you okay?" he asks before gently massaging the back of her neck.

"Do I look okay? I'm…I'm sorry. It's just that, well, do you know what's happened?"

"The FBI didn't listen," he says soberly.

"Philip, why won't they go after Weaver? Ashley and Miranda could very well be rotting under that cement and all they'd have to do is dig it up and everyone would finally know the truth."

"Take it easy, love. You've done your best. Come on. Maybe it's time to move on."

"Move on? While that crud-ball Weaver is still wandering around loose? Never. I'm sure he did it, Philip. Ward Weaver killed those girls. And there are remains in his yard. I'd bet my life on it. He's not even on their radar screen. And you know what terrifies me now about all this? If he thinks he's cleanly gotten away with cold-blooded murder twice in a row, what's to stop him from another and another?"

Philip sees how agitated Linda is and wants to help her get her mind off Ashley and Miranda for a little while. "Listen, how about we go out to dinner?" He notices her quick look of disdain. "I mean, put on your best cocktail dress and let me buy you a nice dinner." He pulls her up from the chair and embraces her, then touches her left ear with his lips. "And afterward, if you've still got some time, how about a little cheek-to-cheek dancing? Come on, it's been months since we went out on the town." He leads her into a dance posture and takes a few rhythmic steps.

Linda cooperates for a moment then pulls away. "The last time we went out dancing was to celebrate. There's nothing to celebrate now."

Philip embraces his wife again. "Yes, there is. We'll celebrate us. Go on, get ready. We'll go in Marilyn. Come on. You need some relief."

Linda sighs heavily, "You're right. I do."

A few hours later, they are seated in the restaurant of a posh downtown Portland hotel. Draped in her finest black evening dress, Linda has her hair up and wears her best pearls. Philip pats her hand

and grins. "You're one gorgeous chick tonight, my love. And I have a surprise for later."

Linda shakes her head. "You know I don't like surprises."

"Oh, I think you'll like this one."

The waiter walks over and they order, but once the food is served, Linda eats silently. Finally, Philip reacts. "Come on, you're supposed to relax. How's your fish?"

"I just walked in there to hand him the evidence and he didn't have the decency to look at it," Linda sputters.

"Come on, what's done is done."

When she is half way through the seafood primavera she continues, "We've got to do something."

Philip thinks for a moment and then jokingly says, "Maybe, maybe we should just sneak over there some night and dig up the slab ourselves."

"Philip, don't be silly! I'm a licensed investigator. I can't do anything crazy and you know it."

Philip keeps trying to inject levity and finally, with a flourish, he folds his napkin up creating a magnificent replica of a lily which he stuffs into his jacket pocket like a clown. Linda finally responds with a little laugh.

Seizing the moment, Philip asks, "Are you ready for that surprise? I've arranged something special that you must come with me to see." Moments later Philip signs the check and leads Linda to the elevator.

Linda now has an inkling of what's up. "Why Philip, you dog, you. You never do anything this romantic."

"I know," he replies. "Trying to find out what happened to Ashley and Miranda has consumed us. I have never seen you in such need of distraction." The elevator stops at the top floor where they find themselves in front of the penthouse suite. Inside, an expensive bottle of wine is jutting from an ice-crammed bucket. While she is still gasping in surprise, he takes her arm and whisks her to the large window that overlooks the bustling city, its lights twinkling seductively. For a while with soft music playing in the background, they stand quietly, holding hands and soaking up the expansive view.

Linda sighs. "A million people out there and nobody notices the obvious. I can't believe I'm the only investigator who sees Ward Weaver as the perpetrator in this case. I know that Valenzuela-Garcia suspects him too. But they won't go after him."

In response, exasperated Philip leads Linda through the suite and into the bedroom, where the bed has already been turned down. When Linda notices her purple negligee already laid out on the bed she chuckles. "That's your favorite one. How did you get it up here without me seeing?"

"Now that is a mystery," Philip chuckles. "Why don't you slip into something a little more comfortable?"

Linda replies, "Don't go away, I'll be right back." She picks up the negligee and withdraws to the bathroom. Philip starts to undress. He puts his jacket on a nearby chair and pulls his shirt over his head. He kicks his shoes off and begins to loosen his trousers when he suddenly remembers the wine. He runs to the other room and brings the wine and two glasses. He pours the wine and hears the door to the bathroom open.

Taking off his trousers, Philip makes a mighty leap to land in the bed. Linda enters, a purple vision of chiffon and silk. She smiles at her husband, but can't help obsessing further, "You know, there has got to be some way to get to Weaver—to make him do something that will demand the task force's attention."

Philip is not willing to let his vision of delight disintegrate. "Linda…come here." He takes her hand, pulls her to the side of the bed and embraces her.

She shakes her head, "I'm sorry, I just can't stop thinking about how to get Weaver."

Philip gently undoes the pins holding her hair up and runs his fingers through the long strands as they fall to her shoulders. He shakes his head. "Too bad you can't just get Weaver to go on national TV and admit he took the girls."

Linda pulls away from him, her eyes excited. "That's it!"

She ponders her new idea for a few moments, then looks lovingly at her husband. She pushes him down onto the bed and leaps on top of him wearing the biggest smile that Philip has seen on her face in months.

■

Early the next morning a re-energized Linda O'Neal enters the *Portland Tribune* newspaper office toting the same documents she had tried to share with the FBI. Her relationship with Jim Redden, the most prominent crime reporter at the *Tribune*, had begun years earlier when they were both guest speakers in a professional investigation symposium. Over time Redden enlisted Linda's assistance for background material to support his article preparations and in true reciprocal fashion he always kept Linda up to date on the various scuttlebutt he was privy to involving the local crime scene. When he notices his old friend, Redden glances up from his laptop and greets her with a smile. "Hello, Linda! Have a seat. What's up?"

Linda sighs and sits down. "First, I want to compliment you for the stories you've cranked out on the missing Oregon City girls. That one a couple of weeks ago about Ashley being abused by her father really added to my perspective on how Ashley felt and how devastating it must have been for that poor child."

Redden nods. "I still don't understand how he managed to squirm away from thirty-nine counts."

"Pretty bizarre, don't you think?"

Redden pauses. "So what's your connection to this stuff?"

"I'm in the family, sort of. My husband is Ashley's step-grandfather; his ex-wife is Lori Pond's mother. So they asked for my help from the beginning. I've been investigating every aspect of the case for six months." She pauses then rushes on. "Why do you think they dropped all those counts and let Roettger take a walk so easily?"

Redden shakes his head. "From what I learned it was a clash of information. The charges got dropped when Roettger's attorney threatened to introduce evidence at trial that would have seriously weakened the state's case. So he got off with probation and was forced to register as a sex offender."

"Would you like to know who was behind the 'evidence' that the lawyer was going to lob in the court's face?"

"Definitely," Redden says.

"Well, there were apparently several other non-related allegations of sex abuse made by Ashley. All of which would certainly impact the poor child's credibility in court. So the prosecutors bailed."

Redden takes a sip of coffee. "That's too bad."

Linda scowls. "Too bad? Jim, it was a vicious revenge. One man was responsible for sabotaging that case and he did it ingeniously."

"Who the hell are you talking about?"

Linda lifts up her folder and hands Redden the documents while asking, "Have you ever heard of Ward Weaver?"

He begins to peruse the papers and replies, "No. Should I have?"

"He and his daughter spent a lot of time with Ashley, yet the FBI seems to be totally ignoring him."

"What makes you think they're wrong to look in other directions?"

"It was the family's observations that started me down this trail. Weaver had been way too affectionate with Ashley. Are you aware that Ashley lived in Weaver's house for several months last year? He took her on a trip to California. She complained of an attempted rape by him, yet her charges slipped through the cracks. Ward's own biological father is sitting on death row awaiting his execution for a double murder in which a young female victim was buried in his yard under a cement slab. And most telling: Ward Weaver poured his own concrete slab in his backyard within a few days of Miranda Gaddis's disappearance. I'm convinced that Weaver is the culprit. Please, look over some of this evidence. Just read. I'll shut up."

As Redden absorbs page after page of Linda's reports and supporting documents, his face tightens. When he comes across a copy of the letter that dog handler Harry Oakes had written about Valorie's death alert at the concrete slab, he shakes his head. "Incredible. Incredible."

She leans over and retrieves a document from the middle of the file and taps it with a forefinger. "Look at his criminal record. See the assaults? Notice the victims all have one thing in common. They were females and most were in their teens. Plus, look here. He was arrested for violating one of the restraining orders taken out against him by his former wives. Weaver is capable of extreme violence. He lives right up the street from the Newell Creek Apartments, so you'd think the FBI would be all over him, but they're not. They appear to be going in different directions."

After studying the reports, Redden looks penetratingly at Linda. "I'm impressed," he says. "This is dynamite. I have to admit, your Weaver-as-perpetrator theory is very convincing. You should take this stuff to the task force."

Linda scoffs. "Yeah, right! Been there, done that. Jim, they won't listen. That's why I'm here. I need your help! Maybe we can 'smoke him out.'"

Redden is dumbfounded. "I don't see how…"

"Let's put Weaver on the front page. Shine a bright light on him. If you'll consider taking this information, incorporating it into your other leads and then writing a Weaver story maybe a little publicity will jerk his chain. Please, Jim, I can't think of any other way to get him."

Redden grins. "Leave me your documents and I'll work up an angle that will pass my editor's muster."

Linda stands up and pats Redden's shoulder. "Thanks a lot, Jim. And please, don't mention me by name in any articles. I'm still conducting my investigation and if my name gets published it could cause people to be alerted. I'm sure you understand… wait a minute!"

"What's the matter?"

"Listen! How about shooting for the moon? Oh yes! Perfect."

"What the hell are you up to?"

"Ambush him. Ambush Weaver."

Redden contemplates then says, "I think it'll work. If he's as much an egomaniac as he sounds, and a sociopath, maybe he'll actually be flattered. He opens his door only to discover a newspaper wants to publish his take on the case. From Mr. Nobody to Mr. Somebody in one instant."

"Please, Jim. Just jump in the car, drive to his house and you can ambush him on his front porch."

Redden is intrigued. He ponders. "Okay, Linda, you can stop the campaign. I'm on board." He checks his wall calendar. "The best shot for ambush interviews comes from catching the subjects totally off guard. So in this case, I'll hit him early in the morning." He points to Sunday the 30th on the calendar. "If my editor approves, I'll drive out to Weaver's and a little after eight, I'll pound on his door. Probably even wake him up. He'll be disoriented enough that he just may give me an interview. "

On Sunday, June 30, 2002, Linda wakes early and waits anxiously, watching the clock. When eight comes, she paces, knowing Redden is on Beavercreek Road arriving near the front of Weaver's house. In her mind she sees him parked off to the side, staring at the Weaver house for several moments before he exits.

And she is right. Clutching his notepad and ballpoint pen, the reporter begins the trek up the sidewalk. He approaches the front porch and knocks. The door opens and within seconds, Redden is invited by Weaver to enter the house.

For the next forty-five minutes, Linda nervously fidgets wondering about Redden's encounter with Weaver. She is hopeful that Weaver will talk to the press, "After all, he waltzed me across that slab." She also is concerned for Redden's safety. What if Weaver becomes violent?

The front door opens as Weaver and Redden begin a slow saunter toward the car, both smiling, chatting. Eventually Weaver shakes hands with the reporter and heads back to his house.

As soon as Redden gets into his vehicle and starts the engine, he begins driving away. During the next few moments holding his cell phone in his right hand he manages to dial Linda's number.

Linda lifts her phone off the hook in half a ring. "Did he tell you anything valuable?" she asks.

Redden laughs. "I think you'll think so. I know I do."

She has trouble containing her excitement and finally blurts, "Please Jim. Come on. What did he say? Tell me everything."

Redden keeps his eyes glued to the road. "It took a few minutes and a lot of hard knocks before he came to the door, but there was Ward Weaver, wearing a dirty white tank top and cut-off jeans."[2]

"Was he accommodating?"

"I identified myself and asked if I could talk to him about the missing girls. He hesitated for a moment, then invited me in."

"Go on."

"We sat on two black couches, angled to face an expensive home entertainment center that nearly filled one living room wall. I noticed two paintings of unicorns hanging in the hall, near the kitchen. Weaver immediately struck me as nervous, but many interview subjects are, especially when you surprise them early in the morning."

"Did he believe you were a reporter?"

"Yeah. I gave him my card to assure him that the interview was on the up and up, and then I asked if he minded if I took some notes. He agreed. So I began asking if he knew the missing girls. He said 'yes', explaining that they were friends with his daughter, Mallori, who attended the same school and is a member of the same dance team. I asked how well he knew them. He volunteered that he knew Ashley very well because she had lived at his house for five months and had traveled to California with him and his daughter just last summer. He said Miranda had only visited a few times. When I asked why Ashley had lived with him, he told me that her mother, Lori Pond, had dumped her at his house one evening on her way to a party and hadn't asked her to come back home for months. At that time, he said his daughter and a former girlfriend were also living in the house. That first visit turned into a series of longer stays before the big five-month stay early last year. When I said this sounded strange, he insisted it was true and said that Ashley lived off and on in his house after that as well. He said that Ashley, Miranda and other children who lived at the complex often visited his house because of its location near the bus stop and because of his daughter Mallori."

"Did he admit to a relationship with Ashley?"

"Weaver said Ashley is a likeable child, but is emotionally immature for her age. But I hit him with another question on the subject and then Weaver seemed to grow even more nervous. After a few silent moments he said he wanted to tell me something but wasn't sure whether he should. I put down my pen and notepad and asked him what it was. To my surprise, Weaver said he had been expecting me to come by. He said an Oregon City Police detective[3] had visited him just a few days earlier to say that I was going to pay him a visit, because I was mad that the police weren't giving me any information about their investigation. He said he recognized my name at the door and on the business card. After your visit on Friday, I had asked several sources about Weaver, and I actually had expressed my frustration with the lack of official information coming from investigators. I have no idea why any of them would tell Weaver that. So I thought he was bullshitting on that point." Redden pauses. "One minute, I need to pass this semi…Alright."

"Why would he say that?"

"I have no idea. Then came another surprise. When I asked him why the police thought I was coming, Weaver volunteered that he thinks he is the FBI's prime suspect in the missing girl's case. Not just a suspect, but the 'prime suspect.'"

"Guilty conscience?" Linda adds.

"Maybe. That gave me the perfect opening. I asked if he did it, if he had kidnapped the two girls. Weaver seemed stunned by the question. But he adamantly denied having anything to do with their disappearances, swearing that he and his daughter considered Ashley part of the family.

"But if that is true, I asked, 'Why does the FBI consider you a suspect?' Weaver reeled off a list of reasons. First, he said that Ashley had accused him of molesting her last year. As he explained it, Ashley made the accusation after they had a petty argument. He said state and local law enforcement officials were notified of the accusations at the time and he was exonerated of any suspicion. Weaver again denied any wrongdoing and repeated the fact that the police looked into the allegations and yet never charged him. Ashley had told her mother last August that he had abused her after the two argued." Redden then imitates Weaver's voice. "'When she first said that, I told her mother to take her to a doctor for an examination to prove that nothing happened. But she never did.' Weaver also told me Lori Pond nevertheless told the FBI about the molesting accusations shortly after Ashley disappeared, prompting the agency's interest in him."

"Is that what makes him think he is their prime suspect?"

Redden shifts his cell phone to the other ear before replying. "No. Although Weaver told me he is disturbed that people might think that Ashley's accusation against him is true, he said it is now becoming common knowledge because of the investigators. He added that investigators crossed the line when they told nearby families to keep their children away from him.

"Weaver admitted that he understands that investigators are under heavy pressure to solve the six-month-old case, but he doesn't understand why they continue to pursue him. He is adamant that he knows absolutely nothing about the whereabouts of the two girls. Weaver claims that he can account for what he was doing when the mothers say they last saw both the girls. He told me, 'I know where I was, and they know where I was, getting ready for work and at work.'

"When I pressed him again about what he thinks happened to the girls, he said he has no idea. He assumes Ashley ran away from home, but he says he does not know enough about Miranda to even guess. Weaver told me he had not met Miranda's mother until after the girl disappeared. 'Whatever happened,' Weaver said, 'I didn't have anything to do with it.'"

"Didn't you find it unusual for him to spill his guts to you so easily?"

"As a matter of fact, yeah. So I asked Weaver why he was telling me all this. He said that everyone that he cared about already knew it and he was mad, because he thought the FBI had crossed the line. As he explained it, he understood why the FBI was interested in him. He knew both girls. He'd been in trouble with the law in the past. He said he'd even spent time in prison after a conviction on assault charges against his first wife. But he added that he has never been charged with hurting a child."

Linda absorbs Redden's account silently for a few moments. "But it doesn't add up, Jim. What is the basis for him feeling he is being looked at as a suspect? According to my own investigation, they were clearly not paying that much attention to Weaver or they would've dug up that concrete slab."

"I'm sorry, Linda, but in all the excitement I forgot to even bring up the slab. But he did reveal a spicy tidbit about a polygraph episode. In spite of denying knowing what happened to the girls, he admitted to me that he failed an FBI lie detector test about one month ago. He said that the FBI told him that he had failed virtually all the questions on the polygraph. He said, 'They told me I flunked 99 percent of the questions, so how accurate is that?' He refused to take a second polygraph test. To quote him, 'At that point, I was like, I don't think I want to cooperate with you any more. I don't know what happened to the girls,' he says."

"Do you think he's just making all of this up to toy with you?"

"It's certainly a possibility. Weaver is a very strange character, no doubt about it. According to him, investigators have tapped his phones, searched his home with trained dogs several times and repeatedly interviewed his friends and relatives. But Weaver said the FBI had crossed the line by harassing his friends."

"Well, what do you think?" Linda inquires.

"By then I believed you had uncovered a real story. I picked up my pen and notebook and again asked Weaver how he knew Ashley and Miranda. As he repeated what I had already written about the girls, I quickly scribbled some notes on the main topics. Then I asked him to tell me again why he thought he was the 'prime suspect.' He repeated the reasons he had said earlier using almost the exact same words. And then he briefly talked about his infamous father, telling me it was unfair for the FBI to be comparing him with his dad. 'He walked out on us when I was three. He hasn't been part of my life since then,' he said. At the end of the interview I thanked Weaver for his time, and told him the *Tribune* probably was going to publish the story soon. He said he understood that."

"Well, what's your say?"

"I could see why he is a suspect. But did Ward Weaver strike me as a total, psycho sex-maniac-serial-killer? No. He came across as what he claimed he was, someone who'd been in trouble with the law, but had been working hard to get his act together. He's just so straightforward. It's hard to believe he would do it, but your investigation is compelling and he thinks he's the FBI's number one suspect. So I'll publish a story on him from that angle and we'll see what it produces."

On July 2, the *Portland Tribune* publishes Redden's account of his encounter with Ward Weaver on the front page under the headline, "Suspect: I Didn't Do Anything." And as Redden had predicted to Linda, Weaver quickly becomes a primary person of interest to the local TV news departments including the ABC affiliate, KATU Channel 2, who dispatches twenty-six-year-old Anna Song to his house to interview him. When it airs on a July 3RD evening newscast, Weaver comes across sincerely and even takes the young TV reporter on a tour through his house, including a stroll across the concrete slab. At this point the public perception is overwhelmingly positive. Most viewers are favorably impressed with his pleasant nature. To Linda's chagrin, the public seems to accept his protestations of innocence in the missing girls' mystery.

But during the following few days, Weaver increasingly becomes the subject of other news stories when local TV stations dispatch their armies of reporters in search of their own Weaver angles. Several call-in radio talk shows begin to toss the Weaver topic around.

Then an article appears in *The Oregonian* where Charles Mathews,[4] the FBI special agent in charge of Oregon, speaks on the issue of the missing girls, "We still have a number of people from a variety of walks of life who are under suspicion." In the same piece Miranda Gaddis's mother, Michelle Duffy, confirms the official FBI stance. "He's not any more of a suspect than anyone else. No one is a 'prime suspect.'"

One week after the publication of Redden's front-page exposé, the story spreads nationally. *Good Morning America, Inside Edition* and other programs court Weaver and he eagerly consents to live interviews where he repeats his denial of having any involvement with the disappearances of Ashley and Miranda.

While his editors seem satisfied with the hornet's nest Redden stirred up, at their urging, he next publishes a follow-up article which shifts the Weaver focus to his children, especially Weaver's oldest son, who is quoted as adamantly defending his father's veracity. "What about me? I lived at my dad's house. I knew the missing girls, both of them, and the FBI has never once even talked to me about the matter. If he's a suspect, why aren't I a suspect too?" He concludes his comments with a passionate promise. "I would turn my own father in to the law in a heartbeat if I ever came to have any doubts about his innocence."[5]

CHAPTER FIFTEEN

Flashing Lights and Getaways

On July 12, 2002, at 3:30 PM, the sizzling summer weather bakes the asphalt surrounding the Newell Creek Apartments. There are no children clustering around outside. The majority of occupants are sealed in their units, windows tightly shut, curtains closed and air conditioners whirring.

Ward Weaver's house across the road is also quiet. Weaver has taken the day off from work and is playing a videogame with his daughter, Mallori. "It's your turn, Dad," she giggles, handing him the controller. While Weaver concentrates on his electronic options, Mallori notices blurring movement outside the window. She rushes over and gasps. "Wow! There's…" she counts, "Two, three, four, five! There's five police cars out there and they all have their lights flashing!"

Weaver drops the controller and races to the window where he peers out. He is shocked to see the big squad cars, one behind the other, slowly lingering near his front driveway.

"Are they coming here, Daddy?"

Weaver furrows his brow and hesitates, eyes glued to the vehicles. "I'm not sure where they're going." He keeps watching them for a few minutes. The police cars unexpectedly turn, one by one, into the Newell Creek complex followed closely by a white Dodge truck with the bold letters, "CRIME SCENE VAN 2" plastered on both sides. Finally he replies, "They're stopped. I...I guess they're *not* coming our way. Put your shoes on and we'll go check out what's going on."

As Weaver and his daughter make their way out the door, they see the three lead police vehicles fan out.[1] One vehicle moves near the front stairway of Lori Pond's building. Two uniformed officers, formidably attired in their riot gear, spring from the car and climb the stairs leading to the apartment near Pond's. A second unit simultaneously rushes to the backside of the building and deposits two more cops. They hold position with hands resting on holsters. The third police car screeches to a halt directly in front of the utility entrance to the building. Its two officers burst forth and quickly retrieve a battering ram and a shotgun from the trunk.

A few seconds later, two police teams arrive at the entrance of an upstairs unit. One of the men raps the front door with a baton. "Open up. Search Warrant," he calls out. "You have thirty seconds to open the door. We have a search warrant." The officers position themselves. After a full twenty seconds of silence, the lead officer shouts a command and a cohort begins attacking the front door with the battering ram. Two whacks later, the door flies open. The team bursts into the living room, guns drawn. "Search Warrant. Down on the floor," they scream as they pour through the bedrooms, bathroom and kitchen. The commander barks into his portable radio. "Secure. Nobody inside. Send in the evidence techs."

By the time Weaver and his daughter arrive, a small crowd including Lori Pond and her daughters has gathered in the parking lot, watching police swarm around a blue Chevrolet while a technician attaches a line from a tow-truck. Lori makes brief eye contact with Weaver then turns her head. "What's going on?" Weaver asks a balding male bystander.

The man shakes his head, points a finger and spits out a gob of tobacco juice before replying. "Take a look," he grunts. "The TV reporters are here. Whatever it is, it must be pretty big. It must be about the missing girls."

"Do you think they'll find them?"

"Not unless they start looking at some of those white slavery rings that have been springing up. They put child porn stuff on the Internet. And that's how they get their subjects—they swoop in to a vulnerable community and when nobody's paying much attention they snatch and grab. They are so slick that girls just vanish, off the street like that." He spits again. "That's my opinion. It sure sounds like it could be white slavers. Maybe they got the girls."

Satellite vans converge and Weaver watches in fascination as various news crews hastily exit, untangling their camera cords, preparing to shoot their video versions of the mysterious unfolding event.

For an hour the apartment is scoured by teams of evidence specialists. They cart off several plastic bags full of material. Meanwhile, the tow truck has hoisted the blue Chevrolet upward and is beginning to pull it away. Just then, an Oregon City Transit bus makes a routine stop on Beavercreek Road next to Weaver's house and the entrance to the apartment complex. A slim, brown haired man of about twenty-five exits and notices the commotion surrounding the tow. He sprints to the site and screams obscenities at the officer supervising the confiscation.

A male plainclothes detective approaches the younger man and flashes a badge. "What's your problem, kid?"

"What's going on here? Why are they towing that car away?"

The officer studies the agitated younger man. "And what is it to you that we're towing this car?"

"It's mine!"

"And you are?"

"Tom Watkins. And that's my car they're taking and I want to know why. It's not illegally parked. I live in this complex and it's parked in my assigned spot. What's the deal?"

The officer scowls. "So you're Watkins. Got ID?"

"Certainly." Watkins pulls out his wallet and plucks out his driver's license, which he hands over.

The detective motions and a pair of uniformed officers approach. Watkins gulps. "Mr. Watkins," the cop says sternly, "I'm going to have to ask you to put your hands behind your back."

Watkins's anger ratchets up. "What? I haven't done anything."

"I told you to put your hands behind your back. Comply now!"

"What the hell are you doing here? No. I'm not going to put my hands behind my back. I haven't done anything."

The policemen pounce on the hapless young man, wrestle him to the pavement and quickly snap his wrists into handcuffs behind his back. "You live in an apartment right near Lori and Ashley Pond, the little girl who disappeared?"

Watkins squirms. "Yes, but I…"

"Quit resisting. Do you remember taking a polygraph test?"

"So what?"

"You flunked."

"So they told me. But that's not my fault. I told the truth on all the questions." The policeman puts his face close to Tom's face. "Know what it means that you flunked? It means you're hiding something, and since you have no verifiable alibi, guess what, pal…you're a suspect. And as such the judge has issued a search warrant for your apartment and your car. Right now they may contain evidence of the crime."

Tom shakes his head. "Come on. I've been told a dozen times that I'm one of your suspects. Well, the last time they just said I was a 'person of interest.' Have I somehow climbed higher on the ladder again?"

"Don't get smart with me, buster! We are investigating a serious crime. You live nearby, you flunked the polygraph and you've had a past history of mental illness."

Watkins seethes. "Who told you that? That's bull! I'm going to get my lawyer. My medical records are private."

The tow truck finally picks up speed and soon the Chevy is gone. "I need my car," Watkins cries, "I just bought a new fuel pump for it."

Ward and Mallori Weaver stand in the crowd of onlookers watching as Watkins is pulled to his feet and stuffed into the back seat of a patrol car. Mallori tugs her father's sleeve. "What's happening?"

Weaver takes her hand and begins walking back to Beavercreek Road so fast that Mallori can hardly keep up.

"Dad, wait up! Why are you in such a hurry?" she asks.

"Damn cops scaring everyone they can get their hands on. I'm sick of them."

Before they reach the street, TV news reporter Pinski Brown approaches Weaver with her cameraman beside her, tape rolling. "Excuse me," she says briskly, "but aren't you Ward Weaver?"

When he notices her microphone Weaver stops, brushes his hair back with his hands and smiles warmly. "Yes, I'm Ward Weaver."

"I saw your appearance on *Good Morning America* last week. Very impressive."

Weaver smiles. "Thanks. I just try to help out the best I can. It's such a sad time for the families now." He indicates the car with Tom Watkins in the back. "But maybe they might be making some progress today."

"Do you mind if I ask you a brief question for our viewers?"

"I guess not."

"You've been telling everyone the FBI considers you their prime suspect."

"That's what they told me."

"So how does it feel to see them finally coming down this hard on someone else? I mean, they've never searched your place and your car like this, have they?"

"They didn't need any warrants, because as a matter of fact, I've always cooperated any time they wanted to look my place over. Even when they brought in their dogs, I cooperated. I want to do anything I can that will help find out what happened to those poor girls. You see, ma'am, I've got nothing to hide, because I was not involved."

Despite the detectives' newest initiative with Tom Watkins, there are no new breakthroughs. The answer to the puzzle seems no closer.

In pursuit of a fresh strategy, Linda launches a search for Claire Stevens, who had developed strong bonds with "stepdaughter" Ashley over the years. Ashley had reportedly confided in Claire frequently throughout 2001. She was very cooperative during an earlier interrupted phone conversation, yet Stevens is lately unresponsive to Linda's phone calls. But this hasn't prevented the dogged detective from repeated attempts to get through. Finally a woman answers the phone.

"Claire Stevens?" Linda ventures.

An agitated voice responds, "Are you from Children's Services?"

"No, no. It's Linda O'Neal, the private investigator. We talked on the phone at length last month. Remember? I'm still investigating Ashley Pond's disappearance. First, I want to apologize for not getting back to you right away. My cell phone battery went out right in the middle of our conversation."

"Yeah, well, I got to thinkin' maybe you hung up on me for some reason."

Linda laughs nervously. "Oh, no, no. I would never hang up on you. Believe me, it was just the stupid battery and then I got on to another lead and had to follow up," Linda explains. "But that won't happen now. I'm on a landline in my office. I was wondering if we could finish up our conversation?"

"This whole Ashley Pond thing has really bummed me out lately."

"I know exactly what you mean. It's almost become an obsession with me."

"I hope you're having better luck in finding the girls than the FBI."

Linda pauses a moment and then says, "The last time we spoke you said that you talked to Ashley about this situation with Gerri Glass. Remember? She was sleeping somewhere else in the house and Ashley was sleeping in Ward's bed. You said Ashley promised you that there was no sex stuff going on. Do you think she was telling the truth?"

Stevens replies, "Yeah, I actually did believe her then. Because she knew what sex was by that time. You know, she wasn't your ordinary twelve-year-old."

"You had no reason to suspect she was…"

Stevens interrupts. "Nope! I thought she told me the truth. It wasn't until later that I heard Ashley said Weaver tried to rape her. And I believed her then, too."

Linda says, "Back when all of that happened, you were convinced that Weaver had tried to molest Ashley. Did you talk to anyone else about this at that time? Let me explain. The reason for me to ask this is, in the case of rape it's very important in the prosecution's case for the victim to have talked to somebody else about it immediately. We don't have Ashley to talk to, so anybody that Ashley talked to becomes the 'first person' in this. It's important to have a second person to corroborate the time line of the events."

"I have a very specific memory of talking to somebody about this. I went to talk personally with her caseworker, the one that was assigned to Ashley when all this molestation stuff with Wesley came up."

"Well, did he take care of it?"

"He never called me back. And then I went to talk to this 'caseworker' just about the Gerri Glass sleeping in the garage incident, basically the same stuff I told you last month. I went back again after Ashley said that Ward had tried to rape her. I contacted him three times. They never even called me back once."

When Linda hears this she is incredulous. She draws a conclusion with broad implications; she feels that there was no DHS intervention. "If only DHS hadn't dropped the ball."[2] But the question that looms in Linda's mind now is where to go from here.

◼

The twenty days that pass between July 12 and August 1 are filled with frustration for Linda O'Neal. She keeps investigating every lead to find the Oregon City girls.

Meanwhile, Weaver's statements have rekindled public interest in the missing girls' saga, prompting stiff competition among TV and print media. Consequently, the investigative staff at the *Tribune* discovers a useful alliance as they frequently turn to Linda to run background checks on assorted characters. Redden's story on Weaver, Ashley and Miranda cause network news correspondents to solicit opinions about the bizarre kidnappings.

On August 1, under a cloudless sky and wearing a wide grin, Philip is standing in front of Marilyn, his red BMW Z-3 roadster with a bucket of sudsy water and a new sponge. *There's something about putting that shine on your lady. Every guy who sees her will crave possession for himself. But she's mine, and I share with no one! Making it all the sweeter.* Philip dreams. As he sloshes the sponge across the gleaming hood, a nearby cordless phone chirps. He answers. "Linda O'Neal Investigations. Can I help you?"

"I need to speak to Linda."

"This is the fifth time you called. She's not home. She's out on a case," he says exasperatedly to his mother-in-law.

"Well, tell her to call me as soon as she gets back."

"I said I would, okay?" When the call has concluded, a pensive and somewhat worried Philip sets the phone back on the driveway, picks up a hose and begins squirting a wide stream across the sports car's soaped-up front end. He sprays back and forth and watches the white foam trickle onto the ground. Then, the phone rings again. He answers again. "Linda O'Neal Investigations. Linda is out of the office for a while. Can I help you?"

"I need to speak to Linda."

"I just told you, Linda's not here. I'll have her call you."

Just then a familiar car pulls into the front driveway with Linda at the wheel. Before she even has time to exit Philip rushes to the driver's side and hands her the phone through the open window. "It's your mother," he whispers loudly. "She needs to get hold of you."

Linda covers the mouthpiece with her right palm before she says, "Philip, I've already talked to her at least seven separate times today."

"What does she want?"

"I think she wants me to make it all better, but I don't think she has a clue about what the 'it' is." Linda places the phone to her ear. "Hello, Mother. How can I help you?"

For the next two minutes Philip watches his wife bite her lip, twitch and look generally upset, while uttering, "Yeah…I see…Okay…It's going to be fine…Really? Okay. You have to just ignore that…Mother, there isn't anything I can do about it. I'm sorry." Linda listens intently before she concludes the call. "Good bye Mom. I love you."

Linda gets out of her car and begins walking toward the house with Philip. He asks, "So what was wrong that she had to call you so many times?"

"I really don't know. She keeps telling me how depressed and sad she is, and she thinks I have some magic solution to make it better. She calls my sister just as relentlessly. Over and over, and..."

"Linda, while you were gone she called your office line at least five times."

"I've agreed to go see her with my sister this evening to check into just how she is. I mean, something's definitely awry. Maybe we can coax her into going out to dinner or something to get her separated from Dad for an hour. Then we can figure out what we need to do to quiet her down so she isn't calling every minute." Linda shakes her head. "It's so sad."

Linda doesn't return from the Hillsboro family conference until nearly 11 PM and as soon as she enters the house Philip asks about her mother. "How bad is it?"

Linda sighs, "Well, I think I may have inadvertently put a halt to the incessant phone calls anyway. She says she never wants to speak to either my sister or me again!"

"Good grief! What the hell went on over there?"

"We told her that we thought if she was really depressed she needed to tell her doctor about it. My God! She still sees him about every week for something, but she's too embarrassed or scared to tell him she's depressed. We tried to explain that depression is a physical ailment that normally responds to medication. But you've got to enlist your doctor's help to go the medication route."

"That's certainly reasonable."

"As soon as we said it, she freaked out. I mean, she freaked out! Her eyes got wide, her voice got shrill. She kept shouting, 'You want me on those funny pills! Don't you? You're just trying to make the real me go away. You're trying to get rid of me with anti-depressants. And you won't get away with it.' We were at the restaurant. Everybody stared. The manager came to our table and suggested we go outside because we were upsetting other customers. You know, I think her doctor must have tried to get her on anti-depressants or something, because she totally lost it."

"It doesn't sound like anything got resolved tonight."

Linda shakes her head, "She hasn't called me one time on my cell phone. Did she call on my land line?"

"Nope. So what's your next move?"

"I just don't know. The situation is going from bad to worse."

■

Linda knows her mother is going downhill and she can't convince her father. She feels equally frustrated with the case of the two missing girls. Meanwhile, she has to press ahead on her other cases. She decides it's time for a lunch meeting with Oliver Jamison. At Tokyo Jack's Sushi Bar, a huge circular counter transports an endless procession of delicacies on a conveyer belt. The counter is surrounded by bright blue tile floors and framed by dark teakwood paneled walls. Linda takes her lunch break from a nearby court session and perches on a tall stool between Ollie and an empty seat.

"Oliver, you really must try the starfish roe with the little star of wasabi. It's to die for." Linda waves a greeting to the chef and picks up a plate of hors d'oeuvres making its way around the station. "You've got to try this black cod with eel grass."

Jamison smiles sheepishly. "I don't know…but, what the heck." He captures a saucer as it approaches on the slowly moving conveyer belt and samples it. "Mmm. Not bad." He chews, swallows then says, "Did you bring the files?"

Linda takes a bite of her black cod, closes her eyes and smiles. "Damn, this is just heavenly, in a fishy sort of way." She absently pulls some folders from her briefcase. "I've got all of them here for you… and the updates on Tom Watkins. And after looking at them I have to agree. I just don't see them having anything to do with Ashley and Miranda. I mean, take a look here." She points to a page. "See? There doesn't seem to be any conclusive signs of sexual predation or violence on their part. Sure, he lived with his buddy right near Ashley, but that's not anything. You don't go from zero to murder and kidnapping in one fell swoop. The steps are always graduated. Ollie, it's highly unlikely that either one of those guys had anything at all to do with this mystery, other than committing the sin of geographical proximity. Now, I know you've got your old cronies available for gossip. Have your police sources revealed anything solid from the big search warrant raid? So far mine haven't been able to point me in a direction about that."

Oliver writes an observation onto his pad then responds, "I don't know about yours, but my sources at the police station have all been skeptical. All those cops and all those hours of intense scrutiny, and they didn't find one shred of physical evidence that linked either of those boys to the missing girls. I mean, Linda, they hauled out six bags of stuff and they went over the one guy's car with a fine-tooth comb. Nothing. It was all for nothing."

"In my opinion it was a trumped up floor show that the FBI staged just to demonstrate that Weaver was *not* their prime suspect. Once we shined the big spotlight on him, we inadvertently shined one on them too. They were forced to react. I still can't tell you if they really have their eyes on Weaver or not."

Linda finishes her first saucer, pushes it aside and plucks a grey one piled high with sashimi and rice from the conveyer belt. She takes a large bite and makes a comment with her mouth full. "What angles are you working?"

Jamison chuckles. "Linda, I don't work angles. Just like you, I'm a private investigator. My mission is to expose the facts surrounding perplexing crimes. I'm at my finest when I can accurately sum up the actions and effects on individuals that crime touches. Victims, perpetrators, investigators, each one is like a tributary of the bigger flow. I sort it all out and explain what I think it means. If you want to characterize my efforts along those lines as 'angles,' well, so be it. But to answer your question, presently I don't really have anything going on. Like you, I'm stalled."

Linda bites the sashimi and gags. "Jeez! This tastes like seaweed."

"It is seaweed," Ollie says, handing Linda a glass of water. "But, oh, so good."

Allison, the final member of the Linda O'Neal lunch meeting arrives, puffing an apology for her tardiness. She takes a seat and grabs a saucer. "What did I miss?"

Linda laughs. "Some great black cod and eel grass." She points to the conveyer. "But if you hang on a minute I see a rerun heading this way. What did you find out that's worth being late?"

"How about a psychic?"

Linda moans, "Good God! A psychic?"

"Oh, but you got to hear this. It seems that Babs Young, out in Lake Oswego, is not just a mere psychic. Oh no, she's a 'psychic consultant' and she gets her information through some sort of extrasensory perception. For example, she was contacted by the guy running all those websites."

Linda nods. "I think I gave you a file on him. He's a strange dude."

"Yes, you did. And yes, he seems strange. But anyway, he contacted the psychic in late April. He said 'I'm a friend of the Miranda Gaddis family and we desperately need your help because law enforcement has let us down. Can you turn your powers in our direction?'"

Linda is confused. "What exactly did she say in response?"

"The psychic wouldn't tell me every tidbit, but she did reveal that she thinks the girls are buried together near Molalla. She says it's a good place to bury bodies."

"Damn," Linda blurts out.

Allison reacts. "What's the matter?"

"Nothing. Nothing. I'm sorry. Go on. So what else did she tell you?"

"Young says that she feels a tremendous connection between the girls' fate and someone on the dance team to which both girls belonged."

Linda pauses a moment to reflect. "I don't know. I believe she 'saw' Redden's July 2 article on Weaver! Or maybe she's for real, I don't know."

"Aren't you including the webmaster in your profiles? He's full of theories on the crime. You've monitored his websites for a few months."

Linda explains. "The Miranda Gaddis family got to feuding with the website guy recently and ordered him to shut them down because they lost confidence in him. I think they suspected him of trying to profit in some vague way from the tragedy. But when he was asked about it, he got real emotional, cried his eyes out. 'I was the only one, the only one to start the volunteer search effort,' he said. 'This is the thank you I get for doing all this work and all these searches.'[3] Oh, he was devastated to be kicked out of the loop. He said, 'All I'm interested in doing is finding Ashley and Miranda, that's all, nothing else.'"

Linda tosses her napkin onto her empty plate, and makes a final comment. "Our Weaver conclusions should have broken this case wide open. Look at what happened. As soon as Redden published the 'Suspect: I Didn't Do Anything' piece, Weaver became a media darling. It turned my stomach watching some of the clips. That guy is super slick. And if the FBI was really after him as much as he thinks they are, why in the hell did they go after those young fellows who lived above Lori? Shake their poor lives upside down? Why not the same treatment for Weaver? What is it about Ward Weaver III that keeps him immune from being hassled too? I just don't get it."

■

Later that night, Linda obsesses over her theory about Ward Weaver's guilt. She's tormented by his arrogance and frustrated that he's living his life "high, wide and handsome." The phone ringing breaks the spell. "Linda O'Neal Investigations."

"Linda, it's Lori, Lori Pond. I'm calling you, because I'm begging for help."

"I've been trying to help, but you've been avoiding me the last few months."

"I know Linda, but they won't let me talk to anyone. But you're a private investigator and you can help me. That's all there is to it. I'm so afraid. I walk around every day, afraid. I look around looking for somebody that…I can't trust. It sounds really weird."

"No, no it doesn't. You're a victim too."

Lori sighs, "I sit home. I am so tired of sitting home. I ask myself why I don't just go out and start doing things, but I can't seem to."

"Are you afraid that there are more people like Ward Weaver out there?"

"I know there is. I've met 'em, throughout my life. My mom tried, but she let people like that into our home. Ask your husband."

"But Lori, Philip wasn't married to your mom when all of those bad things happened. He tried but there was little he could actually do. He had no rights in her house after she married your dad."

"Yeah, I know. I wish we all could have been stronger. Yeah. But my daughter was strong. She was strong in herself...in how she felt."

"I know she was a strong girl. You know, she got that from you."

"Thank you for saying that, but I'm scared of Weaver. Okay? I'm scared. I don't like him."

"I know you don't like him."

"I used to love everybody in a way. No more. Because Ward Weaver...I trusted him and he took my daughter. And so I'm screwed. I am so screwed because I cared."

Linda replies softly, "I understand."

"You do?"

"Of course I do."

"Wow! I never thought anybody ever would."

"We've all made some bad choices in our lives, believe me. You know what you should do? You should take a class."

"Why?"

"You have talents that you need to actualize. You should take a class in painting or yoga. Something that inspires you."

"I'm scared what people will say about me."

"People are not going to bother you."

"I've never had a force standing behind me telling me, you know, 'you are the best. You can do it, girl.'"

"Lori, you can do this. You can do anything you set your mind to. I believe in you, dear."

"Really?"

"Yes."

"Thank you."

"Philip and I have always believed in you and your potential. You can do something positive with your life. You have exhibited such great strength."

"I want to learn. I want to learn so badly." Lori begins to weep and Linda tries to comfort her.

After they hang up, Linda sits there, her head in her hand, feeling great empathy for Lori's obvious pain.

■

Ten more long days arrive and depart. Linda O'Neal detects no progress either from her end or the FBI's.

On the morning of August 11, Linda and Philip sit at their kitchen table, quietly eating cold cereal and toast while watching the news on TV. A female anchor is describing the progress in the Ashley and Miranda search. "After a recent flurry of activity, including the execution of a search warrant at one Newell Creek apartment," she says softly, "officials have concluded no new leads were discovered. The aggressive tactics used lately by some FBI and Clackamas County law enforcement personnel have produced boisterous complaints from many of the area's residents who have declared that lately they are all being treated like suspects in the case, despite no evidence. Our roving reporter, Pinski Brown, discussed the situation with Charles Mathews, FBI special agent in charge of Oregon, today, and this is what he had to say."

Next, Agent Mathews is shown standing outside the task force office with Brown nearby pointing a large microphone toward him. His lined face reveals weariness. "I admit our investigators are still baffled as to how two girls could simply vanish."

Linda's phone rings; she turns the TV down before she answers. "Linda O'Neal Investigations. Oh, hello, Ollie."

Linda's eyes widen and she taps the newspaper Philip is reading. He turns his total attention to eavesdropping on Linda's end of the call. "You've got something new on Ward Weaver? What? Where? I mean..."

Ollie interrupts, "Calm down. It may not be anything. But check this out! I have it on good authority that Weaver has recently put in his notice and, if he hasn't quit already, will soon be leaving that job at the machine shop."

Linda's mind races frantically. "Well maybe it just means he's going to work some place else. In that trade it's easy to get work if you're skilled. But thanks, Oliver. I'll check it out right away. Call me when the Berkley data arrives. I need to go over a few points with you before I write my report."

"Will do. Bye, Linda."

As soon as Linda hangs up, Philip pesters. "What's going on? Did they arrest Weaver or something?"

"I wish. Weaver's given notice at his job which means either he's changing employers, or he's..." She stops mid sentence, struggling to frame the concept in language she can accept. "He may be splitting. Damn!" Linda grabs a notepad from her purse and finds a number before hastily dialing it.

Finally, a groggy female voice responds. "Hello?"

"Is this Jayne Patan?"

"Who's calling please? Do you realize you just woke me up?"

"I'm so sorry dear. It's me, Linda, Linda O'Neal. I certainly didn't mean to wake you."

"I'm working graveyard this month."

"Listen, I won't take but a moment. I just need to run a quick fact by you and get your feedback."

Jayne's voice takes on a serious tone. "Okay. What's up? Something about Ashley and Miranda?"

"Ward Weaver. I just found out he's given his two-week notice at his job. Can you shed any light?"

"Ward's telling people he's moving to Mexico, but who knows if he's telling the truth."

Linda's mouth widens. She sputters. "But...but...does the FBI know about this?"

"I don't see how they couldn't know. He's been moving stuff out of his house all week and storing some of it at his sister's house and the rest in a rented storage place."

A plan begins to form in Linda's mind. Abruptly, she stands and reaches for her purse as she says to Jayne, "Listen, Hon, I'm going to let you get back to sleep. Gotta go. Bye." Linda hangs up the phone, pulls her car keys from the top of her purse and hugs Philip tightly.

"Are you going to fill me in here?" he asks.

Linda picks up her briefcase and purse and heads for the door.

"I'm going to Beavercreek Road and see what the hell is going on at Weaver's house. He may be getting ready to fly the coop to Mexico."

Philip shakes his head. "No way the FBI would let that happen."

Linda tosses her final comment just before she exits the house. "Don't bet your life on that one."

Thirty-five minutes later Linda is in Oregon City. When she finally reaches Beavercreek Road, Linda feels her heart rate increasing. As she approaches Weaver's house, she slows the car to a crawl and cranes her neck for a better look. She comes to a stop when she discovers a pickup truck parked in the driveway half full with cardboard boxes and bicycles. For a few moments she remains still, waiting and watching the truck, wondering if Weaver might be in the house. A pair of teenaged boys in cutoffs and tank tops emerges from the front door carrying a small, white food freezer. When they reach the truck they haphazardly lay it on the extended tailgate and cinch a bungee around it.

Surely, one of the police agencies must have a surveillance team nearby. She pushes her gas pedal and takes the car around several square blocks scrutinizing every bystander, every car. She reaches a conclusion. He's definitely taking off. The scumbag is going to run; no, he is going to tap dance his way offstage! Linda murmurs to herself, "I don't see one officer anywhere within half a mile keeping an eye on that bastard! Nobody's watching him. I can't believe it!"

At that moment, the truck backs out and slowly approaches Linda's car. Ward Weaver is at the wheel and makes a point to look straight at Linda before he suddenly stops. They make eye contact for several seconds neither blinking nor moving. His heavy face is broken by a wry, childish smile; a mocking grin that throws back all of Linda's attempts to bring him to justice. She is frozen with despair and frustration. He hits the throttle hard, tires smoking, and waves a defiant hand out the window with his middle-finger extended arrogantly as the truck disappears.

CHAPTER SIXTEEN

Running

During the next two days Linda racks her brain. *Was Ward Weaver moving or was he being a smart aleck and just going on an errand? Is he really fleeing the county? The state? The country? And what about the FBI or the Oregon City cops?* As she plows through her routine duties during those two days, she is inundated with thoughts of an ecstatic Ward Weaver driving off into the sunset. In Mexico or wherever he is going, he will inevitably create a new life with fresh female victims to prey on. She is overcome not only by a deep sense of frustration, but also sadness. She realizes that the police don't perceive Weaver as a serious suspect, yet they are the only ones with the power to bring him to justice. Her power is limited to what she can stir up.

On August 13, Linda sits in her home office trying to keep her mind on examining a document related to one of her case files. From down the hall she hears the clicks and whirrs of her husband's video decks as he pores through his afternoon workload. Her attention wanders back to the missing girls. She glances about the room and notices the framed photos hanging together on the wall next to her computer station. Pictures of family, her husband and friends all blended together in a gigantic wall-sized montage. When she sees a small snapshot of herself and old friend Ginger as they appeared years earlier, posing stiffly in their sheriff officer uniforms, she smiles wistfully. "Ginger!" she murmurs. Her voice rises, "I have to talk to her."

Linda grabs the phone and dials. A female voice answers. "This is

Ginger. How may I help you?"

"Well, did you win that marathon you were training for?"

"Not exactly. Why don't we meet at the Library at 4 PM?"

Linda glances out her window and notices thickening clouds. She quickly examines her day planner and then makes her decision. "Okay Ginger. I'll meet you out front."

The Oregon City Library, a one story 1970, cinderblock building, is nestled between a movie theater and the city hall/police station. Linda parks her car in the parking area. She makes her way across the lot and looks for Ginger. A gray minivan pulls up and deposits two pre-teen girls decked out in full karate outfits, each carrying a set of bright red nunchakus. They cheerfully dance their way to the karate school down the the street. Linda shakes her head, thinking how Ashley and Miranda must have been equally unconcerned the mornings they met their fate.

Dark billowing clouds conceal the blue skies as light rain drops turn suddenly into a summer thunderstorm.

A voice shouts, "Linda! Linda! I'm over here!" Ginger peers out from the library doorway, only her face visible. Once inside, Linda gets a full view of Ginger's "new look," which is dominated by a full length, flowing saffron robe. Her formerly brown hair is now a pale blond that seems to radiate the bright colors of a narrow crown of flowers that are anchored with ornamental hairpins to the top of her head. She stands at a slight angle, leaning on a thick, hickory cane.

Linda gasps as she tries to absorb the startling sight. "Wow! I almost don't recognize you. What's going on?"

Ginger turns and begins a slow walk down the corridor. "Follow me. I want to get a good seat."

"What's with the cane?"

Ginger laughs sheepishly. "Remember, I was training for the marathon?"

"The last time we were together you were up to six miles a day."

Ginger ponders. "By July 4, I was up to twelve, sometimes even fifteen miles a day. Then my career was brought to a fast conclusion."

"What happened?" Linda asks worriedly.

"Well, I started running mostly during the early morning hours, because it interfered a lot less with work. The weather during those days scorched. As you know, training at dawn in the summer, especially when you're running long distances, is cooler and I wasn't about to put up with the heat."

"And then..." Linda prods.

Ginger bites her lip before continuing. "One morning during the second week in July, I was zipping along the jogging trail in McGiver Park, following my usual route, listening to Spyro Gyra on my walkman, just jogging along, one leg in front of the other. Heart rate was smooth, legs and feet feeling perfect. Then all of a sudden, in one moment, bam! It was all over. Some damned moles had infiltrated the jogging path the night before and I guess I was oblivious or something, because I never even noticed them. But my left foot slipped into a twenty-inch-deep mole hole. Snap! I've never been in such pain."

Linda puts her hand on Ginger's shoulder. "You poor thing. How bad was it?"

Before answering, Ginger gently pulls up the side of her dress revealing a canvas shrouded walking cast covering her whole foot and lower leg up to her knee. "My ankle was shattered. I was running at such a clip that when I stepped in the hole it threw me completely around. When I finally pulled my foot out it was literally facing the other way."

Linda embraces her friend briefly. "I had no idea. Why didn't you call me and let me know?"

"I knew you had a lot on your mind. I didn't want to add to it."

"You're my friend. I could at least offer sympathy."

"They had to put in several pins and other devices to hold my foot together. I was flat on my back for two weeks and just got this walking cast last week. I finally went back to work last Monday. But I get around pretty good for a gimp, don't you think?"

Linda pats her friend's hand. "Ginger, you've always got such a remarkable attitude no matter what happens. You always seem to bounce back."

"The doctor told me my bouncing days are over for good, so no more marathons. And you can't believe how stubborn this kind of pain can be. Damn! I'll be lucky not to have a severe limp when this heals. But in the meantime, Linda, I've discovered a drug free alternative and I've become pain free in less than three sessions. I'm taking you there. Follow me."

They reach a small auditorium with a sign beside the entrance, "Swami Becker, Meditation Priority Session, 4:45 PM, August 13." They enter and Linda notices a dozen or so people, some mingling at the back of the room, others seated. Ginger leads Linda to a pair of chairs in the back row. They sit. Ginger looks toward Linda and whispers loudly, "Okay, so what about you? You said something about being distressed or something. Spill it, will you, before Swami Becker arrives."

Linda takes a deep breath and then begins. "Well, I recently found out that Ward Weaver is flying the coop. He gave two weeks notice to his employer and told his family he was heading for Mexico. So I'm stuck. The FBI doesn't seem to take him very seriously as a suspect. I need to know and you are the only one who can tell me, does the task force know about Weaver splitting the scene? And if so, are they concerned? Last week I witnessed the man removing personal property from the vacated house on Beavercreek Road. And I swear to you, Ginger, I looked high and low and I didn't notice a surveillance team anywhere near."

Just then Ginger turns her attention to a purple gowned, middle-aged man with a scraggly white beard encircling a gaunt, oval face. Very slowly he makes his way into the room, shuffling through every step. "That's him," she proudly exclaims. "That's Swami Becker. My God! He's going to walk right past us."

Linda rolls her eyes and stares at the floor while the robed one saunters by, then she waves her hand in front of Ginger's face, snapping her fingers. "Come on, Ginger."

"You don't understand. Please. Stay for the session. Absorb his wondrous teachings, and you, too, will become free from the shackles of misery that surround all of us."

Linda shifts back to her main concern. "Ginger, please be straight with me. Is the task force keeping tabs on Weaver?"

Becker has reached the podium at the front of the room and bows his head solemnly, which triggers most of the audience with the exception of Linda O'Neal to emulate. Ginger lowers her voice to a whisper. "Well, I have overheard a couple of conversations. Evidently the leaders of the task force seem to think that Weaver is on the up and up. He gave two weeks notice to his employer, then diligently worked those two weeks, always on time, always faithful to the chores. The task force has concluded that Weaver's actions are just not consistent with any profile they have created of an individual who is guilty of kidnapping those girls, despite the fact he lives nearby. They dismiss that whole aspect as coincidence. In short, Weaver doesn't behave in any of the ways a typical person 'on the run' would."

Linda scowls. "So what does that mean?"

"It means they just don't believe he did it. And you're right. They have no surveillance teams watching him move out."

"Well, I'm not buying it. I know he's guilty, Ginger, but I can't do much about it. He'll be out of sight, out of mind."

"I agree, but what can I tell you? In my opinion, it just doesn't look like any of them are willing to go after Weaver at this time. I can't explain exactly what turns them off, but clearly, they aren't looking at him any more or they'd be shadowing his every move. They seem to think he's an okay guy." Linda bites her lower lip. "It would be a lot more okay with me if he were in jail. As far as this 'moving to Mexico' thing, I mean, come on Ginger, that doesn't make sense. Where is Weaver really going to go?"

Becker raises his head, clears his throat and begins to address his gathering of disciples. "It's nice to see all of you back," he says warmly. "Plus, it's nice to see some new faces out there. I hope you're all ready for some enhanced enlightenment today. Let's begin with two minutes of transformational meditation. I want you all to close your eyes and find focus on a happy day in your childhood."

Ginger turns to Linda and squeezes her hand. "Well, Weaver has a half brother."

Linda nods. "Yes."

"He lives in Idaho. It seems like every time that the Weaver family gets into some kind of trouble, they either want to go to California or Idaho. And I don't think he's all that welcome in California any more."

"Oh? What are you talking about?"

"Somebody on the task force interviewed Weaver's mother not too long ago, and, Linda, she didn't have many positive things to say about him at all. It's pretty unlikely he'd be running to Mama for any assistance. So my bet would be Idaho. Idaho is where Weaver sent his oldest son to live. He talked his brother into taking him in. And from what I hear, he's even talked about sending Mallori up there to live with his brother's family."

"So he has mostly Idaho connections right now?" Linda jots a few notes on her pad.

"His son's girlfriend is even from Idaho. He met her when he was living there a few years back."

Linda shakes her head. "I didn't know anything about that. Are they still together?"

"Hell, yes! They had a baby together. He's a year old now. Ward Weaver's grandson. They've probably been an exclusive couple for at least two or three years, and they're both just kids—nineteen years old."

"Do you know what her name is, this girlfriend mother?"

"Her last name is Bowen, I think. I can't recall her first name. But she's like a loyal member of the family. Anyway, she and Ward's son now live in Northeast Portland"

"Why did they leave Idaho?"

"From what I understand, they had to leave in order to be together. Something about a domestic dispute and a restraining order. And you know, the state doesn't lift those restraining orders as easily as they put them on. So, anyway, the most likely place for Weaver to go is somewhere near his younger brother."

"But this is absolutely crazy. You mean the task force is not going to worry about him going? They could be losing evidence."

"Linda, they don't really need to watch him. They trust him. For example, he's scheduled to appear at a hearing, an administrative hearing, at the department of licensing about his invalid driver's license. Weaver vigorously pushed for this hearing. He's gone out of his way to make sure it's going to come down. Nobody in the task force imagines that he'll miss it. In fact the hearing is today. So I guess what I'm saying is, they know where to find him, at least today. And later, well they don't really care."

Before Ginger can continue, Becker's voice vibrates through the sound system. "That's wonderful," he exclaims. "Now I want you all to shake your shoulders. That's right. Shake. Shake all of the evil emotions right out into the air." He laughs heartily.

Linda and Ginger are listening, but only Ginger is involved in the shoulder shake exercise. Linda grabs Ginger's hand. "Where did you say this hearing was taking place on the driver's license thing?"

"At the department of licensing in Gladstone. It's scheduled for about a quarter to five this afternoon." She laughs. "So if they want him, that's where they know they can have him, but I bet they won't be there because they just aren't leaning that way."

Linda looks at her watch. She abruptly stands, causing the Swami to address her. "Yes, child, you have a statement for the group to absorb?"

For a few seconds, Linda glances at the many faces trained on her, anxiously awaiting her answer. She gently kisses Ginger, whispering, "I've got to go. Good luck, Ginger. Keep in touch." Then to Becker and the group, as she rapidly heads for the door she shouts, "I've found the light and now I may go forth!" As the door shuts behind her, many in the group clap and cheer while Ginger sits dazed.

For a moment or two Linda feels more light-hearted, but then her dark thoughts return. What will she do if she does find Weaver? Follow him? If so, where? Linda represses those negative notions as she walks to her car and swears to herself that she will not give up.

■

A summer thunderstorm makes its presence known with occasional cracks and flashes of lightning, but no rain yet. Ward

Weaver's black Firebird is parked in the employees' lot at the machine shop where he works. Ward Weaver's middle son is at the wheel of his pickup with Emily Bowen, his older brother's girlfriend, and her brother.[1] Emily exits and thanks the boys for the lift. She then stands near the black Firebird, glances at her watch and looks around as if she is there to meet someone.

Twenty minutes later Ward Weaver approaches. He tosses her the keys. "I really appreciate you helping me out on this, Emily. After all, it just wouldn't look very good to show up at the hearing driving myself there before I get my license back." He laughs as they get into the Firebird, with Emily at the wheel, and drive off. Within minutes a few drops from the emerging storm dot the windshield. Weaver watches the slender teenager as she maneuvers his tattered coupe in and out of afternoon traffic. "The Motor Vehicles place is the next exit, Murdock," he says, smiling. "Since we're so close, before we go to the hearing would you mind stopping by the house, there's a couple things I need to pick up."

Puzzled, Emily shakes her head. "I thought you got everything all moved out last week."

"Yeah, we moved all the big stuff last week, but there's some papers I need to get to show them."

Emily shrugs. "Okay Ward, but we better make it quick if you have to be there by a quarter to five. It's almost 4:30 now."

The Firebird soon turns on to Beavercreek Road, then pulls up and parks in the Weaver driveway. By now the rain is coming down hard. Weaver heads for the front door of the house and calls out to Emily to follow him in. "Come on, I got something I want to show you. It'll only take a minute." He turns and enters the house, confident she'll eventually take the bait. After looking at her watch, Emily gets out of the car and, feeling the raindrops grow heavy, rushes into the house, shutting the door behind her.

Weaver lingers in a nearby vacant bedroom, completely empty; the only thing covering its blank walls is the assorted sticker collection of his daughter. When he hears Emily he urges her to join him. "I'm in here! Come in. I want to show you something." She enters and reacts to the haphazard decorations. "Is the landlord going to be mad about all those? They won't come off very easy."

Weaver stares at the girl silently for a few seconds and then runs his right hand over the stickers. "I tried to tell her not to stick this stuff to the walls, but those damn kids nowadays, you can't tell 'em nothing." He chuckles and suddenly his mood changes as he sweeps his glance across Emily's torso and fixes a gaze on her breasts pushing against her tee shirt.

Emily always thought Weaver seemed cordial and gentle, some sort of rough-and-tumble teddy bear, but now his long, groping leers begin to make her uncomfortable.

Finally, turning away from her, Weaver approaches the back corner near the closet and standing on tiptoes, tries in vain to glimpse the top shelf. Cupping his hands he calls out a friendly request. "Emily, come over, will you. I want to boost you up to reach what's up here. I think I left those papers somewhere around up there."

"Okay, but we'd better hurry. Your hearing starts any minute." She hesitantly approaches, lifts her leg up and inserts her knee into his cupped hands.

The mood shifts when Weaver says firmly, "Put your arm around me." She is taken aback. Her former misgiving seems confirmed. This is the grandfather of her firstborn. He is family. She can't believe what seems to be happening.

She tries to get him back on track when she says, "It's okay, I can reach it for you, just give me a boost."

Weaver grabs her arm and grips it tightly, forcing it around his neck. A very startled Emily responds by squirming fiercely. "Ward! Stop it! What the hell is going on?"

Weaver's countermeasure literally sweeps the teenager off her feet when he grabs both of her legs and picks her up, like he's cradling her. "Keep your fucking mouth shut!" He carries her a few steps and releases his grip dumping her to the carpeted floor. He straddles her and pins her arms.

Emily screams. "Stop it! Stop! Stop!" He washes her face with his tongue and crude kisses while he fumbles to get her shirt removed.

She fights and kicks with all the energy her one-hundred-twelve-pound frame can muster. But she is no match for Weaver. She tries to reason with him. "I'm part of your family, Ward. You've got to stop this!"

He responds coldly by tightening the grip he has around her throat. She continues to struggle. He intensifies the pressure. Clearly his intent is to literally squeeze the life from her. He squeezes every breath from between her lips, while staring intently into her terrified eyes.

His mood seems to shift from brutish to warm as he inexplicably releases his grip and gently strokes her hair. "If you'll quit screaming and struggling, I promise I won't hurt you. Just relax and I won't hurt you."

Emily decides survival demands capitulation. She remains motionless while Weaver removes every stitch of her clothing, especially savoring the feel and smell of her bra. He continues to fondle the girl while he rolls side to side, gradually completing penetration. With hot, burning tears streaming down her cheeks, Emily clenches her fists.

At the conclusion, he lays quietly on top of her for a few moments. Emily's survival instincts once again overtake her. She squirms violently and screams.

Emily Bowen truly believes that Weaver is hell-bent on murdering her. She braces herself for what she expects will come next.

Weaver by now has taken his weight off her. Suddenly, she sees a window of opportunity. Instinct takes over and she knows she must escape now. She extracts herself from underneath him by pushing off with her hands against his head, then springs to her feet and darts across the room to a hallway that leads to the living room and freedom, if she can just reach the front door before Weaver can intercept her. During her mad dash for liberation, Weaver is struggling to get his pants on. But he is too late, for after grabbing a rumpled blue tarp that was wadded up on the empty floor, a totally naked Emily streaks out the front door hysterically screaming and trembling, into a yard that by now is being deluged with the violent summer storm.

As he drives toward his suburban Oregon City home, he doesn't see the lightning, but Bart Connors hears the ominous thunderclaps. A late afternoon summer storm sweeps through the Willamette Valley depositing its splashes onto the windshield of his year-old Jeep. Beavercreek Road, Connors's normal route home, is turning into the creek it was named after. He switches his wipers to high allowing him to barely make out a towering billboard off to his right. The forty-foot sign displays the images of two girls' faces underscored by a bright red caption, "ASHLEY POND/MIRANDA GADDIS...MISSING GIRLS, $65,000 REWARD!"

As traffic slows, partly because of the rain, partly because of an upcoming red light, he brings the Jeep to a complete stop. Instantly he is confronted with a naked girl who jumps in front of his vehicle and then violently pounds on the car's hood. She clings to a scrap of blue tarp that flaps in the wind. She is obviously very young, perhaps even a teenager. Muddy tears stream down her face as she screams. "Help me! Oh, God! Help me!"

Before Connors has time to react, the girl rushes to the passenger side of the Jeep, swings open the unlocked door and leaps into the front. Crouching down on the bucket seat she pleads to the stunned commuter, "Get me out of here now! Please. He's after me."

Connors looks around and notices a flat black Firebird parked in a nearby driveway, but he sees no one in pursuit of the drenched female. The light changes to green. The surrounding traffic begins to move and an errant horn honk brings him back to reality. He frantically skirts around some cars waiting to make a left turn and accelerates his SUV up the road. The trembling youngster beside him desperately tries to cover her shivering body with fragments of the plastic tarp. "Please take me to a phone," she sobs. "I need help."

Within thirty seconds they approach a small strip mall and she directs him to pull in. She fumbles open the door and jumps out of the Jeep before it comes to a complete stop. Frantically, she sprints to a nearby Joyce's Shoe Store.

Inside the small shop a half dozen startled patrons react to the shrieking nude female wearing only a tarp as a cape, begging to use the phone. A clerk intercepts the distraught teenager and gently leads her to a small office at the rear of the store. Between gut wrenching sobs, the girl manages to dial 9-1-1 and then blurts out, "Help me! I've been raped. He tried to kill me!"

CHAPTER SEVENTEEN

Raped

As the digital clock turns to exactly 5:11 PM, the Clackamas County 9-1-1 emergency line begins beeping in rhythm with the flashing red indicator. Julia Hendricks turns her attention to duty and her fingers open the line. "9-1-1. What is your emergency?"[1]

A hysterical female voice shouts, "Help me! I-I've been raped. He tried to kill me!"

The emergency dispatcher's heart begins to race. "Okay, now try to calm down so I can understand you. Can you tell me your name?"

"I'm Emily Bowen. Please help me!"

"Where are you calling from? Is he still around?"

The female voice screams, "Where am I?"

The dispatcher hears a male voice in the background. "You're at Joyce's Shoe Store on Beavercreek Road."

"Ma'am, do you know where the perpetrator is?"

"I don't know. He was in his house. Maybe he's still there."

"Can you give me an address?"

"I can't think of it, but it's just up the road from here, on Beavercreek Road." She begins sobbing profusely. "Please help me!"

"I am helping. Remember, you're safe now. Just stay on the phone with me. I'm radioing the Oregon City Police. They'll be on their way very soon. Just a minute, please." The dispatcher switches between lines and addresses the radio. "Fifty-two fourteen....We have a rape that occurred minutes ago. Victim location: Joyce's Shoe Store off

Beavercreek Road. She's in the manager's office. Stand by for further."
She switches back. "Okay, I'm back. Go ahead…Do you know who
attacked you?"

"Yes, it was my father-in-law, Ward Weaver."

"Can I get a description?" The dispatcher listens for a moment
then punches some keys and maneuvers her mouse, getting the facts
down before turning her attention back to the rape victim. "Please try
to calm down for me because it's really important for us to catch him.
I'm going to ask you some questions, but you've got to try to hang in
there for me. It's going to be all right. You're safe. I need to talk to the
police car. I'll be right back."

Julia radios the officer standing by. "Fifty-two fourteen, the
suspect is Ward Weaver. Location of incident: south Beavercreek
Road, approximately six blocks north of Joyce's Shoestore. Last seen
by the victim at that location."

The officer responds. "I'm two blocks away from there now.
Proceeding to that location."

The dispatcher returns to the caller. "Did you sustain any
injuries?"

"Yes," Emily cries. "He tried to choke me to death."

"I have an ambulance en route. You're going to be okay. They'll
assist you."

The dispatcher switches to a different frequency, the one used only
by the Clackamas County Sheriff's Department. The computer screen
flashes. The dispatcher responds. "Go ahead sixteen eighty seven."

"This is Detective Fryett, sixteen eighty seven. I'm en route to
interview the victim at Joyce's Shoe Store. ETA, ninety seconds or
less."

"Copy that sixteen eighty-seven." Christine Fryett is the sexual
assault investigator for the Clackamas County Sheriff Department.

The 9-1-1 dispatcher addresses the distressed caller. "Are you still
on the line, ma'am?"

"Yes I am, but so far nobody is here."

"Ma'am there's a police officer about thirty seconds away. I'm
going to keep you on the line with me and as soon as she makes

contact with you, you can hang up and she'll take over. Okay? In the meantime, can you give me a description of your assailant's vehicle? Any information can help."

"It's a black Camaro or something like a Camaro. It was parked in his driveway."

The dispatcher pushes a black button. "All units prepare to copy an 'attempt to locate.'"

Emily interrupts. "They're here. The police are here. I'm going to hang up now. Good bye."

"Dispatch with an attempt to locate suspect and suspect vehicle in rape that just occurred on Beavercreek Road approximately ten to fifteen minutes ago. Suspect's name: Ward Weaver. Five ten, two hundred ten pounds, reddish brown hair, mustache. Suspect vehicle described as black Camaro type."

A few minutes later the officer radios, "Fifty-two fourteen to dispatch."

"Go ahead fifty-two fourteen."

"I've checked the Ward Weaver house and yard and found no vehicles and no subjects in or about the property. I'll do an area check for the suspect's vehicle."

"Dispatch copy."

Another radio transmission crackles into the dispatcher's headphones. "Fifty-two thirty-two."

"Fifty-two thirty-two, go ahead."

"Uh yes, fifty-two thirty-two. I've just spotted a black Pontiac Firebird heading north on Highway 213 with a lone male driver."

"All units copy! Possible suspect vehicle northbound on Highway 213. Fifty-two thirty-two, please provide a cross street."

"Following suspect vehicle onto I-205 at this time, northbound."

"All units copy! Suspect vehicle has now entered I-205 from 213 and is proceeding northbound."

"Fifty-two thirty-two."

"Fifty-two thirty-two."

"Stand by for plate."

"Standing by."

"Oregon plate, Robert Lincoln Tom, 374."

After she types the data, her computer screen flashes the desired information, which she dispenses to the officer. "Fifty-two thirty-two. The registered owner of vehicle, Thomas Gilchrest, advises he sold this vehicle in April, 2002 to Ward Weaver of Oregon City."

"Fifty-two thirty-two."

"Dispatch. Copy."

"Fifty-two thirty-two, please be advised, I am about to initiate the traffic stop south of Strawberry Lane exit. Please assign cover."

"Dispatch to any units in the area of northbound Freeway 205 near the Strawberry Lane overpass. Fifty-two thirty-two needs immediate backup on felony car stop."

At that moment Linda O'Neal is in her car behind the Oregon City Police building. She reaches over and starts the engine. Flipping the turn signal on, she checks her rearview mirror. The image of a huge, white truck comes into her view. When she turns her head for a fuller inspection, she discovers it to be a news van, a six-foot diameter dish mounted precariously to its top. To Linda's surprise the TV vehicle pulls in to an empty space directly behind her car and parks before doors flip open releasing a scrambling cadre of news crew professionals.[2] Linda watches them assemble cameras, connect microphones and tinker with the satellite alignment, then decides to find out the reason for this eruption of media interest. She shuts off the engine and walks to the sidewalk, surveying the group, searching for a distractible staffer. A lean, redheaded teen is setting up some reflector panels. She taps his arm. "What's up?" she gushes. "The presidential motorcade about to arrive?"

The youngster makes no eye contact but does respond. "Na! They just arrested that Ward Weaver guy. Just happened about five minutes ago. We were up on highway 213 covering a brush fire, and they told us to get our butts out here quick to get some footage of the cops dragging his hopefully kicking and screaming sorry ass through those doors into the jail."

Linda's cell phone rings and she quickly picks up. It's Philip. "Linda, they've arrested Ward Weaver. It's on all the channels. They've got a helicopter covering every minute. I just watched 'em put him in the police car. They're taking him to the Oregon City Police station this minute. It's on the TV, live."

Philip pauses a moment, then asks, "Where are you?"

"I'm on the scene," Linda laughs. "If you keep your eye on the TV you just may see me. I'm on the backside of that police station and it looks like they expect Weaver to arrive momentarily. They've got the cameras all set in position a few feet away from me. Put a tape in the VCR and record the coverage for me, will you? I'll call you when I know something. Bye."

Linda lingers for a few minutes watching news reporter Pinski Brown preparing for her live broadcast. "Any moment, ladies and gentlemen," the reporter begins, "we expect Ward Weaver to arrive from that direction being brought in for his initial booking. Stay with us and we'll give you the up-to-the-minute exclusive *Action News* coverage." She becomes distracted by the flashing blue and red lights on the approaching police cars. Linda is staring at them too and her heart pounds when she sees a handcuffed man in the back seat of the lead vehicle. Unmistakably, it is Weaver who sits erect, eyes staring blankly forward. As soon as the car stops, Weaver is ushered out.

While Linda follows close behind, the newscaster, cameraman and sound man proceed in search of a decent angle from which to tape the impending march of the accused from the car to the police station's rear entrance. When she sees Weaver walking by, Pinski hollers at him, "Mr. Weaver, Mr. Weaver, what are you being arrested for?"

Weaver's hands are cuffed tightly behind his back as an officer grips his right arm during the escort. Before they go in, Pinski shouts another question. "Mr. Weaver, does this arrest involve the missing Oregon City girls?" Weaver adjusts his gaze and briefly shoots her a grim glance before he utters a one-word response, "No." Weaver and the officer disappear behind the closing door of the Oregon City Police Department.

∎

That evening, Linda and Philip are in their kitchen, eyes glued to the TV screen, which is tuned to CNN.

Over a garish graphic, a male voiceover intones, "This is Connie Chung Tonight. Live from the CNN Broadcast Center in New York, Connie Chung."

Chung comes into view, and with muted expression begins her report. "Good evening. Tonight, a dramatic development in the story we've been telling you about this week: the mysterious disappearance of two girls in Oregon. Today a bizarre twist has the son accusing his father, Ward Weaver, of being the man behind the disappearances. Ward Weaver currently is in jail being held on a one-million-dollar bond. He's accused of raping his son's nineteen-year-old girlfriend on Tuesday night."

Chung clarifies that Weaver's arrest has nothing to do with the disappearance of Ashley Pond or Miranda Gaddis, but occurred because of the rape of Emily Bowen. Linda is clearly upset. "They have to put two and two together. They just have to!" she says to Philip, shaking her head.

Linda's phone rings. She answers, "Linda O'Neal Investigations."

Her step-daughter Maria is on the line. "Linda," she asks, "did you hear that the police haven't connected Weaver's rape charges with the two crimes?"

"Yeah, it's damned upsetting. You'd think now that they have the bastard locked up they'd dig up the slab in his backyard."

Linda, pensive, taps her fingers against the table next to her. After a pause she goes on, "Remember how effortlessly the search warrant for Tom Watkins's apartment was obtained? They didn't have a shred of any legitimate probable cause, yet they even took Watkins' car to the crime lab. There is nothing stopping them from procuring a search warrant giving them the freedom to search for Ashley and Miranda throughout the Weaver house and grounds based on his son's state-ment. After all, they already have the Weaver property completely secured. It's just a matter of time for them to expand their efforts."

"I don't think so, Linda."

"Why not?"

"Tony and I were at Lori's apartment today; in fact we just got home a few minutes ago. We drove by the Weaver house on our way out and the police took all the tape down. There's nobody there. I swear."

Linda's voice rises. "It doesn't make any sense! Are you sure? They have to find out what's under that slab. We have to get the police to pay attention to it."

"I'm telling you, the cops are not watching the place. Anybody could walk in there. Linda, look, what about our going back to that house and putting up a big sign, right next to the slab that says, 'Here Lies Ashley Pond. Dig Me Up So I Can Find Justice'"

"Good idea. Philip will come too, but wait until tomorrow. By then I'll have time to stir up some news coverage. The FBI occasionally bends a bit when the cameras are rolling. How about it? Tomorrow? Maybe in the early afternoon?"

"Reporters would definitely be good," Maria says. "Okay. I'll go make my sign tonight. What time shall we aim for?"

"How about two o'clock? That'll give the press plenty of time to put our little show on the evening news. I'll call some others to help us out. See if you can get some of our family there too. We'll create what sometimes is called a 'media event.'"

The next afternoon, as Linda had hoped, a few local TV news people position themselves near the Weaver house to witness the event.[3] Philip and Linda stand with a group that includes Maria, Claire Stevens and a few other women, some holding crude cardboard signs that say, "Dig Me Up!", "Dig Here" and "Wake Up FBI and Smell the Coffin!" Linda casts a glace toward Weaver's house and confirms that there seems to be no official police presence anywhere near. She turns to Philip, "What are they thinking? How can they just walk away and leave this place totally open like this?"

Maria approaches holding a hammer and nails in one hand and her forty-eight-inch-wide poster board sign in the other. She proudly displays it for Linda and Philip. "Do you think they'll put mine on the TV news?"

Philip chuckles and hugs his daughter briefly. "Great lettering. The red ink really stands out. How long did it take you?"

"Two hours. I think mine is bigger and easier to read than some others. But even the crayon scribbled on the back of flattened cardboard boxes may help."

For a surreal three minutes, the group disperses to various sites and erects their signs. One tacks the sign, "Dig Here" to a nearby tree trunk. Another's reads "FBI: DO YOUR JOBS!" Maria and Claire Stevens head right for the concrete slab. Using duct tape, Stevens carefully attaches her sign, "Dig Me Up!" horizontally onto the slab itself. As she finishes, Pinski Brown, with a microphone in her right hand, approaches. "Ma'am, can you explain why you're here doing this?"

Stevens continues her duct tape chores as she replies. "Did you notice the odor when you walked up the path? I did. And that's all I have to say."

Immediately, Linda steps into Pinski's path. "It is a weird situation. Can you believe the cops have totally abandoned this place so soon?"

For a moment, Brown soaks up the desperate activities. "If this keeps up the FBI will be clamping down. They can't allow these people to be trampling all over like this. It's ridiculous."

Linda points toward Stevens. "You want ridiculous? Go interview that lady. Ask her about how many times she reported Weaver's abuse of Ashley to the state. Ask her how they handled it," Linda scoffs. Pinski heads off across the lawn in search of her version of the scoop.

Philip's daughter pounds a pole into the ground near the slab before tacking on her tombstone shaped display, "Here Lies Ashley Pond. Ignored by the Police Again." "Suddenly, a white sedan pulls into the open Weaver driveway and screeches to a stop. The black-haired female driver leaps out followed by the lone front seat passenger, Michelle Duffy. While she lingers hesitantly, the driver sprints to one of the trees with a sign nailed to its branch, yanks it down and tears the tattered cardboard in half, then in half again. A couple of the nearby news crews aim video cameras at her in time to record her defiant utterance. "Every time I find a sign put up like this or every time I find a candle put out in front of Ward's house, I will take it down. I will rip up your signs and I will break your candles.

These disgusting signs are here to help mourn the loss of Ashley and Miranda, and we haven't lost them yet, despite what anybody thinks. I refuse to believe the girls are dead and as such I refuse to believe they are buried on this property and I will continue to believe that until the FBI confirms otherwise!"

Philip and Linda look at each other. "Who's she?" he asks.

"She's a friend of Michelle's."

The woman rushes to the concrete slab and rips up Stevens's creation, dangling sticky strips of duct tape every which way. Stevens takes offense and begins a confrontation. "What do you think you're doing?" she shouts as she snatches the sign and pushes the intruder aside.

Reporters swarm to the ripening conflict and soon are surrounding the pair of combatants.

At that moment three unmarked blue Fords arrive and spew six FBI agents onto Weaver's driveway. For an instant, they seem perplexed but eventually fan out in small clumps, approaching each individual aggressively. "You ladies will have to step back off this property," one of them bellows to Linda and Maria. "You're trespassing. All of you are trespassing. This is private property."

Maria bristles and she folds her arms. "Oh, I didn't know you had any jurisdiction here. As far as we've been informed, Ward Weaver controls this property, and he's invited each and every one of us to this property at one time or another. We just chose today to make our visit. Is that a problem?"

By now the black-haired woman and Stevens have been separated, yet in a final act of defiance, the woman yanks up the stem of Maria's tombstone sign and drags it across the lawn toward the street. Maria ignores the FBI man and rushes over to wrestle her creation away from the interloper. With that mission accomplished, she directs her next remark to the group of signsters. "Come on girls, our work seems to be done here for now. We'll be back."

During the next two days, many opinions erupt concerning Ward Weaver's property. Newspaper articles, TV news coverage and local radio talk show commentators climb onto the signster bandwagon.

Each passing hour seems to cast more doubt in the minds of the public about the competency of the officials investigating the case. "Dig me up," becomes a mantra.

The Weaver house is now an attraction. The more adventurous rubberneckers park along Beavercreek Road and wander about the property, peeking through windows, looking under tarps and prowling through yard debris. Even some TV news crews film their stories on the lawn to use Weaver's house for backdrop.

FBI officials have seemingly lost control, having not anticipated the potential damages an unsecured, advertised crime scene could produce. Under increasing public pressure to regain an image of leadership in the case, they contact Frank Jones, the property owner. He informs them that Weaver had not paid rent since June and was soon going to face legal eviction. If he'll agree to post the place with several "No Trespassing" signs, they assure Jones they can provide personnel to enforce the law.

At 9:15 AM on the morning of Sunday, August 18, Jones, accompanied by his assistant, Ernie Taylor, parks his car in the front driveway. Jones notices a pair of TV news staffers parked across the street and comments. "What the hell are they waiting for?"

"Excuse me?" A thirty-something woman walking next to two twelve-year-old girls approaches from the back yard. She startles Jones. "Do you know where Weaver was going to put in the hot tub?"

Jones scowls, pulls one of his "No Trespassing" signs from his briefcase and waves it. "Ma'am, you need to leave this property immediately. You're trespassing."

"But my daughters are the same age as Ashley and Miranda and they made me drive them all the way from Vancouver. They needed to come here."

While the intruders observe from a legal distance, Jones and Taylor selectively tack many of the signs to portions of the building. They push the bulky hot tub frame up against the backside of the house. Taylor notices an unusual odor which triggers him to head for the large storage shed at the northwest corner of the backyard. When he arrives, he is overwhelmed with a sickening stench. "Frank!" he yells. "Frank. You got to see this!"

Jones sprints to the shed where he peers inside. Taylor continues. "Look at those. There must be a thousand of 'em or more." Flies. Thousands of fly carcasses are glued firmly to half a dozen two-foot-long flypaper strips. Many of the insects are still alive and buzzing. Next to the flypaper, a dozen scented, cardboard deodorant trees dangle like eerie Christmas ornaments.

Jones stares briefly at the inside of the shed, and then turns his head in search of a cop. "Where the hell are they?" he mutters. "Where's a cop when you need one?"

Within hours, all public access to Weaver's house is efficiently denied through the use of the "No Trespassing" posters combined with vigorous enforcement provided by the several plain clothes FBI officers. When Jones points out the shed anomalies to them, he is assured that very soon they will be taking strong action. "But for awhile," the agent in charge explains, "we've just got to sit tight until everything is ready." He is reluctant to explain further.

At 8:30 AM on Tuesday, August 20, Linda and Philip sit at their breakfast table sipping coffee between bites of scrambled eggs with toast. While Philip peruses the sports page of the *Portland Tribune*, Linda is poring over a front page story containing a large color picture of Claire Stevens with the headline "Pond Tipsters Got Cold Shoulder."[4]

Linda puts her coffee cup on the table and adjusts her reading glasses. A few moments later she yanks Philip's sports page from his hands to command his attention. "Listen to this," she exclaims. "'Family members and associates of the Weaver and Pond families have described the relationship between Weaver and Ashley as inappropriate. One person said Ashley slept in the same bed as Weaver at his home. Another said Weaver's relationship with Ashley caused problems with his live-in girlfriend, but, the witnesses said, there was little or no follow-up to their attempts to provide this information to investigators.'" Linda embraces Philip. "Somebody finally gets it. Maybe the general public can make the FBI listen to what I've been saying." She pulls back from Philip and examines a different paragraph from the news article. "This is exactly the same stuff I was trying to tell them in June. Listen. 'Claire Stevens saw Ashley frequently and twice told social services representatives that she found Weaver's relationship with Ashley to be disturbing.'"

Linda squeezes his arm excitedly. "Philip, every facet of our case against Weaver has finally found a public forum. This is incredible!" She pulls the newspaper up and smiles. "Look here, they even have the Harry Oakes evidence." She reads, "'According to Oakes he became interested in the Weaver property when his dog gave a death alert in the canyon.' And then later down here they've got some other dog handler, Marty Neiman. Remember him?[5] And someone says Oakes's dog wouldn't alert in a graveyard. Well, I guess we're going to find out if she would, because it says here in a little box at the top of the article, 'FBI To Dig Up Weaver's Concrete Pad. "Listen for the jackhammers," says Oregon FBI chief, Charles Mathews, "Monday. Investigators will dig up the concrete pad behind Weaver's former house as soon as the law allows. We're just waiting to cross all of the T's and dot all of the I's."

"Well, it's about time!" Linda scowls.

Philip says, "How does all this make you feel? I mean, look what's happening. Your investigations have started the ball rolling. It's all finally about to come down."

Linda sighs and takes a tight hold of Philip's hand. "I realize that, but I have mixed feelings. I mean, even with all of this, it won't bring those girls back. Because the real question is why did this have to happen in the first place? If just one person this little girl asked for help had done his or her job—not the letter of the job—but the spirit of the job, this wouldn't have happened."

At 11:15 PM on the evening of August 23, Beth Anne Steele, spokesperson for the FBI Task Force, stands in front of a makeshift podium on Ward Weaver's front yard about to conduct an impromptu news conference before a sparse collection of diehard news people. She smiles politely. Then, squinting from the beam of a camera-mounted spotlight she begins her presentation. "Tonight, we have some special announcements concerning our seven-month-long investigation into the disappearance of first, Ashley Pond, and later, Miranda Gaddis, both victims who lived a block away from where I'm standing tonight.

"For the first time in this case, we are now officially announcing that our exhaustive investigation has finally led us firmly on to this path. Recent discoveries have forced us into the realization that…"

For a moment Steele pauses, trying to think of the exact words that she means to say. She resumes. "We believe that we will find hard evidence at this location. Therefore, at 9:00 AM tomorrow morning FBI agents, assisted by officers from the Oregon City Police Department, will begin executing a search warrant that we just obtained less than an hour ago. The necessity for this search evolved from the dedicated work of dozens of professionals…"

The ferocious roar of a nearby diesel generator interrupts Steele. Then the engine coughs and dies. "…during months and months of frustrating dead ends…"

The engine roars back into life. She turns just as a group of high watt klieg lights strategically attached to twelve-foot poles fire up, casting an incredible glow. There is a pinkish hue in every direction. Uniformed laborers have already connected dozens of chain link fence sections that wrap a barbed-wire-topped iron ring around the entire compound. Another crew pulls a huge tent from its casing and begins erecting it over the concrete slab. More engines fire up. Tractors and backhoes slowly crawl through the new security gate. Green-jacketed agents scurry in every direction.

The next morning Beavercreek Road is empty of traffic. A Cadillac sedan approaches, slows and then stops right in front of the Weaver place. The one hundred seventy feet of metal fencing has become the physical boundary between ordinary and evil. The driver's door opens. A slender, gray haired woman wearing a purple silk pantsuit and wire rimmed sunglasses exits. The TV crews train their zoom lenses onto the lone figure. In her right hand she grips a single, long-stemmed white rose. She reaches the fence and casts a lingering glance at the Weaver house beyond. Then she gently loops the rose stem through several of the chain links and bows her head. She returns to her Cadillac and drives away. Cameras record her poignant departure.

Strangely, the lady's symbolic display of muted respect for the victims profoundly influences the public psyche. By noon that day, the single flower has turned into hundreds of flowers, cards, notes, candles and Teddy bears—each one reverently attached to the fence by someone who was stirred enough to make the special journey. By evening, the hundreds become thousands, spilling over to sidewalk space as the fence gradually becomes transformed into a massive adorned wall of grief. Entire families feel compelled to make the pilgrimage. Residents of the metro area continually stream into the neighborhood, seeking to somehow demonstrate their emotional support for the families of the victims, desperately in search of collective catharsis.

Television news coverage multiplies as well. Three local channels suspend all scheduled Saturday programming and broadcast nonstop throughout the day from their posts directly across Beavercreek Road. By late afternoon, more than a dozen satellite trucks are jammed next to each other as the national networks have also dispatched their news people to join the swelling hordes of media exploiters. The Oregon City girls' tragedy transcends from its humble origin as a regional case of kidnapping and possible homicide. Within a few hours, the story is catapulted into the status of a national phenomenon, people's fixations fueled to a great extent by the emotional residue that TV viewers absorb. Glued to the tube, they watch the event expand into a bigger-than-life pageant, their attention sustained by the suspense. Behind the barricades, the FBI continue their exhaustive search for evidence.

At 9:00 AM the FBI contacts the Pond and Gaddis families to update them. Philip and Linda drive over to the family gathering at Ashley's grandmother's house in Oregon City and join the crowd huddled in front of the TV. The family echoes Linda's mixed feelings. None want the news that they expect, but at the same time they desperately need this ordeal to be over.

At noon the phone rings again. Ashley's grandmother answers and eyes turn toward her. "This is Beth Steele," the caller says. "We think

you need to designate someone to represent your family because…"
Steele falters, and then resumes. "Because there is a lot of media
coverage going on up here, and if we don't provide them with a family
spokesperson, they'll end up pestering all of you mercilessly. That's
just the way they are in situations like this. So, if and when anything
is found, it will be important to give a statement to the news media."

For a moment Ashley's grandmother cannot speak.

Steele says, "Are you there, ma'am?"

"Yes. Okay. Thanks. Can you tell us if they've found anything yet?"

"Nothing yet, but…well, soon. Very soon. That's all I can tell you
at this time. Keep your phone line open. I promise, you'll be the first
to know when we…when we discover anything substantial. Okay?"

"Okay. Thank you." The old woman hangs up the phone and
stands before her family members. Lori Pond sits nearby, holding her
new baby boy in her lap. Her eyes widen. The grandmother shakes her
head. "No, no. Nothing yet. But they want one of us to be ready to talk
to the media when they…if they…"

Maria approaches her mother and drapes an arm around her
shoulder. "Can't you do it, Mom?"

Ashley's grandmother has to fight back tears. "I don't think I'm
capable. I wouldn't know what to say."

For a few moments, murmurs echo from around the room. Finally
the grandmother's husband steps forward and announces, "I'll do it. I
can handle it. I'll talk to them. I'll go up there in a few minutes."

While the rest in the room remain riveted to the continual TV
coverage, Linda offers to drive the old man to the Beavercreek Road
site. Once they arrive, Linda stays near the car and absorbs the unreal
circus-like atmosphere that confronts her. She is amazed at how much
more strongly the live images impact her emotions than the TV
version. Meanwhile, like an obedient soldier, Ashley's step-grandfather
slowly makes the rounds, traveling along the lines of cameras and
reflector shields, offering comments to TV reporters as each snag him
for their individual snippet. His answers are poignant and reflect a
sense of unpolished dignity as he is forced to keep reacting to similar,
inane questions. "How do you feel about what's happening?" Or "Do

you think finding the bodies will bring the closure you seek?" And, "Do you believe Weaver kidnapped your granddaughter?"

During what seems like the twentieth interview, the grandfather notices a man in an FBI jacket standing nearby staring solemnly. "Thank you very much for talking to us," the reporter finally says, motioning for him to move on.

He is intercepted by the FBI agent who softly says, "You need to be with your family right now. Do you have transportation?"

The grandfather feels a chill and then nods as he indicates Linda across the street still standing next to her car.

"I suggest you return to your residence because we're soon going to be making the announcement that we've discovered unidentified human remains."

The old man's mouth drops open and he feels his heart pounding.

"Sir, are you going to be okay?"

"Yeah. All right. I'll go home now. I need to be with Lori."

Gordon Huiras, Oregon City Chief of Police, steps in front of the bank of hastily assembled microphones, his face pale and his expression grim. "We're sad to announce that this afternoon, late in the afternoon, investigators processing the crime scene have discovered what appears to be human remains in the outbuilding behind the house."[6]

A wave of emotion pummels the witnesses of this presentation. Many females literally shriek and wail, releasing mournful sobs that punctuate the rest of Huiras's comments. "The medical examiner has responded to the scene, as you may have seen a few minutes ago, and the remains have been turned over to him. There is not going to be any identification released. We do not know what remains these are. And it will likely be several hours before there's any identification released from the medical examiner's office."

Onlookers collapse into each other's arms, hugging and weeping.

Huiras continues, "Okay, just to repeat, for those of you who couldn't hear, the apparent remains of one body were found secreted in the shed at the rear of the property. The crime scene investigation will continue into the evening. Right now, we're engaged in trying to remove the concrete slab behind the house. There are also other areas of interest in the property that the investigators will be moving to next, after they finish the investigation around the concrete slab. We'll probably cease work later this evening and then start again tomorrow morning."

Linda and Philip exchange warm embraces with several of the people still assembled at Ashley's grandmother's house and promise they'll return in the morning to give additional moral support, pledging to participate in their vigil during the Sunday session.

By noon the next day, Beavercreek Road has literally become a parking lot requiring a crew of uniformed traffic officers to assert control. Long lines of vehicles inch past while heads crane from open windows, anxious for any peek at the flower-laden, fifty-yard-long monument. Every news crew is on the air with nattily dressed correspondents holding microphones, pontificating endlessly.

At 2:45 PM the gates are briefly pulled open to allow a medical examiner van on to the property, creating a burst of apprehension among the throng of observers.

Fifteen minutes later, Chief of Police Huiras once again stands before the maze of clustered microphones and remains silent for a few moments while television technicians adjust their sound mixers and lens apertures. Then, with a long face, he begins a speech. "First of all, I'd like to express my appreciation to the many hours of hard work that our dedicated investigators have spent trying to bring this case to a conclusion. Now, with regard to the remains that were removed from the Weaver property yesterday afternoon, the medical examiner has preliminarily concluded that those remains were placed in the shed approximately one month ago, on or about July 24. The body had been tightly bound with quarter inch nylon cord and then covered with several layers of plastic."

Huiras's anguish begins to invade his delivery, so he stops talking for a few moments, takes a deep breath and continues. "The plastic was secured in several places with twelve-to-twenty inch strips of tape. Then the remains were bound in a ball-like configuration and stuffed into a microwave oven factory carton."

Some TV reporters begin weeping.

"The medical examiner has further concluded that before the

remains were placed in that shed, they had been stored in an environment consistent with extremely low temperatures, perhaps a cold storage bin or a home freezer, because there was absolutely no insect activity. At this time I would like to turn this over to Agent Charles Mathews, the man in charge of the FBI's investigation."

Huiras remains in front, but steps slightly aside to make room for the weary Charles Mathews, whose uncombed white hair and rumpled shirt speak volumes about his present state. He leans toward the microphones and with hushed tones begins. "Sadly, I am here to report the findings of the Medical Examiner. They have made a positive identification from dental records of the remains that were discovered in the shed near the rear of the property."

For a few seconds Mathews hesitates while every single person watching him speak literally holds a breath. "They were found to be the remains of Miranda Gaddis."

Later, Michelle Duffey would express to *People Magazine* reporters the heartbreak she felt at that moment. "It's hard knowing she was right there the whole time."

A shock of emotion stuns the crowd, releasing tears, mournful wails and embraces. Mathews just watches, absorbing the cathartic wave for several moments. As the sobs begin to subside amid fluttering handkerchiefs, he clears his throat. "And finally, I am here to announce that we have just discovered a second set of remains under the concrete slab behind Weaver's house."

This time several in the crowd drop to their knees, overwhelmed.

"The remains of this second victim were fully clothed, bound with cord and pushed into a three-foot steel barrel. The barrel was sealed and wedged among two additional barrels in a straight configuration directly beneath the concrete that was poured over the top in an approximate three foot by twelve foot strip."

Many in the audience continue to shake their heads in disbelief, tears still flowing.

Mathews gestures toward a white van, adorned with the words "Medical Examiner" that is moving through the gateway and onto Beavercreek Road. "An autopsy will be performed immediately but the medical examiner has explained that it will take at least a day or longer before a positive identification can be established. There's nothing left to say at this time."

Later that night, Linda is tossing and turning so much that Philip awakens next to her. "Hey baby," he says softly, "what's the matter?"

She buries her face into his neck. "I can't sleep. I can't even think. I'm so damn wound up. I can't take much more of this. I'm having so much trouble letting go."

Philip holds her close. "I am so proud of you. I mean it. You are one determined cookie," he says in a voice filled with emotion. "You got him. Yes, you. You got him."

"But part of me still hopes that it's not Ashley," Linda cries.

By 5 PM Monday, most of the TV crews have disbanded. The crowds have dissipated. Most of the microphones have been disconnected and carted away. Yet a handful of dedicated journalists are still on hand to witness Chief Huiras[7] slowly walk to his usual spot, pausing politely to facilitate the technicians before beginning a formal statement. "As you know, we recovered some remains yesterday under the concrete slab. The medical examiner has provided us with some preliminary findings that I think it only fair to share with the public. The body had been stored at another location consistent with the environment of a cold storage unit or a deep freeze prior to burial beneath the slab. The medical examiner[8] has also concluded that the victim had elevated blood alcohol content[9] consistent with a person consuming five to six shots of straight whiskey prior to death. The medical examiner has determined that these are the remains of Ashley Marie Pond."

CHAPTER EIGHTEEN

Dark Revelations

After Ward Weaver has signed over permission for the authorities to search his Beavercreek Road property[1], he paces in his Clackamas County jail cell. As the police search for Ashley and Miranda's bodies, Weaver's agitation is noticeable. Looking deep in thought, Weaver scowls. He has to be aware that the horde of camera crews are all descending on the crime-scene, and are all asking questions about "Ward Weaver." Suddenly he slams a fist against his cell bars. "Damn!" his voice resonates in the corridor.

At 6:30 PM on Sunday, August 25, Weaver is told he has a visitor and taken to the meeting room. A few minutes later his attorney, Hal Williams, sits across a conference table from him and explains what charges may be filed if the police find evidence on his property. Aggravated murder, kidnapping, custodial interference and sexual assault of a fifteen-year-old child are all included on the list. These charges would be in addition to the rape and kidnap charges he faces over the Emily Bowen assault.

Weaver asks if the media is broadcasting what's happening. Williams informs his client, "Every TV station in Portland plus a few national networks are on the scene and don't look ready to leave anytime soon."

Weaver insists he has to make a telephone call to his sister. She had taken temporary custody of his daughter, Mallori, at the time of Weaver's August 13 arrest. Ward wants to tell his family his version of the events.

Reminding him that all jailhouse phone calls are tape recorded, Williams argues against it, suggesting instead that Weaver can tape record his comments from the sanctity of the conference room. The tape can then be delivered to his sister for playback to his daughter. The authorities have no jurisdiction over such recordings, Williams says, because of attorney-client privilege policies.

Williams's investigator, Sue Putnam, pulls a cassette recorder from her briefcase, punches the record button and hands the device to Weaver who spends the next fifteen minutes reciting his complex version of the transpiring events about his relationship to the missing girls.

Later, Weaver tells his sister about the tape he made for her and Mallori. When she asks why she hasn't received it, he tells her that the lawyers won't let her have it, because it would make them witnesses for the prosecution. On September 24, the sister mentions the tape in a phone call to Oregon City Police Detective Greg Fryett, complaining that Ward said that the tape would hurt him.[2]

■

Investigators and Clackamas County prosecutors have the bodies but have very little physical evidence linking Weaver directly to them. On August 29, even before Ashley and Miranda's funerals, West Linn Detective Jay Weitman arranges to subpoena bank records for Weaver's check and debit card transactions.[3] Purchases of concrete, plastic sheeting, cleaning chemicals and tools used for cement slab construction are especially scrutinized.

The time between Weaver's August 13 capture through the afternoon of August 29 is filled with collective grief by the entire Portland area. Residents feel they have been through a difficult ordeal. First one of their children disappears with not one clue. Then, a second. Then months of searching and praying and hoping, but no solution. Finally they find the victims and begin to organize the prosecution. The families of Ashley and Miranda are grieving, but by the twenty-ninth, the citizens of Oregon City are in desperate need of their catharsis. So area churches, with the cooperation of police, FBI and local dignitaries, organize a public memorial to take place that evening in the Oregon City High School gymnasium. In ninety-degree heat, mothers clinging to their middle school aged daughters begin lining up at 4:00 for the 7:00 PM service. Within two hours the ranks swell to three thousand.[4]

Linda O'Neal and her husband Philip are part of an entourage surrounding Lori Pond and her relatives that form a long car caravan snaking its way behind a police escort. "We've all got to cry with the crowd tonight to help the community's healing process," Linda remarks stoically.

Two gigantic video screens have been mounted on the roof allowing an overflow crowd to witness the event via television coverage.

Anna Song, the familiar Channel 2 newswoman, offers a touching eulogy. "Tonight we all share one thing in common," she begins. "We did not know Ashley and Miranda, but we wish we did. We also wish that we could go back and protect them from this tragedy." After confessing an emotional involvement with the evolving drama, Song offers an astute observation. "It's touching to see how many people have cared. You who are here and those who are strangers to these girls placed flowers, mementos and personal messages on that makeshift memorial on Beavercreek Road. I think the most poignant message I found on that fence was a simple red sign with black lettering. All it said was, 'Why?' I believe that is the question we all struggle with tonight."

The very next morning, according to a report published in that day's issue of *The Oregonian*, Oregon Child Welfare Department officials admit that Ashley Pond's molestation charges against Weaver were sent to the wrong police agency the previous summer. A spokeswoman for the State Department of Human Services says the report had been faxed to the Clackamas County Sheriff's Department in error. It turns out that agency claims no jurisdiction over Oregon City, where the molestation was reported. Further, after an exhaustive document search, the Clackamas Sheriff's Department cannot find any records of receiving the report.

Officials of the Human Services Department didn't call to make sure the Clackamas Sheriff's Department received the referral and are looking into whether or not it was followed up later. Unfortunately, their current policy doesn't require follow-up of any kind, although it is encouraged. But practically speaking, budget cuts severely hamper any meaningful efforts.

On August 31, 2001, a report concerning Weaver's sexual abuse of Ashley came into the Multnomah County child abuse hotline. This tip came from someone at the Clackamas County District Attorney's office.

Current policies require that the report was to be sent to the Oregon City Police. Records show that it was diverted to the Clackamas County Sheriff's office instead. Ashley's accusation file contains a fax cover sheet indicating that the report had been sent to the Clackamas County Sheriff's office, accompanied by a supervisor's sign off verifying that the caseworker indeed had sent the referral. But on Thursday, Clackamas County Sheriff Pat Detloff voices his alarm when he claims his office never got the report. "We have no record of that in the files at all," Detloff says. "That should tell you something. Maybe it didn't get sent to us."[5]

These inconsistencies trigger Oregon's governor to order a review of the state's handling of the case. The appointed committee promises a complete report within ten days.

The concrete slab continues to provoke confusion and concern. Oregon City Police Detective Greg Fryett becomes determined to find the exact time it was poured and establish evidence of Weaver's involvement.

Fryett manages to secure an appointment for an interview with Ward Weaver's sister at the police station. On August 30 at 2:13 in the afternoon she arrives at the windowless conference room alone and is invited to sit at a table across from Fryett and FBI Special Agent Rob Morgan. Within a few minutes the soft-spoken policeman succeeds in coaxing a long statement from the troubled woman.

As her information pours forth the detectives simply listen intently, taking notes.

Ward's sister insists that there had been a blue tarp covering the spot for the slab for a couple of months prior to June. She says that she told Ward at the house that he should start pouring the cement for the walkway because it was going to get really hot the next week. According to Ward's sister, the forecast for the following week called for one-hundred-degree temperatures. Ward's intentions for the concrete were connected to installing a used hot tub. The concrete would provide a stable base for the heavy structure. Ward's sister looks at Fryett and then firmly reminds him she is positive that Ward had not poured any cement until June or July.

Fryett asks, "Is it possible Ward might have started pouring the cement as far back as March, not June or July? Is it possible?"

The sister shakes her head. "It wasn't possible because he had that blue tarp up starting in February or March. And it wasn't until I came back from my trip to Mexico in May, that I know for sure the cement hadn't been poured yet. You see, my birthday is in May and I specifically remember being at Ward's house for my birthday on May 20. And on my birthday there was no digging, no barrels, no tarp and no cement poured."

Fryett interrupts. "I'll tell you what bugs me the most about this cement slab business. I mean, really, two girls from next door mysteriously disappear and suddenly your big brother is digging a big hole. Do you see what I mean?"

"I told him I thought it was a bad idea to be pouring cement with them girls missing like that. In fact, I even teased him then about our father. You probably know about it, but he's on death row for killing a girl and pouring concrete over her grave. Hell! I told him that coincidence alone would probably prompt 'em to break up the cement and check for the girls anyway. Ward told me to mind my own business and said he was going to pour the cement anyway and he didn't give a goddamn if the police came to tear it up. 'They aren't gonna find nothing,' he says. 'They ain't gonna find nothin.'

"Ward kicked Ashley out in November 2001 and he never once let that girl return to his house. After November, the only times I ever heard him mention her was when he'd be cussing about her. You know, he'd call her 'fuckin' bitch,' stuff like that. Now I told him it weren't right and all. I said, 'Ashley's just a little girl and you shouldn't call her those names.' You know what's funny detective? After Ashley disappeared, my brother never mentioned her name again."

Agent Morgan consults some sheets on his clipboard. He finally says, "Many of us are confused about whether or not Ward used a freezer in his house. Was storing frozen meat part of his regimen, do you think?"

"Sure, he had a freezer for a long time, maybe five years. Probably did store a lot of meat. And it was a locking freezer too. Nobody could get into it without him because he always kept it locked and he always kept the key in his front pocket."

"Was there only one key?"

"Oh, Ward was very weird about not losing keys. But just in case, he had a copy of every key he owned and kept them on a ring in his backpack. That backpack was at the center of his life. He kept everything important in it. In fact, it was on the front seat of his car the day he was arrested. Anyway, they towed the car and after a few days they released it to me. Officer Valenzuela released the backpack to me personally. And it had them two sets of keys inside. Then when they was putting that big fence up around Ward's house, I got a call from Frank Jones, the landlord, wondering if I had the keys to the house. So an hour later I gave him both sets of keys. The thing was, he said, otherwise the police would have to break down the front door to get in. So the freezer keys would have been on those rings and that means the landlord should still have them."

"Are you getting along with Ward's oldest son?"

"No, he's a bit mixed up these days. I kind of feel sorry for the poor kid. He doesn't contact me at all anymore, and we used to be close."

"What about Ward? Did he and his son see eye to eye?"

"They hadn't been."

"Do you think Ward and his son were in cahoots on killing the girls?"

"No way, it's just not possible. Those two never got along. Hell! They could never agree on anything, so how could they do something this terrible together?"

"Have you had any contact with your brother lately?"

"On the Saturday morning when they first started digging for the bodies, Ward called me real early. He wanted to know if I knew where Mallori was. He also told me 'the shit's going to hit the fan.' And then he got real pissed and said, 'My son Francis is in the middle of this. And that kid is thinking he's going to get him some reward money. God damn it, my son is in on it!'"

The sister continues her rambling for another hour. Just before she is ready to leave she seems to remember one more thing. "This morning Mallori took me aside and was almost in tears. She said, 'I've been trying to tell you. In July, I was going through my dresser looking for my Walkman and I found Miranda Gaddis' s school binder in the bottom drawer, covered up by clothes.' I asked her if she was sure it was Miranda's and she says, 'Oh yes. Because it has all of her school papers and pictures of her little sister.' Apparently there were other pictures in the binder as well."

"What ever happened to that binder?"

"Mallori said she intended to return it to Miranda's mother. It was the only right thing to do, she said. She said she told her daddy she'd be right back and then Ward asked her where she was going and why. When he found out she was giving that binder up to Michelle, he told her no—that they should do all that later. Mallori told me she put the binder back in her room and left it there in the drawer, back under some clothes."

"But where is the binder now? Do you have any idea?"

"At the beginning of August, when they were packing everything up to move out, Mallori found that damn binder in one of the boxes they moved to the storage room in Gresham. So I suppose it's still there."[6]

Fryett and Morgan next consult with the Oregon State Medical Examiner, Dr. Clifford Nelson, who reveals the gruesome details surrounding the condition of the victims' corpses.

Ashley Pond's body was located in a metal barrel approximately three to four feet beneath the surface of the ground. Above the barrel containing the body was a layer of crushed rock and above the layer of crushed rock was the slab of cement.

Ashley was completely clothed with one exception. She had been buried with no shoes or socks. A beige rope had been coiled around her neck and under her knees, binding her body tightly into a fetal position. Several layers of clear plastic sheeting with "PPI" in dark letters stamped on it were wrapped around Ashley's crumpled remains. Doctor Nelson stated that Ashley's body was mummified without any evidence of "bug activity." He was convinced the body had to have been in a sealed (closed off) environment consistent with "placement in a freezer," prior to being buried under the earth. Precise cause of death for Ashley (and Miranda) could not be determined, Dr. Nelson said, "due to the desiccated state of the remains."[7]

The remains of Miranda Gaddis were found in a shed upon the property. They were bound tightly and encased in black plastic sheeting inside a box that itself was wrapped in clear plastic sheeting. The sheeting was secured by clear tape. That package had been placed inside another, larger microwave oven box, which was also wrapped completely in clear plastic sheeting and secured tightly by clear plastic tape. The remains were unclothed except for her socks.

According to bank statements of Weaver's debit card transactions, on February 16 six sixty-pound sacks of mortar mix and a finishing trowel were purchased from a store near his house.

His interview with Weaver's sister results in Detective Greg Fryett obtaining a warrant to search her house and the public storage facility containing Ward Weaver's belongings. Fryett is authorized to confiscate clear plastic sheeting with the PPI logo, a freezer, a microwave oven, beige colored rope, black colored plastic, tape, a finishing trowel, digging tools, clothing belonging to Miranda Gaddis, white Skecher shoes belonging to Ashley Pond, school books, notebooks and paperwork written by or involving either victim and any videotapes.

Another subpoena is served on KATU TV. Fryett wants to see any video footage that showed the inside of Weaver's house while he was living in it, particularly any shots showing his freezer.[8]

Meanwhile, Detective Weitman begins his search for Weaver's keys. He obtains a search warrant to sift through the property Weaver had in his possession during his arrest and discovers many keys.

Weitman also contacts Weaver's landlord who surrenders more of Weaver's keys.[9]

A few days later, Detective Fryett receives a strange call from a male identifying himself as Paul Myers. Myers claims to have inside information about Ward Weaver. Anxious to hear the man out, Fryett arranges for a 9:00 AM conference at police headquarters where he and Rob Morgan sit, listening to Myers's tale.

"I want to talk to you about that shed," he says. "I knew Ward had my tow-bar in his shed. When I needed it, Ward was locked up. So I just went over on my own to look for it, but there was a police officer at the house and he told me they weren't allowing anybody on the property. So I hung around and waited until they got done with their search warrant stuff. After they all left, I went to the shed and looked for my tow-bar. It was right there in plain sight."

Fryett ponders, then makes a drawing depicting a rectangle representing the shed. He asks Myers, "Draw for me the approximate location of where your tow-bar was."

Myers does and then hands the pencil back to Fryett who asks, "When you were in the shed, did you notice anything on that shelf on the right hand side?"

"I don't remember if there was a shelf in the shed or not. Just a few bags of clothes is all I remember." He points to the drawing. "Also there was an old dresser on the left wall, but I didn't look through anything. I just wanted to get my tow-bar."

"Did you see any fly strips hanging in that shed?"

"Fly strip?"

Morgan taps the table and says, "You know, long strips of sticky paper, the flies bump into it and get stuck. Think hard about it. Fly strips."

"I don't remember."

Fryett changes the subject. "Have you been friends with Ward Weaver for a long time?"

"I've known Ward for years, oh, maybe ten. I first met him when we both lived at the same trailer park. Then off and on over the years we'd do stuff together, help each other out here and there. But right now, I can't say for sure that I'm still friends with him, under the circumstances. I mean, I think he's guilty in regards to that stuff involving Emily."

■

The family organizers want Ashley Pond's burial service to be as private as possible. No reporters, no TV cameras. Linda O'Neal and her husband Philip along with the other mourners assemble at Ashley's grandmother's house that Saturday morning and comfort each other.

At noon, a large airport shuttle-type vehicle glides to a stop in front of the house. Linda notices that it is solid black. "It looks like a giant hearse," she says. "You can't even see through the windows."

Two Lincoln stretch limousines pull up behind the bus, one white and one black. Within minutes the vehicles are full and, escorted by police squad cars, begin the procession to the funeral chapel. Linda and a few dozen others follow behind in their cars, headlights glowing.

There are no empty seats during the formal service. Lori and her family sit in a secluded section off to the right. Chief of Police Huiras, Valenzuela-Garcia, Fryett and several other police sit with Linda in the back row.

Songs are sung, informal speeches given and several prayers offered. Then the tribute video that Philip and Maria made is played. For several minutes the audience absorbs still images of Ashley moving to the soft hum of the soundtrack. Tears flow stronger when the still images morph into home video clips. There she is, in full action, that beautiful child being silly, jumping into the water, carrying her baby sister piggyback, riding her skateboard and giggling incessantly.

The official service concludes. The mourners make their way, single-file, past the table holding a white urn between a pair of recent portraits. Each stops briefly to say "good bye," before exiting.

In minutes only immediate family remain. Some take their turns to approach the urn and lay ceramic hearts on the top edge. When they've finished, the hearts form a perfect circle around the contents. Lori is the last one, but when she reaches the table she collapses onto her knees, sobbing.

An hour later they reassemble at Sunset Hills Memorial Garden, the West Portland hillside cemetery where the interment takes place. Ashley's stepfathers serve as pallbearers for the encased urn and they march across the hillside up to the freshly dug hole with a canvas pew anchored nearby. Lori and her surviving daughters sit on the pew, their eyes focusing nervously on the hole as the urn slowly slides in. By now the crowd is closing in. Standing at attention behind the grave, Chief of Police Huiras and ten of his officers observe.

Alex Chase, the youth and families pastor at Oregon City Christian Church, had been designated to officiate. He speaks from a spot next to a mound of brown soil piled onto a tarp next to the grave. "We are here to honor, give tribute and remember a very special young lady. This service isn't about me. It's not about the investigation. It's not about the events of this past week. It's about a young girl, very special to each one of you. But I want you to remember something. You are assembled together here not because somebody died, but because they lived, and that's the best perspective I can have. We are only here to remember life.

"Ashley Pond was born on March 1, 1989 in Milwaukee, Oregon. She was raised, however, mostly in Oregon City and was a student at Gardiner Middle School. She was very devoted to her mom Lori, and there were four very special people in her life. They are her two sisters, her grandmother and her baby brother, whom she never got to meet, but whose coming birth stirred her love.

"Ashley was involved in dancing. She loved the dance team and this little girl knew how to have fun, she really did. She loved to do gymnastics. She had her own brand of gymnastics. She'd been doing her brand of somersaults since she was a little girl. She liked to rollerblade. She liked embroidering with her grandma. She liked camping, fishing, playing *Nintendo*. Most of all, she loved karaoke. I've heard it said that she and Lori could break up the audience with their rendition of *Achy Breaky Heart*. She was a loving, giving, very caring young person.

"She loved babies. From the time when it was almost dangerous for her to be packing a baby around, she always had a little kid on her hip or she'd have one in a stroller that she'd be pushing around. She loved that. Ashley was full of energy, and she gave pretty good hugs.

"As we are now about to commit her to this grave," Chase continues, solemnly, "I am reminded of what Euripides said three thousand years ago when confronted with similar circumstances. He said, 'what greater pain could mortals have than this? To see their children dead before their eyes.' Let us pray that all little girls in this cruel world will somehow find their safe havens. Our Father, Who art in Heaven..."

The minister next picks up a medium-sized shovel and scoops up a few ounces of dirt which he scatters onto the urn. For fifteen minutes the shovel is passed from one mourner to another, as each takes a turn at pushing the blade into the soft stack of earth and then raining down their contribution into the grave. Linda doesn't participate and can barely bring herself to watch the sad ritual.

"This concludes our service here today," Chase says, "But you may stay and observe the closing of the grave, if you wish."

Sorrowful eyes watch as a cemetery attendant lays strips of green sod on top and gently presses them into place.

For another half-hour, Ashley's family members, friends and police officials remain surrounding Lori and her girls. Reluctant to leave, they all still cling to the event, as if by stretching out the experience they can avoid the future recognition that Ashley is forever gone from their midst.

Three days later, Ashley's friend Miranda Gaddis is buried in a private ceremony with no press coverage. Michelle Duffey later gives an interview to Anna Song in which she tells the reporter that most nights she cannot bring herself to go back to the apartment she shared with her daughter. She often has nightmares about Miranda. "Once in awhile I remember bits and pieces of them and it just scares me, and I know that I'm hoping that she didn't get hurt or suffer too bad."

CHAPTER NINETEEN

Finger-pointing

U p until the funerals the sympathetic public furnished the mothers with gifts: homebuilders offered rent-free housing, merchants gave various goods, cash donations paid the funeral and burial expenses. However, once their public support begins to wane, the mothers feel the sharp recoil of reality surfacing at every turn.

The public now seems to affix some blame for the Ashley-Miranda tragedy on the mothers. Letters to the editor, call-in radio talk shows and national TV personalities voice heated opinions and harsh, snap evaluations of Lori Pond and Michelle Duffey. The media microscope examines their lifestyles and past activities with a judging eye. Within days, local press coverage and talk show buzz shift from a tone of respectful condolence to one of recriminatory finger-pointing. How ironic, considering Ward Weaver, the perpetrator, sits in jail awaiting justice.

Detective Viola Valenzuela-Garcia sees recently released medical examiner reports showing Ashley had an elevated blood alcohol level at the time of death. Garcia is stunned. She confronts Lori Pond with the evidence, wanting to know how the child was able to consume that booze before leaving the apartment at 8:00 AM

In response, Lori revises her version of the morning that Ashley disappeared. She says she and Dave were up fighting until 4:30 AM. Ashley also got up then, saying that she was hungry. Lori claims to have told Ashley to make herself a Cup-o-Soup and go back to bed.

Lori protests, "Ashley could not have gotten the alcohol at home, because I count my beers and none were missing."[1]

Garcia continues probing, "Well, while we are on the subject of questions about the night before Ashley disappeared, your daughter told us that she had spent that night at your friend Hillary's house. She told us this the day after Ashley left, so her memory was sharp and she was very sure. Yet, Lori, you told me on that same day that your two younger daughters had gotten up and gotten dressed and then they woke Ashley before they left for school. You can see why I am confused here. It sounds like you have no idea what really happened at your apartment that morning."[2]

The new pressures increase Lori's depression. After surrendering her surviving daughters to their respective fathers, she, her boyfriend and their infant son take refuge thirty miles east in Estacada, where they obtain an unlisted phone number. For weeks she refuses any contact, even from family.

Soon the Clackamas County Grand Jury is convened to begin examination of evidence linking Weaver to the girls' homicides. One of their first subpoenas is for the audio recording Weaver had made for Mallori in the jail conference room. Did he confess on that tape? In a vigorous counter-attack, Weaver's attorney, Hal Williams, quashes the attempt with a successful motion, claiming the tape is protected by "the right against self-incrimination, the right of attorney-client privilege and the right to the assistance of counsel."[3]

The continuing police investigation of the Weaver property concludes during the first week in September when custody of the home is returned to Frank Jones, its owner. After being featured on the local TV news, Jones is barraged with requests from the public who want the entire compound destroyed. Somehow, they collectively feel if the evil place is torn down, maybe the community's healing can finally begin in earnest. After several days of consideration, Jones agrees to the demolition. Pacific Land Clearing Company donates their services and on September 9 they raze the buildings at 10:00 AM. By 5:30 PM every scrap had been hauled away.[4]

On Friday September 13, the director of the Oregon Department of Human Services submits the special report commissioned by the Governor. *The Oregonian* says the report confirms the most egregious mistakes that contributed to Ashley Pond's becoming a crime statistic. In 2001, Ashley's first abuse report was not referred to the Clackamas County Sheriff's office until September 18, eleven working days after it was phoned in to the abuse hotline. Although a computer entry indicates that the report was referred via fax to the sheriff's office on September 18, no documents confirming the fax could be found. The sheriff's office denies ever receiving the fax.

The complaint had not been screened despite the agency's strict rules requiring every report to be screened within five days. The staff at DHS, the Clackamas County branch, was unable to find abuse reports and other documents related to the Ashley Pond complaints. It took until January 17, 2002, more than a week after Ashley's disappearance, for a supervisor in that Clackamas County branch to sign off on an employee's handling of that first abuse complaint from September.

No written protocol existed at the time for abuse committed by a perpetrator who is not a family member and who lives outside the victim's home. The hotline staff on duty that night determined that the report didn't require immediate attention because it indicated Lori, Ashley's mom, was aware of the allegation and Ashley was not living with Weaver.

A devastated Governor admits the State of Oregon was derelict. "It is clear from this review that mistakes were made," he says, "and that the system established by the department to meet its responsibility to abused children failed Ashley Pond."[5]

Anxious to unravel several inconsistencies, on September 23 Detective Fryett and FBI Special Agent Rob Morgan interview Mallori Weaver at her attorney, Tom Regan's office. Seated around a conference room table are Morgan, Fryett, Regan, Ward's sister, a DHS employee and Mallori Weaver.

Fryett begins, gently asking Mallori, "How is school going for you this year?"

"I'm doing good in school so far, I've got straight A's. I got the lead solo part in chorus and I can't wait until we do our first concert."

"That's just wonderful. I'm real glad things are starting out well for you this year. Now, how many brothers do you have, Mallori?"

"I have three brothers. Two live with my mom, and my oldest brother lives with his girlfriend."

"So, does the youngest one ever stay over at your house?"

"Once in a while, like maybe on a weekend."

"What about your middle brother," Fryett inquires. "How often does he spend the night?"

"Oh...once or twice a month, usually on weekends."

"On those weekends, when they stay over, where do they sleep?"

"Usually they just fall to sleep watching TV in the living room. Sometimes they sleep in my room if I don't have anybody staying over, but I usually have a friend over on weekends."

Morgan asks Mallori, "Did Ashley Pond spend the night a lot?"

Mallori and Ward's sister make brief eye contact before the teenager replies. "Ashley stayed at my house for a couple weeks towards the end of the year when I was in the fifth grade. When we were sixth-graders it was different. Ashley stayed with us almost the whole sixth grade school year. She didn't move back to her house until just before seventh grade started."

Morgan nods. "What was the sleeping situation when she was around? I mean, where did you all bed down at night?"

"There are bunk beds in my room. After Gerri moved in, her daughter had the top and I had the bottom. When Ashley came to live with us, she took over the top bunk and then Gerri's daughter moved to the bottom bunk with me. Gerri slept in my dad's bed. She was my dad's girlfriend then."

Fryett's interest is piqued. He asks, "With your dad? You mean Gerri and your dad shared his bed?"

"Not all the time. After Ashley told a bunch of lies about my dad, Gerri started fighting with my dad, and then she got mad and made him sleep on the couch. By then, Ashley was gone from our house. She didn't come around any more."

"She never returned?"

"Not for a few months anyway. My dad was real mad at her for a long time."

"So they patched things up and she started coming around again? Is that it?"

"Well, I guess you could say my dad wasn't so mad at her any more."

Detective Fryett scans through a few pages in a manila file folder and stares at a certain page for a few moments before he goes on, "Mallori, I want you to think back for me, think real hard and try to remember when Ashley was living with you. Did you ever see your dad and Ashley laying together or sleeping together? In his bed, maybe, or like on the couch cuddled up?"

Mallori shakes her head. "Nope. Never!"

"Not ever? Not even one time in all those months? Are you sure, Mallori?"

"Well, I guess I did see Ashley in my dad's bed, sometimes. A few times, maybe."

"What about alcohol? Did your dad keep liquor in the house?"

"Of course."

"Did Ashley ever drink any of it?"

"The only time I remember Ashley drinking was when we were over at her mom's house. She really liked wine coolers."

Morgan summarizes. "Okay, so when Ashley was part of the household, there was also Gerri, her daughter, you, your father Ward, and weekend visits from your two brothers. Anybody else?"

"Just friends. A lot of my friends hung around, especially on weekends."

"Must have been pretty crowded at times. How well did everybody get along? How about Gerri and Ashley? What do you remember? Were they close?"

Mallori laughs. "Are you kidding? Gerri couldn't stand Ashley."

"Why do you suppose that was?"

"I think it had a lot to do with Ashley always trying to break her and my dad up. She made a lot of fights happen just by making up stories."

Fryett interrupts. "A few minutes ago you mentioned something about bad things Ashley was spreading about your dad. What kind of bad things?"

Mallori squirms and hesitates. "Ashley said it was the same kind of bad things that her real dad did to her. I remember. We were alone, up on the dirt hill behind my house. Ashley asked me if I'd take hold of her hand. I thought that was really weird. Anyway, she grabbed my hand and she said, 'Your dad did to me what my dad used to do. Your dad raped me. Your dad did the same thing to me as my real dad, he raped me.'"

For a moment there is stunned silence. Finally Morgan resumes. "How did you react to all of that?"

While Ward's sister grips her left hand, Mallori takes a deep breath. "I didn't really know what to do. So I went down the hill to the house and Gerri was there. She asked me what was wrong and so I told her what Ashley had just said to me."

"What was her reaction?"

"All she did was tell my dad what I told her. Right there, in front of me! She was screaming it. 'Rape, rape, rape,' she kept yelling. And my dad, well, he just went outside and smoked cigarettes."

Fryett consults his notes, whispers a quick comment to Morgan and asks Mallori, "You said Ashley went back to live with her mom. Did she ever return?"

"Not for a few months anyway. My dad was real mad at her for a long time. After a couple of months went by, Ashley started hanging with us again, but she didn't move in, she just came around. Like she'd come over in the morning and then we'd go to the bus stop together."

"Was this something you did frequently?"

"Oh she came over maybe two or three times a week, in the morning. Then we walked to the bus stop. And then one day she was gone."

Morgan changes direction with his next question. "Did Miranda Gaddis come around your house much?"

"She didn't visit every day. Maybe every other day or so. Sometimes after school we'd hang at my house and sometimes over at hers."

Fryett asks, "Can you shed any light about a notebook of Miranda's?"

"You mean a binder, Miranda's binder. Well, after Miranda disappeared I found her school binder in my toy box."

"Your toy box."

"Yeah, in my bedroom. It's made out of cardboard and I keep it there in my room, for my play phones, my Barbies, my balls and other stuff. After I found it I carried it to my dad who was working on a car out in the driveway. I showed it to him and I said I was going to go over to Miranda's and give it to her mom. I knew she'd want to have it. It was originally my binder, but last year Miranda traded me something for it. Then she was using it at school. I know she was using it, because I saw her carrying it to school up to the time she disappeared."

"How did your dad react when you showed it to him?"

"He said for me to put it away. He said he didn't think Miranda's mom needed that kind of pressure right now. He took it from me and I guess he put it in his bedroom or something. I didn't see it again until we were moving our stuff and I found it in my box of school supplies in my daddy's room." Mallori pauses. "Or maybe it was in the toy box. I'm not positive exactly where, but I did see it when we were moving."

"What was in this binder when you discovered it?"

"Photographs, and I saw homework with Miranda's name written on it."

Fryett refers to his notes again. "Do you know where the binder is right now?"

"It should still be in my toy box, I guess. In my attic, or I mean my aunt's attic."

"Do you know Cindy Pearson?" Fryett asks.

"Cindy was out here from Idaho. She was here two weeks and she spent the whole second week staying with us in our house. She has a boyfriend, I think his name is Billy. He lives over in Idaho and she sure missed him. She called him from the phone booth every single day she was at our house until I finally went down and bought her a phone card. From then on she called Billy from my house."

Morgan writes on his pad then says, "Do you know Billy's last name? How about his phone number?"

"No way. I didn't call him or have anything to do with him. He's Cindy's dawg."

"Tell me about when Cindy was hanging out at your house."

Mallori closes her eyes briefly and giggles. "A lot of fun. That week Cindy stayed with us was a lot of fun. We went swimming in the backyard pool. We watched a lot of movies. We ate a lot of pizza. I don't know, I just remember it being a lot of fun."

Fryett chuckles. "Sounds like party time to me. Any drinking take place? Did Cindy drink any alcohol?"

"The last day she stayed at the house. She drank a lot of wine. And that's not all she drank either. Later she was drinking something from a tall glass. I don't know exactly what it was, but she sure got drunk fast on it. She got so drunk she fell flat on her face when we were walking from the pool to the house. Anyway, inside the house we made popcorn in the microwave."

Morgan raises his eyebrows. "Microwave. What microwave? Tell me about this microwave."

"It was just a microwave oven. Alice Adams bought it and brought it over to the house sometime between the time Ashley and Miranda disappeared."

Morgan is excited. "What brand microwave was it? Do you remember its size?"

"I don't know anything about microwaves. We just came home one day and Alice was setting it up in the kitchen."

Fryett takes a turn. "Let's get back to Cindy. You made popcorn with the microwave, then what?"

Mallori laughs. "Cindy puked. She threw up all over our house. And finally my father had to pick her up and carry her to his bed. She was so out of it. Anyway, my dad told me to go to the bathroom and he was just setting on the bed next to Cindy, who was upset and crying."

"How was Cindy dressed then?"

"She was wearing a bikini-top and shorts. I came back from the bathroom with a wet towel and Dad took it from me and told me to go to my room. He said he was going to try to get Cindy to calm down. Anyway, I did go to my room and for about two hours all I could hear was Cindy yelling and wanting me in there. Finally at some point my father told me to grab my stuff and come into his room to be with him and Cindy. He said I could lie on the floor. So I did and I slept on the floor below Cindy, in my father's bedroom."

"So before you went to sleep, how long do you figure your dad was alone with Cindy in his bedroom?"

"Oh he was probably alone in there for five or ten minutes."

Fryett seems confused. "But what did you do then, during those five or ten minutes?"

"I was in the bathroom. I was drinking in the kitchen. And for a while I was even in the front room watching a movie on TV. Anyway, Cindy was making so much noise, I kept going in and out of Dad's room to check on her, and every time I went in there Cindy would say, 'Stay here with me.' But my dad made me leave, so I did."

The interview of Mallori consumes another hour. When it is over, Detective Fryett retrieves some documents from his briefcase and hands one to Regan for Mallori and the other to Ward's sister. "These are grand jury subpoenas," he explains. "They are for the same day and time. All you have to do is show up and tell them what you told us."[6]

As they exit Regan's office, Ward's sister tells Mallori to wait for her in the car then motions for Fryett to follow her down the hall where they have a brief private conference. "I'm concerned about my niece," she says. "Mallori is under a lot of pressure."

"I'm sure she is. How can I help you?"

The woman lowers her voice to almost a whisper, "I talked to Ward at the jail Sunday and Detective Fryett, he is convinced he's going to be out real soon. Is there any chance that he could be let out?"

"Only if someone comes up with a million bucks bail. Do you know of anyone who would risk that kind of money?"[7]

Ward's sister shakes her head. "No, no. But you don't understand. I'm not afraid of my brother for myself. I've always been able to handle Ward. But I am concerned with what he might do with Mallori, particularly because…because," She falters.

"Why should Mallori be afraid of her own father?"

The woman pulls a pair of hand written documents from her purse. "I think Ward is trying to intimidate us. We each got letters from him this morning. Can I read you a couple of his comments?" She unfolds the sheets.

Fryett nods. "Sure."

"This is from the one he addressed to Mallori." She reads, "'I do not want you having any more contact at all with Jayne Patan. She is saying all kinds of lies and having the police take our stuff away because of her mouth. Stay away from her. Don't even call her. Daddy is going to deal with her eventually. Same with everyone else talking shit. You just be the good girl that you always have been.'"[8]

Fryett grimaces. "You say she just got that letter today?"

"That's right, and you just handed my niece a subpoena for her to testify against him. You can't blame me for being a little worried, can you?"

"What about the letter he wrote to you?"

The sister reads from the second letter. "'Blake called and said he was going to write to me. Give him a call and see if he is still going to. If he is, tell him I need for him to do it extremely soon.' And extremely is capitalized and underlined." She resumes reading from the letter. "'I have some things I think he would enjoy doing very much. Revenge kind of things. Nothing that would get him in trouble. People want to run their mouth about things that they have no idea about. Let's see how they like a dose in return. I think he will enjoy doing this. You will enjoy it too, seeing it being done. I really need for you to keep trying to get a hold of him.'"[9]

Ward's sister hands the letters to the policeman. "And there's a lot more. Go ahead, take them, read the contents and put them in your file or whatever. This stuff is frightening, because frankly, Mallori didn't tell you everything she knows. I think she thinks her dad maybe did have something to do with what happened to Ashley and Miranda and she's very scared."

CHAPTER TWENTY

Charges and Countercharges

The Clackamas County Grand Jury spends a week reviewing the claims concerning Ward Weaver's connection to the murders of Ashley Pond and Miranda Gaddis. After hours of testimony from witnesses, including his own children, former landlord, even one of Ashley's teachers, on October 3 they issue an indictment.

The next day Weaver is arraigned through closed circuit TV, never leaving the jailhouse. In the courtroom, the two mothers watch the proceedings from the front row, disappointed they can't look Weaver in the eye. The judge summarizes seventeen counts to the disheveled defendant seen on a TV monitor, offering little response except when he repeats his plea, seventeen consecutive times, "Not guilty, your honor." There are multiple counts against Weaver, including aggravated murder, abuse of a corpse, sexual abuse of minors, attempted aggravated murder and first-degree rape.[1]

Evidence that the state's child services failed to intervene before tragedy struck prompts the governor to demand some quick changes in DHS procedures. By October, every recommendation from the September report is implemented, forcing an intense strain on manpower and finances. The new rules establish strict standards, dictating how caseworkers document and follow up on reports to police. The new rules require supervisors to review incident reports sent to the police daily and set time limits for screening reports; staff workers are now only allowed three work days to screen reports.

Three working days becomes the new mantra for the Oregon State Department of Human Services rehabilitation. Determining whether the child is safe, checking to see if there are other children in the abuser's home who may be at risk, checking the agency's computer databases for information about the families involved; all must be done within three working days. Supervisors must now sign off on child abuse reports within three working days or if a child welfare worker does a field assessment of abuse allegations, the supervisor has only three working days upon a report's completion to submit it. The most stringent new rule requires DHS to forward allegations of sexual abuse from outside the home, so-called third party abuse, to law enforcement officials within one hour of receiving them.[2]

Six weeks after the new policies begin, the bureaucracy of Oregon politics finds its first scapegoats. The first hits are leveled against a caseworker and a supervisor, who are placed on administrative leave. It is alleged that the mishandling of several calls made to the agency concerning the well-being of Ashley Pond created the foundation for tragic events. After two weeks, the suspensions evolve into outright terminations.[3]

Later in the fall, the state releases two reports, one internal and one by a consultant, both designed to study the broader issue of state-wide responses to child abuse reporting and case handling.[4]

A day after the report, the director of Oregon's four billion dollar state social services agency resigns his post. He simply says, "I am tired and I don't see any light at the end of the tunnel."[5]

Meanwhile, Ward Weaver is becoming increasingly worried about his relationship with Mallori, claiming DHS is dragging its feet where visitation is concerned. He attacks legally with the assistance of his attorney and surprisingly wins a small victory when a Clackamas County Circuit Court judge rules that Weaver is entitled to jailhouse visits with Mallori.[6]

Soon after Ward Weaver's first visit with Mallori, Detective Fryett receives an intriguing phone call. "This is Officer Fryett, can I help you?"

A soft spoken female is on the other end of the line. "I was told you're in charge of the Ashley and Miranda investigation."

"I'm one of many looking for evidence. Do you know something about the case?"

"Well, my daughter goes to the middle school. She was a classmate of the missing girls and she's friends with Mallori Weaver. Today she came home from school with a photo of Miranda Gaddis and her sister, and some other things that were supposed to belong to Miranda. And she says she got them from Mallori. I watch *CSI*. These could be evidence. What do you think?"

Fryett is already jotting notes onto his pad. "I think I need to talk to your daughter, right away. What's her name?"

"Jessica Thompson. I'm Penelope, Penny Thompson."

An hour later Fryett is seated in Thompson's living room across from fourteen-year-old Jessica, who sits on a couch next to her parents and two teenaged female friends. Jessica holds several paper objects in her lap. Fryett begins. "I've been told that Mallori Weaver is a friend of yours, Jessica. Is that correct?"

The slender teenager smiles. "Yes. I've known her since fifth grade." She glances at the other girls. "Well, we all have. We all hung out together."

"Your mom said Mallori gave you some things that might have originally belonged to Miranda Gaddis."

"Yes." She holds up a photo of Miranda and Marissa Gaddis, arms locked, smiling. "And these too." Jessica shuffles through small heart-shaped papers, each covered with the mess of adolescent handwriting, and holds them up for the policeman's inspection. One contains the slogan, "Dance Rocks," and the other two have boys' names scrawled with garish circles surrounding them, maybe a secret crush.

Fryett accepts the papers and examines them for a few moments before he asks, "Anything else?"

Jessica gives Fryett a homemade calendar. On one side, the words, "March, 2002", written in bold cursive, headline the page. Fryett stares at it and notices the dates March 1 to March 7 have been crossed out with an indelible black marker. On the opposite side, "2002 Dance Schedule" has little notes and reminders scribbled with some of the dates. Fryett looks up, asking Jessica, "How can you be sure that these items originated from Miranda Gaddis?"

"At school I sat next to Miranda at fourth period career development class. That's where I saw them. She had her binder in class."

Janice, one of the other teenagers interrupts. "Actually I'm the one who made that calendar, and I made it for Miranda on March 1st in study-hall. See I wrote it all with my pink marker. She loved it so much, I gave it to her, and she liked it, so it was definitely hers."

Jessica says, "I definitely saw those papers and that calendar in Miranda's binder. I did."

Fryett looks at the calendar again before he asks, "When? This is really important Jessica, try to remember for me the last time you saw Miranda with this?"

"I saw the heart-shaped papers and the calendar in Miranda's binder on March 7th. I know exactly that was the date, because we both looked at it together when she was making plans for spring break. You can see her notes there, on the calendar, see where she drew the green line? The fifteenth to the twenty-second?"

Fryett studies the calendar for a moment. Jessica continues. "I know it was March 7th for another reason too. The very next day was when Miranda disappeared. March 8th. None of us can ever forget that date."[7]

Fryett becomes excited with the notebook evidence. He's close to getting his hands on another piece of solid physical evidence linking Weaver to one of the murdered girls. If only he can complete the chain of custody. Being aware that Mallori will soon be removed from her aunt's custody and placed into foster care, Fryett knows his window to question Mallori is short.

He spends half an hour with the child confirming his hunches. The detective shows Mallori some photographs of a notebook that had been confiscated in an earlier search of Ward's sister's residence. "Have you seen this notebook before?"

Mallori studies the photos for several seconds. "This is my notebook in the pictures."

"Your notebook? Look at the picture again. Isn't it the same notebook that had belonged to Miranda Gaddis? The one from your toy box?"

Mallori is emphatic. "No! This is not Miranda's, it's mine. It's a totally different one. It's mine."

"Okay. It's yours. Did you ever give anyone at school some paperwork or photos that you found in Miranda Gaddis's school notebook?"

Mallori looks at the floor for more than a beat or two. At last she answers. "I did give Jessica Thompson some stuff from the binder. You never said not to. You only asked me where it was. You didn't tell me to give it to you. Did I do something wrong?"

"No, no. I'm just a bit confused about some of this. Can you help out here? I need to know about that notebook. Was it the same one you told me about from your toy box?"

"Yes, the same one, the one my dad told me not to take down to Michelle Duffey's after Miranda was gone."

"I'm just having a problem with your motivations for distributing Miranda's papers and pictures like that. You do realize, don't you, that those things are evidence in the case."

Mallori offers no response and nervously stares at the floor.

Fryett hesitates for a moment. "I have a lot of respect for how well you handle these challenges young lady. I mean it. There's going to be a lot of junk coming down and some of it will be in your direction. I want you to take my card with my cell phone number. If you ever decide you want to tell me anything more, anything at all, I want you to call me any time day or night."

Once back in his office, Fryett calls the DHS supervisors to express his concerns. His last interview with Mallori left him unsettled. He ponders if Ward Weaver is somehow enlisting Mallori to serve his schemes; maybe Weaver had orchestrated this dissipation of notebook evidence too. In any event, Fryett determines he needs to stop Mallori's jail visitations, fearing the more she sees of her dad, the more damage he can inflict. He urges DHS to schedule Mallori for a CARES Northwest interview before any more contact with her dad is allowed.[8]

While charges, countercharges, rumors and innuendos fly back and forth, Lori Pond continues her self-imposed exile with her baby son and her boyfriend, Dave Roberts. She gives her phone number only to her mother and her lawyer, Gina Gordon.

Miranda's mother, who had been on television a lot when she was trying to find her daughter, also becomes reclusive. She moves her surviving daughters to a suburban town near Salem, where they won't be plagued by people she feels are trying to profit from Miranda's death and to give her other children more attention. Her family members complain that she has cut off all access to them, screens all phone contact through an answering machine and refuses to return any calls.

Even though closure evades the grieving mothers, the intrigue of the Ashley and Miranda case and the fate of the survivors stimulate more media interest. But the mothers now turn down all requests for interviews.

The isolation policy prevails for weeks until one day Lori's mother gets a call from a producer for Montel Williams who is passionate about producing an episode of the syndicated TV show devoted to a subject that she feels strongly about, "The Damage That Murderers Do to Their Victims' Families." Montel wants to pair the mothers with Mary McCarty, the mother of young Barbara Levoy, who had been buried beneath concrete in Ward Weaver's father's yard back in 1981. The audience could discover insights into the healing process. The producer insists that talking about the lack of closure should somehow bring it about. Just bringing the painful topic into the open and letting it wash through the psyches of the troubled women will help cleanse their spirits. His final sales pitch proves persuasive. "And besides," he reminds, "Don't forget that this will be good for the mothers. A free trip to New York City, where they'll be put up in a beautiful Manhattan hotel, taken around town in a limousine, plus they'll gain several hundred dollars for the appearance fee. Please, tell them it will be most therapeutic for both of them to be on the *Montel* show and they can have a break being in the Big Apple too."

Lori's mother successfully conveys the urgency of the producer's message to her daughter, who reluctantly agrees. A week later Lori, her attorney Gina Gordon, Dave Roberts, Michelle Duffey and her best friend Francie Walters are in an airplane bound for New York.

After a swift limousine journey that gives the Oregonians fleeting glimpses of the urban landscape, they are deposited into a midtown Manhattan hotel. Feeling somewhat abandoned, Gordon, Roberts and Lori sit together and polish off a bottle of honor bar champagne while gazing through a large window at the bustling sidewalks below. They had hoped high spirits would accompany such an exciting trip, but the tragedy's memory is never far from their thoughts. The opportunity to attend a Broadway musical or to visit famous city landmarks or just order room service has no effect on their sullen dispositions. Lori and Dave stare out the hotel room window, complacent that their only impression of New York is from the safety and privacy of the twenty-seventh floor.

On the morning of the taping, they are all whisked to Montel's studio where they wait in the green room with associate producers and other guests. One of those guests is Mary McCarty, who sits in front of a vanity mirror nervously brushing her hair. Lori recognizes her from the promotion photos on the nearby bulletin board, which depicts her as a victim's mother. McCarty's daughter, Barbara Levoy, had been violently murdered by the elder Ward Weaver and her remains covered by a concrete slab. Lori's heart aches for the older woman. Approaching McCarty, Lori introduces herself.

McCarty invites Lori to sit beside her. Within minutes they feel comfortable talking and exchange phone numbers. Miranda's mother walks in and takes a seat beside them.

"It's a strain on you," McCarty says to the pair, "and you don't get any rest. Every night you try to block it out but you dream. I've lived a nightmare for eighteen years and I'm still waiting. But as long as he is on death row, breathing, I will still be haunted. I am hoping I will at least see him die, before I do." McCarty looks at Lori. "We all have something in common. The same family destroyed our families."

"I know exactly what you mean," Lori responds. "Your Ward Weaver did the same horrible things to your daughter that our Ward Weaver did to mine."

Michelle Duffey speaks as if she is in a trance. "'Our Ward Weaver,' is like 'our cross to bear.' It's a burden that we'll have to carry until... our own deaths."

With tears in their eyes, the three women nod, finding some solace in shared misery.

Just before the taping is to begin, Michelle, perhaps strained to the breaking point by all the heartbreaking events, refuses to participate. She spends the taping session as a member of the studio audience leaving Lori Pond to interact with Montel on the air. Lori attempts to talk about the effects of Ashley and Miranda's deaths with him, McCarty and Dr. Helen Smith, a forensic psychologist. With sincerity, she comes across as overwhelmed, grieving and baffled about how to forge ahead with her life, her pain multiplied by the lack of closure created by the slow criminal trial against Weaver.[9]

Having no TV in his jail cell, Ward Weaver never sees the *Montel* episode. With no newspaper privileges either he isn't able to read the dozens of articles that spew forth from the local presses which portray him in an unsavory light. Nevertheless, he is still able to digest the gist of these accounts through the only outlet at his disposal, the jailhouse rumor mill. Weaver's only human interaction comes from the correction officers who deal with him. They feed him bits and pieces of what they hear being said about him and over time, he becomes infuriated at what he perceives to be the unlawful, distorted representations of his views.

Weaver writes a hand-written two-page letter to KATU reporter Anna Song, who had earlier interviewed Michelle Duffey several times. He says that he is fed up with the half-truths and lies that are being printed. He also complains about a violation of privacy, because his thirteen-year-old daughter is being identified in some news reports. Then he offers a bizarre transaction, which he claims, can "set the record straight," and give them an "exclusive scoop." He wants them to send a camera crew and videotape his take on the case. But

FBI File Photo

FBI File Photo

Ashley Pond was twelve years old when she disappeared from a bus stop, on her way to school.

Miranda Gaddis went missing in the same location almost two months to the day after Ashley's disappearance.

Photo courtesy of Bob Ellis, The Oregonian

Oregon City police Detective Viola Valenzuela-Garcia, displays a poster seeking information about Ashley Pond, who went missing on January 9, 2002.

Digital photo services courtesy of Al Kruper, AK Photo, Fanwood, NJ

Authors Philip Tennyson and Linda O'Neal were step-grandparents of Ashley Pond. Linda O'Neal, a Private Investigator, was asked by the Pond family for help in Ashley's disappearance.

Ward Weaver appeared on the National news and declared himself a prime suspect in the girls' disappearance while declaring his innocence. Although seemingly ignored by the police and FBI, Weaver became a prime suspect in O'Neal's investigation.

Dog handler Harry Oakes and his Search and Rescue dog, Valorie. Oakes alerted the FBI and the police to Valorie's findings.

Unidentified person wearing a "Missing" t-shirt depicting the missing Oregon City girls.

Newell Creek Village, where both Ashley and Miranda resided prior to their disappearances.

Portland Tribune crime reporter Jim Redden was instrumental in getting the public's attention focused on Ward Weaver III.

Ward Weaver, Jr. father of Ward Weaver III, has been on Death Row in California, since 1984, for kidnapping, rape and murder.

Oregon City Police Chief, Gordon Huiras annouces that human remains found in a shed at Ward Weaver's house are of Miranda Gaddis and another body was also found. On the fence, which was erected by police in preperation for the search, are tributes to Miranda and Ashley.

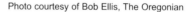

The shed, at Ward Weaver's house, where the remains of Miranda Gaddis were found. Nearby, Ashley Pond's remains were discovered under a concrete slab. Weaver's father, Ward Weaver, Jr. disposed of his murder victim in the same way, using a concrete slab under a deck in California.

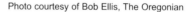

Photo courtesy of Bob Ellis, The Oregonian

Photo courtesy of Fredrick D. Joe, The Oregonian

Ward Weaver is shown being escorted to a Clackamas County courtroom in November of 2003. The mustache and shaved head is one of several guises Weaver sported while in the pre-trial phase of his captivity.

Michelle Duffey (center, left), mother of Miranda Gaddis, and Lori Pond (center, right), mother of Ashley Pond, listen in a Clackamas County courtroom, as Ward Weaver is arraigned on charges of killing Miranda and Ashley. Duffey and Gaddis are surrounded by friends and family in the courtroom.

Two unidentified pallbearers carry a large urn containing the ashes of Ashley Pond to her burial site at the cemetery where she was laid to rest.

Linda O'Neal and Oregon City Police Detective Viola Valenzuela-Garcia sit side-by-side at Ashley Pond's funeral services.

Lori Pond stoically watches in an Oregon City courtroom where Ward
Weaver's motion that he was mentally unable to aid in his defense was with-
drawn.

Ward Weaver holds a pho-
tograph of his daughter,
Mallori Weaver, during his
plea and sentencing.

Though he had bragged that he would beat the
charge, Ward Weaver, in a sudden reversal,
plead guilty to the kidnappings and murders of
Ashley Pond and Miranda Gaddis.

Lori Pond (left) and Michelle Duffey (right) hug after Ward Weaver was sentenced to life in prison for the murders of their daughters, Ashley Pond and Miranda Gaddis.

A memorial to Ashley Pond and Miranda Gaddis on the lawn near Weaver's home, where their remains were found.

A sign asks, "WHY?" on the fence surrounding the Weaver residence. To this day, Weaver has remained silent on the real motives for his crimes.

he'll talk only if they pay him an interview fee. They'll get more than their money's worth, he contends, even if they have to pay a hefty amount, because during the interview he intends to "prove the incompetence of the FBI and the Oregon City Police."

Admitting that writing such a volatile letter forces him to disregard the advice of his attorney, Weaver nonetheless offers to grant exclusive access throughout his murder trial "to only the highest bidder." "My attorney has kept me under a gag for my own protection," he writes. "Well, enough is enough! I have decided to come out and give an exclusive interview with only one news source, and I would like it to be you, Miss Song."[10] Weaver does not provide further details about his claim in the letter to Song, other than to say that the Clackamas Country District Attorney's office has "paperwork" proving the incompetence of investigators "cost a little girl her life."[11]

To demonstrate his dedication to his new policy, Weaver declines to meet with a reporter from *The Oregonian*, and waits for KATU and Song's reply.

KATU responds to Weaver's query with an emphatic "No." They would never offer Weaver or anyone else money to talk. But, if he changes his mind on that issue they would be receptive to sending Song to hear him out with tape rolling and would certainly consider putting some of it on the air.

After *The Oregonian* publishes an account of Weaver's scheme, his youngest sister dismisses his letter as a "money-making ploy," based on lies. Calling his letter a "good dose of Ward Weaver head games," she says she hopes no one pays her brother for an interview.

Soon, it's a week before Thanksgiving; a time which is especially hard on grieving families. During that period, Lori calls Linda. "You know what? You're a very, very exceptional woman," Lori exclaims when Linda picks up the phone.

"Thank you. That's very nice of you," Linda says gently.

"No Linda, every time you see me, you give me a hug. And no matter if I turn my head, you give me a hug. I respect that. I respect that. So if I'm the biggest dork in the whole world…"

"No you're not. Don't say that about yourself."

"I never said I was. I said 'if.'"

"Oh, you said 'if.'" Linda laughs, "I must have missed that."

"You know what my idea of love is? It's strong understanding. And you're right. I should think highly of myself and then my kids will think highly of themselves. But I can't even think about how to proceed with my life. All I ask myself are questions about Ashley, over and over again." She pauses and rushes on in a stream of consciousness, "Why do you think Ward Weaver killed my daughter? I know why. Because he was an arrogant asshole."

"Because he couldn't get what he wanted? I mean, I don't know why. I have no idea."

"No, because Ashley started doing good in her life."

"And she didn't need him anymore?"

"Exactly."

"And he had to be needed?"

"I never liked him. But she used to like him. He must have had some kind of charm, because a lot of people liked him."

Linda bursts out, "I don't think he's going to have much chance to use it on anyone else, frankly."

"You're right," Lori agrees. "I don't know what kind of charm he has. He's a jerk. I'm so sorry."

"You don't have to be sorry."

"Yeah, I do. Yeah, I do. And the reason why I do, is I wish I would have known. I really wish I would have known. What was really going on with Ashley, and all the stuff?"

"All the stuff?"

"Yeah. It seems like it was all so terrible. I wish I would have known..."

Finally, during Thanksgiving week, the Clackamas County court gives Ashley and Miranda's families something for which to be grateful. They finally set a trial date for Ward Weaver. The previously issued indictment charged him with killing Ashley and Miranda, raping Emily Bowen, molesting her young relative, Cindy, and attempting to molest Ashley Pond. Judge Herndon presides over a hearing originally scheduled to consider setting a bail amount for the defendant. When that issue is raised, neither side calls witnesses. And it lasts as long as it takes to say, "Hell no," according to one Oregon City attorney who witnessed the proceedings, which he claims took "less than five minutes." In a surprise move, next the judge declares September 16, 2003, as the trial date. Earlier, Herndon had poured over a thirteen-page affidavit, the contents of which set a strong tone for the prosecutors' plan of attack. Although much of the evidence is circumstantial, there is one significant piece of physical evidence linking Weaver to the slaying of Miranda Gaddis. His fingerprint is discovered on a piece of packing tape used to seal the box in which Miranda's remains were found.

The affidavit, listing details why Weaver should not be released pending trial, is made public and provides previews of the prosecution's case against Weaver. It includes statements from his oldest son Francis, who claims to have heard his father say he killed Pond because "she deserved it." Also in it are the medical examiner's records and evidence that the plastic tarp that enshrouded both corpses and the barrel containing Ashley's remains originated at Weaver's place of employment. However, no reliable witnesses have been found who saw either Ashley or Miranda after they separately disappeared on their way to school. Using Weaver's credit card transactions and store receipts, the district attorney's affidavit summarizes the purchases made two days after Miranda disappeared, including sacks of concrete mix. An FBI agent is quoted in the affidavit, certain he saw the freshly poured slab on March 15. On that same day two search dogs had shown mild interest at the back of Weaver's house. However, investigators did not close in on Weaver until the August 13 rape of Emily.[12][13]

So many different avenues of the Ward Weaver-Ashley Pond-Miranda Gaddis tragedy dominated the airwaves and newspaper pages for eleven months. It is no surprise when the story is overwhelmingly voted the "Top Oregon News Story" for all of 2002 by an annual survey of newspapers and broadcasters conducted by the Associated Press.[14]

Weaver's sister, who assumed sole custody of Mallori the day her dad was incarcerated, but only until an arraignment date could be made, had done her best to provide a suitable, stable home for her niece. But in October she is able to convince the DHS that too much is coming down on the young girl, that she needs a more permanent sense of stability. The arrangement is extended to mid-December when Mallori is placed into an official "foster home," where she is supervised and loved by experienced surrogate parents.

Realizing Mallori is a potential fountain of information for the case he is building, Detective Fryett schedules an early January meeting with Mallori's new foster mother at the Gresham office of the Department of Human Services. What effects have her jailhouse visits played on Mallori's young psyche? Has she changed her previous opinions now that she has been free of Weaver's direct influences? Does she reveal her innermost feelings about him to her new mom?

Grace Quigley, a forty-something well-groomed woman, greets the detective in the small conference room. After some small talk, Quigley studies Fryett's face before she asks, "Do you have a solid case against Mallori's daddy? Does he have any chance of getting off?"

"No, Mrs. Quigley, I don't believe there's a chance in the world that he's getting off. Why do you ask?"

She bites her lip and goes on. "Mallori seems to talk freely and highly about Ward, saying that he's 'one in a million,' at least that's what she said when she first came to stay at our house. A few days later, there was a time when we were in the kitchen and Mallori wanted to confirm that what she was holding in her hand was a skillet. Mallori then started rambling on and on about her dad supposedly being accused of hitting some woman over the head with a skillet. Mallori told me she didn't think it was possible for her dad to do such a thing because the impact would have killed the victim, not just injured them."

Fryett ponders, jots down a few comments, then, asks Quigley, "Has Mallori bared her soul much, so to speak? Do you feel she's revealed some of her inner conflicts to you?"

"I think so. For example a short time after the skillet incident, she felt guilty. She was convinced God could never forgive her. When I asked her why, she admitted she's been drunk before, not just once but many times. And she thought this was really bad, yet what was worse, her father in each instance had been the source of the alcohol. I mean she's only thirteen!"

Fryett shakes his head. "So did Mallori's opinion of her father continue to disintegrate over time?"

"Oh yes, especially after she returned home from one of those visits to the jail. She was very upset. When I asked her what was wrong she told me Ward had been happy to see her, but was feeling bad about what he'd done. She said, 'If he didn't do anything wrong, how could he feel so bad?' And then Mallori learned from the TV news accounts about the fingerprint evidence, her dad's print being found inside the microwave box that Miranda's body was in. I think it was then that Mallori had to come to terms with a reality she had been avoiding, that her dad, indeed, was involved in Miranda's murder."

"So in your judgment, this realization depressed her?"

"Absolutely. For instance, a short time later she wrote a poem, which Mr. Weaver has already received. It was quite disturbing, because it went on and on about her wondering if she could ever trust her daddy again. Would she ever be able to have a friend stay overnight at her house again?"

Fryett scribbles onto his notepad, then looks up. "Any other incidents you can think of along these lines?"

"She told me about a time when a friend had been staying at the house, and that her dad was accused of raping her. You see according to Mallori, her dad thought she was asleep on the floor below them during all of this, but in fact, she was wide awake and heard every disgusting moment. But she didn't put it all together until she learned about the rape charge, again by watching the TV news stories."

"Did she mention who the victim was by name?"

"She called her Cindy. I don't think she mentioned a last name. Later, her voice was emotional when she told me, 'If he's capable of doing that, then he's certainly capable of killing Ashley and Miranda.'"[15]

CHAPTER TWENTY-ONE

Remembering Ashley

Thursday, January 9, 2003, marks the one-year anniversary of the day Ashley Pond disappeared. To commemorate the sad occasion and to offer the family and community a chance to express their good-byes to a young girl whose brief life was so prematurely snuffed out, a memorial service is scheduled on the abandoned Beavercreek Road property where Weaver's house once stood. Organized by Claire Stevens, Ashley's stepmother, the event attracts more than a hundred people, including news crews from television stations and reporters from newspapers.

Stevens asks Linda O'Neal to help greet the arriving mourners. They hand each a slender candle, a bottle of bubble-soap and a wand. Linda's husband, Philip, also attends, trying to videotape the event.

Lori Pond, her mother, sisters and daughters, assemble among the dozens of sweatshirt clad thirteen-year-old girls, all trying to keep their candles lit in a chilly January wind.

Michelle Duffey watches from the sidewalk, a safe distance from the assembly. When asked why she doesn't join the others, she insists she isn't yet ready to set foot on the evil place, because she hasn't fully healed yet.

Stevens had purchased a young magnolia tree for the event, which she intends to plant as a symbol of life and growth near the spot where murder and destruction had so recently taken place.

Flickering candles provide a moving backdrop. Linda O'Neal

begins the service holding a shovel and standing beside the magnolia tree. She says, "We are here tonight to remember the lives of two young girls that touched so many and have left an impact on this community. We think tonight of Ashley and that day exactly one year ago that changed so many of our lives. Because of everything that has unfolded in the last twelve months we are seeking the healing that is necessary in order for us to continue our own lives. We come together tonight to plant this tree. We recognize that the life that expands as this tree sprouts up then climbs many feet into the air, will come to symbolize, in a small way, the spirit of Ashley Pond. The fact that we stand near the very spot where her physical life tragically ended creates a poignant irony, yet we hope the tree will bloom for years to come. Just as this tree grows, we pray our knowledge and acceptance of life will expand."

Linda hands the shovel to Claire Stevens who then says, "Thank you, Linda. And now if Lori Pond will step forward, I'd like you to help finish the planting of this wonderful tree as a symbol of growth, new life and hope."

Lori walks over, grasps the shovel and distributes some soil onto the tree's base. Then she says in a strengthening voice, "I need to do this. It's helping me, as I hope its helping all of you. It's part of the healing process. My daughter was initially buried here. And now we plant this tree in belief of growth and hope. Thank you."

While a couple softly harmonizes the lyrics of *Tears in Heaven* in the background, Stevens briefly embraces Lori, now brushing away a few tears before she addresses the crowd. "I'm Claire, Ashley's step-mom. I want you all to know how special Ashley was to me. I thank God every day that I got the opportunity to have Ashley in my life, even though it was shorter than I had hoped. My fondest memories of her are of the summertime when she would spend most of her time with me. Every time she was over, she would pretty much take over caring for her sister and her brother. I didn't have to do anything. She just did everything with those babies. She dressed them, burped them, fed them and rocked them to sleep. She was a great sister and they still miss her."

The teenaged girls in the audience begin to cry as they listen to the two speakers closely. Pausing for a moment, Stevens smiles and then continues her tribute. "I remember Ashley as a great swimmer. You could not get that girl out of the pool. She swam from the beginning of the day till the end. I don't know. I think that every time I look up at the sky and I see the stars, that Ashley is there. I also think that when I look out on the ocean, she's there, too. When I look at the moon, I can see her. And when I look forward to the magnolia flowers that will bloom from this tree as time passes, it fills my heart with the spirit of Ashley."[1]

While the musicians continue singing their soft ballads to the strum of guitar chords, for another twenty minutes several female classmates of Ashley take turns offering touching eulogies and personal anecdotes that portray their departed friend's uniqueness. Then Claire and Linda hold up their soap bottles and wands and Claire adds, "Do you all remember that little bottle of bubble solution like this one, and that little plastic wand that Linda gave you earlier?"

Linda watches as the crowd nods collectively.

"Well I want each of you to open your bottle and dip your wand into it until it becomes completely submerged. Okay now everybody, follow what I do."

Claire withdraws her wand from the soap and raises her hand high in the air, continuing. "Let the wind push through the wand and create bubbles. As they travel past our faces, let us continue to remember dear Ashley Pond, and let the bubbles become spiritual vessels carrying our prayers, our thoughts, our love and our joy skyward."

Linda O'Neal steps forward and offers a final comment. "And as they float upward, for me, and I hope for you, those bubbles will represent the spirit of Ashley ascending to her place in Heaven."

People dip their wands and the bubbles flow. Over and over thousands of round bubbles climb upward, softly illuminated by the candlelight.[2]

For the months while Linda was deeply involved with the

investigation, things seemed quiet with her mother. Then, one day she gets an engraved invitation. It was from her parents and announces the occasion of a gala event to honor John and Florence's golden wedding anniversary. Linda is pleased that despite her mother's deteriorating state of mind there will be a celebration, but she has a difficult time forgiving her mother's previous actions. A few weeks later, her father shows up and finally confesses that though things are quiet the situation is worsening.

He pleads, "You can't know what it's like. Your mother used to have a bad spell every once in a while, but recently she has been having her good days only once in a while. I just live for the days when she is normal. This anniversary party has given her something to hold onto, and she's done the planning with the help of a party planner. The planner hired an accordion player, and lots of food, and a special cake. We've only heard back from a small handful of people we mailed stuff to."

"She just is acting so strangely, people are put off."

John considers her statement. "Yes, she has driven off most of her friends. That's probably true. And you're right, even the relatives have stopped coming by. Maybe that was my fault. I was trying to shield them from how bad it's gotten and maybe that played wrong. Your mother needs you and she needs your sister and she needs this party."

"Look Dad, I'll try to help and you can count on us to show up. I know it's important."

On the Saturday afternoon of February 15, 2003, the grand occasion commences in the Hillsboro Grange, a 1920s era barn-like building surrounded by towering firs and nestled behind a huge gravel parking lot. Only a few family and friends are present.

The afternoon proceeds with her mother, Florence, chatting non-stop to captive hearts, but not making much sense. Their nods and forced smiles belie their true thoughts. Then everyone eats, and eats again.

During the next few weeks Linda spends a lot of time visiting and talking on the phone with her mother. She has become much more tolerant with her mother's sometimes disjointed calls, as if her frustrating pursuit to bring the perpetrator of Ashley and Miranda's tragedy to justice has made her more patient.

In late January 2003, DNA experts drop a bombshell in Ward Weaver's direction. After profiling Weaver's DNA, then comparing it with a sample taken from his oldest son, they conclude there is no blood relationship between the two. Weaver had married Kathryn Diaz believing she was pregnant with "his" child. The fact that she was not, now disclosed nineteen years later, shocks him and also devastates his son, whose reaction is to repudiate the older Weaver's past actions. He vows to testify in the murder trial against the man he's called "dad."

The impact of this news prompts Ward Weaver to suspend his previous demand to be paid for an interview. In early February he again writes to KATU-TV reporter Anna Song, telling her if she brings a camera crew to the jail, he will answer any and all questions. Song agrees and comes to the jail. Her two hour conversation with the accused murderer is promoted by the station with the title "Inside The Mind of Ward Weaver," and will be broadcast in seven segments over three days from February 23 through February 26, 2003.

Meeting with Weaver she asks him point blank if he killed Ashley and Miranda. "No," he tells her curtly. "I did not."

"But if you didn't kill Ashley and Miranda, then how did they end up in your backyard?"

Weaver reminds the young reporter that the public has had open access to his property for two months. Regarding the concrete slab under which Ashley had been found, he contends that the hole for the slab had been open for two months, implying that many people could have placed her into the barrel, and then into the hole.

"Why should we believe you?"

"You know what," he responds testily, "I honestly don't care. Because I put up with so much bullshit because of all this. I put up with so much crap, because everybody believes I raped these little girls."

Next Song challenges the prisoner about his fingerprint found on the microwave box containing Miranda's remains. Weaver's spin on that issue changes the location of the print. Fryett's sworn affidavit points out that the print was discovered on tape inside the plastic that covered the box. But Weaver maintains his print was on the outside of the box. "They found Miranda in a box, wrapped in plastic, wrapped in another box, inside another box, wrapped in plastic, and the only fingerprints of mine they found were on the tape on the outside of all that."

When Song solicits a comment from Weaver about his alibi for the mornings the girls disappeared, he admits being home during the time in which both girls vanished, but has an explanation. He tells her that since he gets up at 8 AM, the overall time-frame precludes any possibility that he would have had time to harm Ashley and then Miranda and still get through his morning routine allowing him to arrive at his workplace by 9:00.

"Do the math," he says. "Mallori catches the bus at 8:20. Twenty more minutes for me to take a shower. Five to get dressed. That's forty-five. Twelve to get to work. That's fifty-seven minutes. That doesn't leave a hell of a lot of time to kidnap someone, rape them, murder them and get rid of the body, and get to work on time."

His explanation seems plausible until it is compared to the police's interview with Weaver a week or so after Ashley disappeared. According to Weaver at that time, on the morning of January 9 he had encountered problems with his burglar alarm. He was at home late that morning, not arriving at his workplace until about 9:30. When Song points out the contradiction, Weaver explains there was a simple misinterpretation about the day. "It was two days before Ashley went missing that my burglar alarm screwed up on me. They got it wrong. It's as simple as that.

"I did arrive at work a half an hour late the day Miranda disappeared, but that was on account of 'my alarm clock,' who's my daughter Mallori, being at her mother's house that morning. And while we're on this subject, I only took her to her mom's one time the night before, not twice. So anyway, without her there to wake me up, I didn't get up until 8:30 and I had to get my ass in the shower and get dressed, go get my car warmed up and I was at work by like 9:10."

When Weaver is asked about the freezer, he attempts to convey his sense of outrage over the police's confiscation of the appliance and makes a bizarre comment. "I'm also aware that they've taken my freezer. And they're going to pay me for a new one, because I'm pretty sure whatever chemicals they're going to use to test the blood that, you know, that's inside that thing, is going to make it so I'm probably not going to be able to put food back in it again."

The TV reporter shakes her head and says, "Wait! There's blood in the freezer?"

"Food. You know if you put your meat in there. Blood. Hamburger and steak. Yeah!"

"So you never stored Ashley and Miranda in your freezer, then?"

"No, I did not. The only thing that's ever been in that freezer is food from the store. Period!"

With autopsy reports showing Ashley with a blood-alcohol level of .17, the State Medical Examiner concludes that she had likely consumed quite a bit of alcohol before she died. The young reporter asks Weaver if he had ever fed booze to the young girl.

"Yeah, I've given her alcohol," he admits.

"So was Ashley ever drunk in your home?"

"Drunk in the house?"

"Because of the alcohol you had given her?"

"Fall-down drunk? No. Maybe a little...tipsy. She didn't weigh that much so I didn't give her...give her that much. I gave her alcohol on probably, maybe, three occasions. So, she got a little...well, maybe classified as a little drunk. But not fall-down, staggering drunk. She was fine."

Turning to Weaver's state of mind when Miranda disappeared, Anna Song confronts the accused about his police report which claimed his ex-wife said he had been very upset when the second girl went missing. Three weeks before Miranda disappeared, she had cautioned another girl not to spend the night at his house during a birthday party for Mallori, because Ashley's previous molestation allegations indicated Weaver might molest her, too. Was he angry enough to kill Miranda over that?

Weaver's response is emphatic. "I never had any problems with Miranda. Never! And someone said I got mad at Miranda for that?" He giggles. "Okay. No. The comment was…and I did not get mad at Miranda. I was mad at the parent. One of the girls was not going to be allowed to sleep over because of Ashley's accusations. And I said, 'Fine. If she's so worried about her daughter why is she even letting her be here?'"

Song pulverizes Weaver briefly when she brings up the volatile subject of his oldest son's DNA mismatch which meant that the young man was not the accused killer's biological son. She reminds him that his sons, his daughter and his ex-wife had all testified against him during grand jury proceedings. For the first time in the TV interview Weaver seems genuinely shaken.

"My eldest is a pain in my butt, but I care about him. He's my oldest. He and I have been butting heads since he was five. Now they compared his DNA with mine and found there was no match. That fucking destroyed me to find that out in here. Actually it was probably good that my ex and I weren't in the same room when I found that out, or I'd probably fuckin' killed her."

The irony of Ward Weaver's father sitting on Death Row in California awaiting execution for a double homicide prompts Song to request a comparison of this Ward with his dad. He falters before managing to utter a bitter response.

"I'm just irritated that I'm more like him than I thought I was. I could wind up where he's at, and that's really, really not a happy thought. And my mother! I can't stand her. In fact, there are two people that when they die I'm having a kegger on their grave. That's my first ex-wife and my mother. And I'm going to invite everybody, even if I don't know 'em."

"Why did you have such a poor relationship with your mother?"

"Step-father. Because of the things she allowed him to do to us. And I'm not talking sexually. I'm talking physically."[3]

Public reaction to Ward's interview when broadcast is over-whelmingly negative. The outcry for justice increases. Hal Williams,

Weaver's attorney, seems to be livid having his client spilling his guts like that without permission or guidance from counsel. He had vociferously advised against any public statements. A competent attorney, like Williams, could never countenance such a display of outrageous blather, which would further taint the potential jury pool in the Oregon City community. Later, when he confronts Weaver about the unsanctioned interview Williams complains that he had heard a promo on the radio about it which began, "Tune in tonight folks for our exclusive series, 'Inside the Mind of a Murderer.'"

Weaver seems proud of his performance but concerned about how it is being promoted by the station, and particularly upset about what Williams had told him about the broadcasted title of Song's interview. The next morning he asks a county jail worker if she had watched the Anna Song interview. When she admits to having seen the show, he then queries what they called it.

"I think 'Inside the Mind of Ward Weaver' or something like that."

"Well my attorney told me they called it 'Inside the Mind of a Murderer.'" His voice takes on a razor's edge, "If that bitch, Anna Song, did that to me, I will cut off her fucking legs."[4]

The worker stares at him, startled that Weaver has let her see his violent nature. Weaver's habit of talking at length about his case and his blatant disregard for his attorney's advice to refrain from commenting provoke widespread clamor in the media and public. Weaver's actions pose an extraordinary challenge for his defense. Criminal defense attorneys often must strike a balance between advising clients about what's best for them and respecting their clients' rights to make decisions. Most of the time clients listen, but here was a case where the attorneys were totally pushed aside. One question surfaced in the minds of many, "What is Weaver up to?"

To discover a plausible explanation, it is important to examine how Weaver's ego became the central force in his downfall. Linda O'Neal, who had bet that Weaver's distorted personality would feed on fame, had triggered the avalanche by maneuvering his very first press interview with Jim Redden. It was just as Linda had hoped. Weaver openly declared himself a prime suspect in the two girls' disappearances. Within a week Linda's bet paid off when he became "well-known," and talked about everywhere. He soaked up the spotlight in numerous interviews with reporters in which he delivered delicious, salacious details concerning his close relationship with Ashley Pond. Linda watched each one with interest, gathering details about his psychopathic mind. Each interview gave Ward an inflated sense of his own importance. In one he even had the audacity to point out the concrete slab behind his house under which Ashley's remains were later found. His desire to discuss his case with reporters and to make what appear to be self-incriminating remarks seems to fill him with a bizarre sense of accomplishment.[5] While basking in the spotlight, Weaver is out of his lawyers' control.

The last week in March, 2003 proves eventful for the case when his lawyers finally decide to throw in the legal towel. When confronted with their motion to be dismissed from defending Ward Weaver an exasperated judge of the Clackamas County Circuit Court reluctantly agrees that they have given their all in a most difficult situation. Recognizing the irreconcilable differences that now dominate the attorneys' relationship with their client, he gives them their walking papers.[6] The cost for the seven months of legal work that essentially has to be redone from scratch is a staggering $141,000, all billed to the taxpayers.[7]

Michael Barker and Peter Fahy, prominent area lawyers with extensive experience in capital crime cases, agree, if reluctantly, to become Weaver's court-appointed advisors.[8]

The trial date is reset to June 2004. Barker and Fahy claim it will take a year to prepare the new defense. Ashley's family is devastated when they realize that they will be forced through another whole year of uncertainty with their closure having been hijacked by Weaver's tactics. Holding back her tears, Lori Pond attempts to handle the frustration. "I feel he should pay for what he did. In time I believe justice will be served." Michelle Duffey, who must be equally heartsick, declines to comment. During the court session, sporting a newly shaved head, Weaver appears on closed-circuit TV and quietly nods to the judge when he tells Weaver that by agreeing to a delay he will waive claims of violations of his constitutional right to a "speedy trial." Weaver says he understands.

Linda O'Neal and Philip, who have watched the proceedings, get up to leave. On her way out of the courtroom Linda comments, "To wait another ten months for justice." She continues, "I find this very disappointing. Where are the people's rights for the 'speedy trial?' Certainly the citizens have a right to have the accused brought to trial in a speedier manner than this? I've seen this attorney-merry-go-round game dozens of times before. I guarantee you, before June he'll be coming up with something else to avoid paying up for what he did."

Afterwards, a disgruntled prosecutor on the case gripes to a TV reporter, adamant that his office was fully prepared to proceed with the September, 2003 trial date. Outraged by the delay, first Lori Pond and later Michelle Duffey each file notice of intent to file suit against the agencies they feel are culpable in the deaths of their children. The Oregon State Department of Human Services receives its letter from Ashley Pond's mother stating that her attorneys are considering a wrongful death suit seeking compensation for the fate that Ashley suffered at the hands of Ward Weaver.

When word of the notice comes out, Pond tells *The Oregonian*, "I just believe that if they had listened to us in the very beginning, my daughter would still be alive."[9]

Emily Bowen follows the trail blazed by Pond's lawyers a short time afterwards saying that she may include the Clackamas County Sheriff's office in the list of agencies that failed in the investigation of Weaver. Eventually, Emily[10] and Michelle Duffey[11] each sue DHS for $1.5 million and Lori Pond sues for a whopping $9.75 million.[12]

When Linda's phone begins ringing the night the article breaks, she already knows who it is. Lori Pond's reactions to the unhealed pain in her life place her in emotional turmoil. For weeks she has been calling Linda, always in the wee hours. The calls are long and convoluted.

As soon as Linda says hello, Lori's emotional voice begins a conversation. "I thought when I sued their asses it would make me feel better, but it doesn't. They just don't get it. The one thing people have to understand is that you're a child, even if you're like a child being made fun of and that ticks me off. Because, it's like those children are just like society, and it pisses me off.

"And as a mother, you're trying to get something out of them and they're just like, 'no, no, no, no, no, no, no.' Bull crap! You know, as a mother, that there's something that you have to get but you won't get it, because they're not going to tell you the truth. Are they, Linda? Well your daughter lived, mine didn't. Mine didn't. Tell me."

Linda knows that it is not the time to debate the issue, but to try to calm down the anguished woman. "You're right."

"I'm sorry, Linda. I can't stop thinking about Ashley tonight."

"That's okay sweetie, I understand."

"I loved my daughter and she sat there and endured probably more than I ever could."

Lori pauses, then blurts out, "I don't want to get in trouble for anything."

"What do you mean?"

"I'm just saying what everybody else has told me. 'Don't say anything', you know. If I tell it all that makes them think I'm the wacko. Because throughout all this they say, 'shush shush shush. Don't say anything.'"

"Lori, just tell the whole truth. To hell with what they say. The important thing is the killer of your daughter doesn't get away without the punishment he deserves."

"But anything I say can hurt. Ward is an asshole. Use it against me. I don't even give a flying crap. He hurt my daughter and that's just it."

"And you want to do everything to see him convicted, so you don't want to talk about anything?"

"But I just said it. You can use it against me. You know what? Anything I say that you're tape recording it, they're going to use it against me in the trial. Oh yeah. That's news. He's a jerk. He killed my daughter. Okay? That's all I have to say."

Linda is having her usual trouble following Lori's distressed rambling. "Why?"

"Because I just said it."

"You're not supposed to say that to anyone?"

"I don't think so. But I just said it."

"I can't imagine that saying that would be a problem."

"I don't know. If that S.O.B. gets off though...I don't know what I'd do. I don't like him. I don't want him. And God won't want him, either. So he's in a new realm of life. He's not allowed."

"Lori, don't worry. We're not going to let him get off."

"Yeah but I'm pissed. Sometimes I get really pissed."

"Do you think you'll feel better, when he finally gets convicted? Do you think that will be any sort of relief to you?"

"No."

"Yeah, I didn't think so."

"I mean, death is death."

"Yes, it won't bring her back."

"No it won't. That's my girl. I want her home. She's a lady and she's one constructive little girl. I mean, if you sat there...if you, Linda, sat there and said to Ashley, 'I need fifty cents,' and it was the only money she had, she'd give it to you. It's one hundred percent true. I'd do it too. That's the kind of people we are. And Weaver took advantage of her naïveté."

Linda tries to help Lori see that she is finally grappling with the truth. "That's right, that's what predators do, they take advantage of people—people's weaknesses."

"I hope to shout that this doesn't come to..." Lori breaks off and takes a breath trying not to break down. "He's murdered my daughter, and I know it. He took advantage of a young child."

"He did. Yes, he did, because he couldn't have gotten away with it with adult women."

"He tried."

"He tried?"

"Obviously. Look at the nineteen year old he tried to strangle. I'm mad."

"I think you should be."

"Yeah, but despite his being caught, I can't seem to pull myself together."

"After a tragedy like this, it takes time. Just take one step at a time."

Lori sputters. "But I'll need to talk about it forever."

"I can imagine."

"He's an asshole. Can I say that again?"

"Yes."

"Asshole! Asshole! Asshole! He took the life of my child, just because, why? Asshole!" Lori breaks down into tears, sobbing. "I'm really mad."

"I know, honey. I know." Linda comforts her.[13]

CHAPTER TWENTY-TWO

Woe-stricken Days

Linda continues to divide her energy between her private investigation cases, serving as a frequent telephone advisor for Lori and the problems of her own mother. When the summer months arrive, Linda's mother's calls are finally reduced to a manageable level. Although she finds it upsetting to hear the repetitions that invade her mother's speech, by now Linda has become much more patient with the aging matriarch and tries each time to turn irrational chatter into a meaningful connection. Though her mother's hold on reality has grown very tenuous, her mom's childlike conversation often brings laughter that hasn't occurred between mother and daughter since Linda was a child.

At sundown one day, the phone rings at the usual time. Linda picks up, preparing mentally for her mother to be confused, agitated and wanting a ride home. This is the most distressing time of day for Linda, because her mom will often beg her to come and take her home, having no idea that she already is home. Linda is surprised to discover this call is from her father. A direct call from him is unusual, because he normally calls only when her mom needs something. His fifty-year marriage has molded him into a cheerful attendant, a good soldier. He says, "Your mother and I have overnight reservations at the coast for Saturday. You know how we love the beach. So we need someone to come over and feed Pee Wee. Just on Saturday. We plan to be back home by noon, Sunday. What do you say? Can you help us out here, Linda?"

"Saturday? Sure, okay. Any special time?"

"Late afternoon would work. Maybe you could also take the dog for a little walk."

"Definitely. Anything else?"

"If there's not enough dry dog food in the kitchen cupboard, you'll find an extra bag in your sister's old bedroom. You still have your key to the house, right?"

"Of course."

"Oh, and I'll call you when we get back from the beach to check how things went."

On Saturday Linda arrives at her parents' house and greets their dog Pee Wee. When she discovers only an empty dog food bag in the cupboard, she wonders why her Dad wouldn't have put a fresh bag in there. Then she remembers that he said there were extra bags in the room down the hall.

Linda makes her way to the room, pushes open the door and steps back, spellbound. She discovers mountains of new clothing everywhere, hundreds upon hundreds of dresses, blouses, pants, sweaters, skirts, coats, bathrobes, pajamas. Linda is amazed and confounded. She navigates her way around piles stacked six feet high in all directions. Sorting through the closest one, she quickly notices that the original price tags are still attached to every item. Adding the tags up as she goes, she rummages through nearly a thousand dollars worth before she decides to stop counting. Towering piles cover every square inch of the room, except for the small path that twists between them.

Linda goes to the wardrobe closet and tries the sliding door. An avalanche of more clothes tumbles out landing on her head and shoulders. Hot tears fill her eyes.

Linda shakes her head and says, "Oh my God! Oh my God!" It takes her several minutes to get a grip on just how overwhelming a discovery she has accidentally stumbled onto. Then it dawns on her. This is no accident. Her dad must have used the dog food malarkey to get her to see what has been happening. Linda realizes that her overwhelmed father is finally crying out for help.

Linda checks out other rooms confirming her suspicions. The master bedroom, plus two guest bedrooms are all filled with piles of women's clothing, most of it never worn. She marvels at how the rest of the house, the living room, the dining room, the family room, all appear normal at first glance.

Next she ventures into the master bathroom half expecting to find more clothes. On a hunch she pulls back the shower curtain and discovers dozens of brand new bottles of shampoo all lined up in neat rows around the edge of the tub. She tries to open the top drawer to the linen closet. She yanks and tugs and eventually gets it to slide. There are so many towels, she loses count after eighty-five.

The other bathrooms are also overloaded with supplies. Dozens of new towels, many more full shampoo containers, full hand lotion bottles and hundreds of bars of soap each still in their paper wrappings. Linda tries to make some sense of what is becoming increasingly senseless. What the hell is happening? How did all this stuff get here? Has her mom become a serial shoplifter? Has her father let her buy out the mall? Why would he have let her purchase a hundred extra bath towels? Her dad kept a lid on the disintegration. So many secrets! Linda's mind flashes back and forth. "How could I not have recognized how bad my mom's disengagement has become?" she asks herself.

She next decides to employ her best snooping techniques honed from years as a private detective. The first place you always go to find the hidden truths? The garbage. Within minutes she's out behind the garage, carefully lifting the lid on a thirty gallon green vinyl can. She tips the can spilling the contents onto the sidewalk in front of her and sifts through each item, holding it up and making a mental note. Empty ice-cream cartons, beer cans, soup cans, more beer cans, more soup cans and more ice cream cartons. Nothing else. The contents speak volumes about her parents' current plight.

The kitchen becomes Linda's next objective. Throwing the refrigerator door open, she scans the contents. Twelve cans of beer, twenty-four kinds of salad dressing and a four-weeks-past-code-date bagged, mixed salad. That is it. No milk, no juice, no eggs, no fruit, no cheese, no leftovers. Linda turns her attention to the freezer compartment and when she pulls it open she smiles. Every inch of space is crammed with square half-gallon cartons of ice cream. She pulls some of them apart and notes the flavors: strawberry, chocolate, vanilla, rocky road, pistachio, orange sherbet. Next, she decides to check out the pantry. She finds only chicken noodle soup. She counts, ten, twenty, fifty; by the time she stops she's up to three hundred and ten cans. And every can is identical to every other: store brand chicken noodle soup. Linda's head spins; she wonders if this is some bizarre alternate universe.

Linda goes back to locate the dog food and feeds Pee Wee, then heads for home to await word from her dad.

At precisely 12:05 Sunday afternoon, while she is elbow-deep in washing breakfast dishes, the phone rings. Linda wipes her wet hands on a nearby dishtowel and picks up. "Linda O'Neal Investigations."

"Hi, Linda. It's Dad. We're back."

Linda tries to be upbeat. "So, how was your trip to the beach?"

"It was good. The weather was beautiful."

"Did you go to your favorite restaurant?"

"Yeah, we went out to dinner."

"What did you have?"

"Oh, I had liver and onions. And your mom, I—I don't remember what she had, and," he blurts out, "neither does she." They both laugh, concealing their concern. "So, did you have any trouble with Pee Wee?" he asks.

"No, no. Pee Wee was fine. I did have some shocks, though, when I got inside your house," Linda says loudly.

"Shocks? What are you talking about?

"Dad. You told me there was extra dog food in Sis's old bedroom. The bag in the kitchen was empty. When I went to Sis's room, I found a lot more than dog food. There's enough stuff in there to open your own store! What is going on?"

She hears her father's sharp intake of breath. "Well, your mother likes to shop. And I've taken her shopping a lot, I guess. And the stuff just, I guess it just builds up after awhile."

"Dad, you're supposed to be the one that's well. Why would you allow her to purchase hundreds and hundreds of outfits? None of them have ever been worn."

He gives a heavy sigh then goes on. "Well Linda, as you know, handling your mom is difficult these days. But I've found a surefire way to calm her down when she starts really getting out of hand and it works every time. I just say, 'Let's go shopping. We'll go to the mall and buy you some nice things, and then we'll get some ice cream on the way home.' She suddenly becomes calm as a purring kitten, and she still gets the biggest damn kick out of the whole experience. Driving up, walking in, looking through the clothing racks and don't forget the thrill of watching the clerk wrap up the purchase, it all makes her happy. And after we get home, for hours she's content. It works wonders, better than any pill."

"But why so much?"

"The more your mother gets upset, the more times I've been taking her shopping, and that's been a lot lately. I guess it just got to be too much. But remember, it makes her happy. And that's the only important thing in a situation like this. Besides, what else can I do? Sometimes, now, she throws horrible tantrums. When that happens, sometimes I can't calm her down. I have to let her go out and buy stuff. I haven't found anything else that works."

"What about all those towels, Dad? And there must be a hundred unopened bottles of shampoo."

"She loves picking out towels. To her they are ultimate luxury. So many textures, colors and print patterns. Sometimes, your mother spends an hour running her hands through the stacks, touching the fabrics, even smelling some of them. And as for the shampoo, I guess she never wants to run out. So what if she's overbuying them? It's way cheaper than a nursing home. Your mom and I still have good times, we really do. It's still working," he explains.

"Dad, don't you see how sad this all is? Maybe you can't, because you are so close to it all the time. But this is wrong. You're not helping her. I don't know what will help, if anything can, but this doesn't."

Silence fills the line.

Linda has been in emotional chaos since the revelation in her parents' house. To her, it is so incredibly sad. The humanity has slipped right out of her mother while she wasn't looking and she didn't even get the chance to say good-bye.

Finally, she says, "Okay Dad, if you want to spend your retirement funds on a hundred thousand dollar wardrobe that keeps mom mellow, who am I to argue? I suppose it's really none of my business. But there's something else I saw yesterday. Let's talk about nutrition. I looked through the kitchen when I was at your house and all I could find was about three hundred cans of chicken noodle soup."

"But Linda, chicken noodle soup is good for you. That's what they feed you when you get sick. It makes you better. It's good for you. And besides, Mom doesn't cook any more. You knew that."

"I knew nothing of the kind. What's going on? You said just a few weeks ago that Mom was cooking dinner. What's the real truth?"

Her father hesitates for a few moments. "The truth? The truth is she hasn't really been cooking anything in quite a while. I can't have her around the stove or she might burn the house down."

"Has it been weeks or months, Dad?"

He sighs. "Months. And you know I never did know how to cook, Linda. Remember that time when I tried to make you kids macaroni and cheese?" He laughs nervously. "And I burned the macaroni so bad there were little macaroni-shaped spots in the enamel sauce pan. Well, I never did learn to cook, but even I can heat up a can of chicken noodle soup."

"Dad, it's full of sodium and it is definitely not something you should be feeding Mom all the time. It could deplete her immune system more. And you know I'm wondering what you're feeding her the rest of the day. I looked in your garbage can, and I was appalled at what I found. There were a dozen empty ice cream containers. That's six gallons of ice cream. The only other trash was empty chicken noodle soup cans and your beer cans. That shows me how much things have slipped, and frankly, I'm worried about both of you."

"I'm sorry, but it's all I can do. I'm doing my best. Come on, Linda. Why do you think I had you look for the dog food? I know I need help but I don't know what to do."

"I feel guilty, because I haven't been here for you, Dad. What can I do to help you?"

Linda's father falters a bit, desperate to come up with a logical-sounding plan. Finally he says, "Can you help me get rid of clutter? Your mother will never miss it, really. I know because she can go into our bedroom, see the piles of clothes you saw, and come out complaining that she has nothing to wear. She can't find one change of clothes among hundreds of new outfits. The stuff becomes somehow invisible. It's weird. If we can get rid of all of it, she won't miss it and that would be a big help."

"Yeah, all right, well, I'll talk to Sis and if you can engineer getting Mom out of the house again for another weekend, maybe we can come in and pare it down a bit."

"No, pare it down a lot. I'm telling you, if every room is empty, she won't notice, Linda. She won't."

"You've got to come to grips with the situation. We've got to make some big changes, more than just cleaning up the clutter. What about trying the Meals on Wheels Program? I can call them tomorrow. They deliver a hot meal every day to elderly people, no questions asked. They'll come out five days a week with a good meal."

"How much will that cost me?"

"Let's not worry about that now…the most important issue is getting you and Mom on a more sensible diet. I'll call you tomorrow after I talk to The Senior Center."

The intervention reshapes her parents' agenda enough to foster a period of relative calm. Linda and her sister's big purge results in four truckloads of donations to homeless shelters. Somehow, at least for the time being, their parents keep their lives together. The daily hot meals, and of course the shopping trips contribute to the continued, if fragile, stability.

The new routine includes weekly visits from both daughters with additional meals, personal attention and companionship.

At the same time that Linda is coping with her parents' problems, she discovers that there still are issues in the Ashley Pond case. The terminated DHS workers who had not followed-up on Ashley Pond's molestation complaints against Ward Weaver are both reinstated to the DHS work force. The administrative law judge presiding over the pair's emotional plea for a second chance concludes they had been improperly persecuted. He upholds the agency's decision to strip one of her management position. But he recommends that she be returned to work at a lower post.[1]

Linda quickly realizes that when Lori finds out she'll surely see it as another blow to gaining justice for Ashley and it will become the primary venting topic of the next call. Sure enough it is. "Hi Lori. How's it going tonight?"[2]

"Wouldn't you just know it, Linda?" Lori is almost screaming. "Those rejects both got their stinking jobs back and with all the back pay too! My food stamps for Ashley got cut off the first of the month after I reported her missing. Where's my back pay, god damn it?"

Linda sighs and tries to divert Lori to an issue she can do something about. "How are your daughters doing these days? Are they still living with their dads?"

The ploy works. "Yes, and I will do anything to get to see my kids, at this point in time."

"Have you set a date for them to come home?"

"School starts next month, right after Labor Day and I want them back home in time for the new school year."

"That's great news!"

"I know, but it's the time 'til then I can hardly stand...without them, without Ashley."

"You should go with me to the beach next Tuesday."

"Oh, I don't know. You're my friend, but other people I don't really feel comfortable with...that's hard. I mean I just love you Linda. And you're so sweet, and you give me a kiss on my cheek. I love that."

Linda chuckles warmly.

"Don't laugh at me, please."

"I'm not laughing at you."

"Because that means a lot to me, I mean, if somebody gets respect,

I feel that's respect. I mean, if they do that. And if you're not going to do that, fine, I'll give it right back. And if you don't do that it means we're not friends. I'll fight for it. You don't have to tell me. I'll fight for it. I really will. Linda, I don't want to hurt anybody. I don't want to hurt nobody. Maybe I'm afraid of being stupid, okay? Maybe I'm really stupid."

"No, Lori, you're not stupid. You just have a lot of problems right now and I understand that."

CHAPTER TWENTY-THREE

Nefarious Plotting

M eanwhile, inspired by a conversation with an Oregon City
Detective about what constitutes criminal "custodial interference," Ward Weaver sits in his Oregon City jail cell plotting his
next move. Soon he demands an audience with a sheriff's department
representative. On October 7, 2003, he is placed in the jail's
conference room. While Emily Tsao, a reporter for *The Oregonian*,
takes feverish notes, Weaver articulates a new complaint to Detective
Maurice Delehant.

"It seems when I was arrested in August that my daughter and I
were already living at my sister's at that point. In fact, we were living
there since the first of August. When I got arrested, Clackamas
County stepped in and took custody of my daughter who was already
living in another county so they had no grounds to do so. I was
arrested in another county, in another city. She was not with me. At
that time I was her legal guardian and Clackamas County had no
grounds to step in and take jurisdiction of any kind. They had no
jurisdiction to start with, you know."

Delehant nods. "So what's the issue here, Mr. Weaver?"

"They had no right to take my daughter. None. She wasn't in
any danger. I was her legal guardian. And she was at my sister's.
Nobody called DHS and said, 'Mallori's being abused.' So, I got to
thinking, and that's why I called you. Because I was reading those
original charges that they had against me where they were originally

going to charge me with interfering with parental rights. And then I read this custodial interference thing and so that's what I asked you about. And kidnapping. That was something I read somewhere in another case. Because it doesn't mean that you have to take the kid out of the house, just keep the kid from going somewhere. So I want to charge them with kidnapping, too. Custodial interference and kidnapping."

"Are you serious?"

"Hell yes. I've got rights, you know."

"Exactly who do you want to make these charges against?"

"I want to file charges against several DHS workers and their supervisors as well as the DHS Directors."

Delehant jots a few notes before he looks up. "Is that all?"

"I'm also going to be filing civil lawsuits against some of those individuals."

"Just so I understand, when did all of this happen? Was this prior to the arrest for the murder or ..."

"Prior."

"So they came in prior?"

"They came in on the nineteenth, according to the paperwork I have. They filed the petition on the nineteenth of August. I was arrested on the thirteenth and they took custody of Mallori then. I didn't get indicted for the murders until October."

"Okay."

"They didn't discover the girls' bodies until a week or so after."

Delehant is confused. "How's that?"

"They didn't discover the girls' bodies until a week or so after. After they'd already taken Mallori. So, I mean, it has nothing to do with the Ashley and Miranda thing, as far as their reason for coming in like that."

Delehant asks, "Were you in custody when they took your daughter?"

"According to the paperwork, yes."

"So you were technically in physical custody of the jail."

"Yeah, I was right here."

"Okay. And who was designated then to care for your daughter?"

"Mallori? My sister."

"Did you have an agreement with her to care for Mallori?"

"It was a verbal one."

"How long?"

"For years."

"Okay, so where did she go after the state took custody of her?"

"She stayed there."

"At your sister's house?"

"Yeah, she stayed there. But they were looking at her mother for her to go to instead of my sister."

"So where did she end up staying? Did she end up with your sister? Or did she go to her mom's?"

"Well right now she's in a permanent foster home."

"Okay."

"So DHS interfered with Mallori and my life when they stepped in and took control of Mallori. My sister had no say in anything. Even though she is my daughter's legal aunt. She was staying at her house with my permission. But they wouldn't let my sister make any decisions for Mallori."

"Did the judge, I mean when did they actually talk about the taking of the child into protective custody?"

"To my knowledge there was no discussion of why they were even in court. There was no discussion of why we were there in the first place. You see that would be like you getting arrested for DUI and your kids are over at your mom's. And then they step in and say, 'Okay well he's in jail for DUI. Let's take the kids.'"

Delehant is exasperated and shakes his ahead. "No it's not. What it's like is someone gets arrested for aggravated murder of two kids."

"No I didn't."

"Okay, I didn't say you did, but that's just what you got arrested for."

Weaver is incensed and his voice rises. "No!"

"Initially, it's what you're charged with, right now." Delehant pauses and takes a deep breath before continuing. "Okay, you got arrested on Ballot Measure Eleven crimes, which are violence charges that carry stiff mandatory sentences, and not the same as a DUI. Those are not the same as a DUI."

"It wasn't the kids and it wasn't the murders."

"Okay."

"It was the alleged rape of Emily. You got it?"

"I got it," the detective says grimly.

Weaver repeats, "The kids were not what I got arrested for."

"You got arrested on the rape first?"

"Yes."

"Okay, then later on you got charged with the murders."

"Yes, and they took her before I was charged."

"When were you charged with the murders?"

"October 4."

"And they took her when?"

"August 19."

"Okay, so when were you indicted?" The detective is obviously having trouble keeping cool.

"October 4."

"Okay, it took them until then, but you were in custody on...?"

"I was in custody on the rape. On the thirteenth of August. They took my daughter on the nineteenth of August. They found the girls what, a week or so later and they indicted me on October 4 and my paperwork says it was the twenty-fourth and the twenty-fifth of August when they found the girls. So you see, when they took my daughter I was not charged with a Ballot Measure Eleven crime. So they can't use this as an excuse to take my daughter."

Delehant writes more comments onto his pad before asking, "So who's your attorney for Mallori and you through the court?"

"Mallori has her own attorney. His name is Tom Regan. My attorney for the custody battle now is Robin Banks. It was Faith Sawyer."

"Okay and Faith?"

"Faith screwed me. I'm filing a complaint with the bar association against Faith for malpractice and incompetence. In fact, she had me stipulate to something that costs me my rights to any decisions about Mallori, and so I fired her. And now my attorney is Robin Banks."

Delehant stands up, closes his briefcase and offers a final comment to the prisoner. "It's not likely that charges are going to get filed because of this."

Weaver smiles. "I know that. But you have to get paperwork started somewhere."[1]

During the month of October, Weaver continues to organize his strategies and confounds his attorneys by writing a flurry of letters trying to bait media interest in his case. Portland's KPTV Channel 12 is the first to bite, sending reporter Kelley Day to the jail for a three-hour videotaping session.[2] During the interview, still sporting his shaved head and goatee, an animated Weaver offers an exciting new slant when he postulates a previously unmentioned conspiracy involving motorcycle gang drug dealers being responsible for the deaths of Ashley and Miranda. Weaver refers to a box full of police reports to claim that the girls were killed by people he knows wanting to implicate him. "I do know how, and I do know why and I do know whom, but that's something that I'm not willing to give out at the moment," says Weaver.[3]

As he rambles on, Weaver repeatedly refers to dozens of police reports and other documents supplied by his court-appointed attorneys, even proudly displaying autopsy pictures. He claims to know some of the people involved in the conspiracy, admitting he had pissed them off in the past. "Drugs were involved," he tells Day. "It's drugs. It's money. It's a mess." Although he criticizes all news coverage, he is adamant that the *Portland Tribune* is doing a hatchet job on him, because the *Tribune* had identified him as a suspect in July 2002, nearly two months before law enforcement officials found the girls' bodies. But during Weaver's interview with Redden for that article, it had been Weaver who declared himself a suspect.[4]

The judge's reaction to this latest Weaver publicity overture is swift and decisive, if not altogether constitutional. He's had enough. "Further publicity regarding this case will make it increasingly difficult to select a fair and impartial jury," he says, "and will be unlikely to significantly enhance the public understanding of the proceedings." He imposes a strict "gag order," prohibiting Weaver and his attorneys, the prosecutors, investigators and witnesses from disclosing any information about the case to the news media until the end of the trial.[5]

Weaver's reaction to the judge's decision is muted, since no reactions can be reported, but Weaver's relationship with his second legal team deteriorates rapidly. Courthouse gossip portrays a brewing conflict centered on Weaver's determination to testify in his own behalf at trial. Jim Redden speculates that Weaver's recent public statements may conflict with the private admission he has made to one of his attorneys. If that is the case, the lawyers could not ethically put him on the witness stand if they believe he would be likely to commit perjury. It's the worst possible ethical dilemma that could face a defense attorney. And he couldn't talk about it in public.[6]

The issue boils to a head a few days later when Michael Barker and Peter Fahy file a motion before Judge Herndon to be dismissed from defending Ward Weaver any further. On November 21, Ward Weaver is brought to a Clackamas County courtroom in shackles. Lori Pond and Michelle Duffey sit silently a few feet away with their lawyers, intently watching him being escorted to his seat. Tensions run high, because this is the first time since his incarceration that Weaver has been in person at a hearing. The young mothers desperately want to look the alleged killer of their children in the eye. He ignores them.

When the hearing commences, Barker and Fahy tell the judge they have reached the end of their patience regarding ethical considerations, plus they claim that their relationship with their client has been fractured beyond repair. The lead prosecutor in the case counters, "It should be obvious to the court by now that this defendant does not intend to submit himself to the control of any attorney. There is simply no likelihood that the defendant will magically reform himself to yet a third set of court appointed attorneys."

Because both arguments are compelling, the judge seriously considers the merits, then he concludes he must force the defense lawyers to stick it out. As he puts it, "Some clients are more difficult to represent than others." Addressing Weaver directly, the judge continues, "There's a lot at stake. You are fighting for your life, I understand that. The state is not required to appoint an indigent defendant an endless string of attorneys...It's an absolutely flawed strategy." The motion is firmly denied and the attorneys are told to continue to do their best in representing their client despite the difficulties they are encountering.[7]

During these months, Mallori Weaver is often a point of contention between her father and those trying to help her. Despite Detective Fryett's vigorous attempts to disrupt her mandated jailhouse visitations with her dad, Mallori dutifully shows up every three weeks. Subjected to Weaver's non-stop sniveling, rationalizing and protests of innocence, his daughter is growing up, physically and emotionally, and her skepticism enlarges. She gives lip service to his expressions, but inside her doubts and frustrations grow. By November, Mallori is seeing her dad approximately once every month. Her December visit causes a great disruption because during that session Weaver is especially vociferous, talking at length about the unfairness of the charges against him, wildly protesting his innocence. He must sense he is losing Mallori's devotion, so in a desperate ploy to engage her he pulls out gruesome autopsy photos from his box of papers and displays them to her. Somehow, his logic has convinced him that if she'll stare at them long enough and listen to his rebuttals, she will be swayed. He will have reignited her loyalty and she'll once again believe in him. Yet those who found out about his tactics wondered if he was up to something else.

Ultimately, showing those photos to Mallori backfires, becoming the final straw for her. Pushed beyond the point of ever wanting to lay eyes on him again, she bravely takes action on her own behalf. Mallori writes an emotional letter to the presiding Family Court judge, whose jurisdiction includes the visitation mandate. Mallori pleads to be excused from any further obligations to see her father in jail. Ironically, the previous day the judge received another letter, from a Department of Justice employee. This letter carries the force of an "official recommendation," and focuses on Weaver's violation of rules, the most important of which was the absolute prohibition of discussing any aspect of the murder charges with his child. After careful consideration the judge announces her ruling. The visits are terminated. Mallori will now be free to rebuild her life with no more personal contact with Ward Weaver forced upon her.[8]

Weaver's attorney, the weary Michael Barker, says, "Weaver will be bitterly disappointed by the ruling. The visits were extremely important to him. It's going to have a decided effect on his mood." When he is given the news, Weaver reacts with anger that turns into what appears to his jailers to be either deep despair or a valiant attempt to portray deep despair. With Weaver, no one can be sure.[9]

At 9:02 PM on January 11, 2004, Ward Weaver is taken from his Clackamas County jail cell to the common area of the cellblock. A deputy hands him a bar of soap and a disposable razor as he reminds the inmate he has only an hour to finish his shower and shave. Weaver is then to return the toiletry items before going back to his cell.

Half an hour early, the guard notices Weaver has already returned to his cell, and he becomes concerned. Prisoners always use every minute of their recreation time, time when they can move around, away from the closet-like barred cubicle in which they are incarcerated the other twenty-three hours a day. It isn't like the normally gregarious Weaver to sit sullenly in his cell. The jailer approaches and what he sees makes his heart race. A weeping Ward Weaver is perched on a stool dripping with blood, both hands clutching a batch of hand-written letters to his chest. Incoherent mutterings can be heard between intermittent wailing. Tears stream down Weaver's face.

The guard shouts for assistance and within moments the prisoner is stretched on the floor just outside his cell, surrounded by correction officers. Weaver continues crying and thrashing about as his guards restrain him. "You can't have my babies," he shrieks, "I want my babies back." He tries to pull away from any attempts at treating the superficial lacerations on his left arm. Looking closer, the guards see he has crudely attempted to carve his daughter's name into his flesh with the purloined razor. Surprisingly, he had only reached the third letter when the profuse bleeding prompted him to quit. The guards finally subdue him enough to apply direct pressure to the wounds. A few minutes later a nurse is summoned to the scene and she applies antiseptic before encircling the damaged arm with a gauze wrap. The guards ask her to inspect Weaver's chest where she discovers deep scratches, likely made with the razor's blade. Resisting the nurse's attempts, Weaver resumes screaming. "Take my heart!" he cries. "I need to remove my heart, to make the pain stop. Where are my babies? You took my babies!"

Weaver's injuries are deemed not to be severe enough that an ambulance will be needed. Instead he is transported to a nearby hospital in the back seat of a patrol car, continuing to sob and whine loudly during the entire trip. Two hours later he is returned to a cell in the medical block, patched up and quiet.[10] For now the jailers plan to keep a "suicide watch" over him, just in case he really is cracking up. However, jailhouse scuttlebutt promotes the theory that the accused murderer is involved in some kind of ploy.[11]

Within weeks Weaver's attorneys file a motion claiming Weaver's emotional condition has deteriorated so much that he has become unfit to stand trial. "We are unable to communicate further with our client about the case," Weaver's attorneys explain. "We cannot inform him of decisions or suggestions and get or gauge his response. Also, Weaver has fired us." This new announcement compels the judge to demand an independent mental evaluation of the accused man. When that has been completed, a competency hearing will be scheduled where both sides will have the chance to make their cases.

Next, the lawyers for Weaver submit a psychiatric report saying that Ward Weaver is unable to assist in his defense. "He refuses to talk to his attorney and me. He dismisses the idea he is in jail for murder. Weaver's condition could improve significantly after two months at the state hospital in Salem."[12]

The independent psychologist reports, "Malingering is a term used when people initially fake or exaggerate physical or psychological symptoms for some type of gain." He concludes that Weaver is fit to stand trial.

The prosecutors are adamant. The lead prosecutor declares, "Weaver's behavior is the product of the most lucid of minds." He and his colleague maintain that Weaver's murder trial should proceed on schedule. "By pretending a mental illness, the defendant could be rationally and dispassionately engaging in behavior that he perceives as his best and maybe even his only chance to save his own life."

The judge shakes his head and sternly addresses the prosecutors. "It seems to me that the state's position is simply ignoring all the other clinical evidence that is overwhelming in this case of this man's profound mental illness that has been diagnosed by at least three clinicians. Am I supposed to disregard all that?" He then agrees to rule on the issue as soon as possible.

In a surprise move, Weaver's attorneys launch a series of motions starting with a demand for a change of venue for the murder trial. At the same time they file a request to withdraw from the case if the judge rules that Weaver is fit to stand trial, because they can't communicate with him.

A few hours later the judge passes the word that he is ready to make his ruling.

Before an audience of about thirty people, including Lori Pond, Linda O'Neal, relatives of Ashley, plus reporters, assembled in the courtroom, their hearts pounding with anticipation, the hearing begins. One man whispers, "Look at that monster," as Weaver takes a seat next to his lawyers. From then on Linda watches Weaver who sits motionless for most of the hearing, staring at the floor, shoulders hunched.

Offering a final plea, prosecutor Landers tells the court that Weaver's actions are a short-term attempt to get what he wants, to derail the criminal proceedings.

The judge nods, then strikes his gavel, clears his throat and says, "Ward Weaver does suffer from a mental illness or defect. Therefore it is my ruling that he will be transferred to the Oregon State Hospital. I also hereby remove Weaver's June 1, 2004, trial date from the court's docket. I order him to be transported to the state mental hospital in Salem where he will undergo three months of observation and assessment as well as treatment. The hospital will report to the court in three months on Weaver's fitness to stand trial."

Many of the hushed courtroom occupants burst into tears. Linda O'Neal scoffs.

"Weaver's malingering is a transparent ruse only to be accepted by panty-waist anti-death penalty liberals."

Wiping away her own tears, Lori Pond is clearly disgusted. "Will we ever get justice for what he did to our daughters?" she cries. "It's just not fair. The asshole is just working the system one more time."

The judge's ruling provides for Weaver to be treated for up to three years. He concludes sadly, "If this is the course that the psychiatrists recommend in three months, it is likely that the current charges against Weaver will be dropped, to be refiled at such time that he might be found competent to aid in his own defense."[13]

CHAPTER TWENTY-FOUR

Falling Dominoes

On January 9, 2004, the second anniversary of Ashley Pond's disappearance, Lori Pond files a 9.75 million dollar "wrongful death" lawsuit in Federal District Court against the state for its negligence. Lori must wait for that suit to work its way through the system, praying for some form of justice.

In Oregon, the Attorney General has jurisdiction over cases against the state's interest. His spokesman deflates hopes when he reveals that the state had filed a motion for the claims against the state in the Pond case to be dismissed. Clackamas County is expected to file a similar motion.

Finally, on June 21, 2004, the judge writes in his decision that he accepts the argument that the state and the state's agencies are immune from wrongful death claims in federal court. He also dismisses three federal civil rights claims made against the state and the Department of Human Services saying that, "Although the state did not increase the level of Ashley Pond's safety, it also did not decrease it." The judge explains his court has no jurisdiction to determine whether the department took appropriate action to protect Ashley when it learned that Lori Pond had not reported Ashley's allegations of sex abuse to anyone for more than two weeks.

Philip feels outraged. "Damn," he mutters to Linda upon learning of the details. "More white-washing!"

Linda pats his hand. "Sweetheart, if they allowed every crime victim that was wronged by a serial felon of some kind to collect damages, there'd be no end to litigations."

"But there has to be some culpability somewhere out there for what happened to those little girls. It's just not right!"

Linda forces an ironic smile. "Yeah, it reminds me of that scene in *The Grapes of Wrath*: 'Who do I shoot?' the poor guy cries out when they come to run a bulldozer over his house."

The spokesperson for the Department of Human Services attempts to lay the issue to rest when she says, "The death of Ashley was a tragic event. We hope that today's decision can help all parties in the case move on, and hopefully bring closure to the Pond family."[1]

Emily Bowen's lawsuit becomes the next domino to fall. The attorney Emily had employed to file her similar federal suit against the state retreats. "The case law makes our case moot," he says. "It would have been futile to go forward."[2]

Meanwhile, Ward Weaver is at the Oregon State Hospital. His treatment by the staff is gentle compared to that received from typical jailhouse officers. In a hospital, you are considered sick, and the goal is to evaluate your ills and make you better. "This is a hospital, not a prison," says the superintendent.[3]

The life inside for four hundred sixty so-called "forensic patients" is a daily routine of treatment, meals and activities such as shooting pool, playing ping-pong and bingo, watching television and listening to music. Patients are rousted from their beds about 6:00 AM and are put to bed by 9:00 PM. Wearing their own clothes, those deemed non-violent remain unrestrained and have total freedom to move about the unit from bedroom to gymnasium and other shared spaces. Patients in Weaver's category are generally confined to the top two floors, Wards B and C. These ancient rooms were immortalized by the 1975 movie *One Flew Over the Cuckoo's Nest*, which was filmed in them.

The wards are divided into Buildings 47 and 48. In 48 B and C, about thirty patients on each floor share a long hallway with bedrooms and common areas where they dine, rest and are entertained with continual programs flashing from a large screen TV. On the other side, 47 B and C, are a gym, a law library, a chapel and recreation area. The most important section contains the nearby treatment rooms, where patients must meet frequently with medical staff to have individual progress encouraged. Twice each day patients are allowed to exercise in the outdoor yard, where they can toss around a basketball or jog along a walking path. Classes are attended for part of each day. Once a month they go outside for a fire drill. According to an article in *The Oregonian*, all four hundred sixty patients in this unit have been charged with or have been convicted of crimes. The majority of them are found guilty but insane. Sixty to eighty patients like Weaver await trial but have been deemed mentally incompetent to aid in their defense. These particular patients are referred to as "370s," based on Oregon Statute Number ORS161.370, which points out they should be treated not punished. Ward Weaver is said to enjoy the daily bingo games the most and is reputed to use as many as six cards at a time to enhance his chances at success.

On July 27 the judge receives a package from the hospital evaluators. Will the report support a basis for keeping Ward Weaver indefinitely for mental treatment, or send him back to the court system to answer the murder charges? The judge promises he'll study the documents carefully and then hold hearings where he'll make a ruling on the mental illness aspect. The first of those he schedules for August 25, where the primary issue will be whether or not Weaver is mentally fit to stand trial on charges of killing the Oregon City girls. If the judge determines him mentally fit, he will schedule a second hearing to determine which lawyers are to represent the defendant for the remainder of the prosecution and a trial date. Weaver's lawyers, by this time, had asked to withdraw from the case numerous times, but the judge's decision on that had been put on hold while the psychiatrists in Salem coaxed Weaver through their diagnostic hoops in search of his sanity, or lack thereof. Yet another hearing will take place specifically for ruling on the change of venue.

The summer heat and the agony of Ashley and Miranda's families continue unabated. For Linda, it is exacerbated by the worsening mental condition of her mother.

On a Saturday evening in mid-August, a frantic call is taken by a female dispatcher at the Washington County emergency call center near Hillsboro, Oregon. "911. What's your emergency?"

"Someone came into my house and pushed me aside and I ran over here to my neighbor's house and…please! I'm scared. You've got to help me."

"Okay ma'am. What's your address?"

The woman relays the information.

"All right, stay on the line for me ma'am, for just a minute while I get the police en route." The dispatcher turns her attention to her radio console. "All units in the area of 194 NE Haverstack, respond to a possible home invasion robbery."

The radio speaker crackles. "Eighty-six-sixty-five, I'm en route."

"Eighty-six sixty-five you're en route at 20:39 hours."

"Eighty-six sixty-four. I'm en route to cover eighty-six sixty-five."

"Eighty-six sixty four, copy. You're en route at 20:39."

"Eighty-six-sixty. I'm also en route. Do you have any suspect information?"

"Eighty-six-sixty stand by for suspect information."

"Can you tell me anything about the intruder? The fellow that pushed his way into your house? What he looked like?"

"Oh I don't know exactly."

"Was he a white male or a black male? Was he in his twenties or thirties? What do you think?"

"Well let me think a minute. He was a white man, I guess, maybe in his thirties.

"Please hold on a minute, ma'am. I'll be right back." The dispatcher again shifts to her console. "All units responding to 194 NE Haverstack, copy suspect information. We have a white male, possibly in his thirties who has pushed his way into a house, shoving the caller aside. The caller escaped to the neighbor's. The suspect is apparently still in the victim's house at this time. Repeat, suspect is described as a white male adult, possibly in his thirties. No further description."

Another call interrupts. "Eighty-six-sixty, am arriving 194 NE Haverstack. I'm going to need a dog here."

"Eighty-six-sixty, copy. Is there a canine unit to respond to 194 NE Haverstack?"

"Eighty-six-forty, I've got the dog and I'm a block away, en route code three to 194 NE Haverstack."

"Eighty-six-forty, I show you a block away at 20:42."

"Eighty-six-sixty-five. I'm 10-97 as well."

The dispatcher responds. "Eighty-six-sixty-five, I show you at the scene at 20:43."

"Okay Mrs. Billings. An officer just arrived to contact you so I'm going to let you go now."

"Okay. Good-bye."

Within five minutes of the 9-1-1 call for help, five police cars have rushed to 194 NE Haverstack. A group of officers, guns drawn, disperse around the property while several others cautiously push open the front door and aim their halogen flashlights toward the darkened hallway. They inch their way forward, shouting, "Police! Police! We have the house surrounded. Come out with your hands up!"

The cops burst through one bedroom, but find it empty. When they arrive at the next one they discover an elderly gentleman curled up under a heavy layer of blankets, sleeping, until the beams of the flashlights landing on his face trigger a quick awakening. When he realizes that several gun barrels are inches from his face, he shrieks. "What the hell! Help! Help!"

"Take it easy, Mister," one of the officers says, as he switches the room light on. "Who are you?"

"I'm John Billings. I live here. What's going on? Who are you?"

"Hillsboro Police. I'm Sergeant Williams. We just took a call that there was a home invasion robbery in progress at this address. Is there a woman living here with you?"

"My wife. Oh no. Where is she? Did she call you?"

"Is there some reason for your wife to have called the police?"

"Sergeant, my wife doesn't need logical reasons for anything she does. She's got old-timers disease."

The policemen holster their weapons. The sergeant says, "You mean Alzheimer's disease?"

Linda's father nods. "Half the time she doesn't even know I'm her husband any more, and we've been married for fifty years."

The sergeant speaks into his walkie-talkie, "Eighty-six-sixty. Have contacted the owner who says caller has mental defect."

While the police wind down the bogus call, Linda O'Neal receives a phone call. "Linda O'Neal Investigations."

"Hello Linda. This is John, John Vandehey."

"John? It's been awhile since we've touched base. How's the old gang out at the 9-1-1 center?"

"We're all fine. But a strange call just came in, and I thought I ought to let you know that there's something going on at your parents' house. I don't know the specifics, but it started out as a home invasion robbery call, and…"

Linda's eyes widen and she gasps. "Home invasion? At my folks' place?"

"We ended up with eight police units responding out there because it sounds like your mother left the house, ran down the street and made the 9-1-1 call from a neighbor's. She said someone pushed her and she got out of the house. Several officers went into the house with their weapons drawn, and they apparently woke up your dad. But at the moment, they didn't have any idea what was really going on. I mean, it could've been a burglar who put some pajamas on and slipped into the bed to disguise himself or something. Those kinds of things happen. Anyway, I think it's all straightened out for now. But you might want to give your parents a call just to reassure them or calm them down because that's really a very dangerous situation. A home invasion call like that could have resulted in shots fired. I'm sure it must have been quite a traumatic experience for them. I know it was for the cops."

"Thanks a lot for the tip, John. And I will get a hold of them right now. By the way, call me again when you just have some time to chat.

It's been too long."

"I will Linda. Take care, and good luck. Bye-bye."

Within seconds Linda has dialed her parents' number. Her father answers. "Hello?"

"Dad? What's going on?"

"Nothing. Why do you ask?"

"I just heard that the police were there, something about a home invasion. Can you level with me here?"

"Oh yeah, it was nothing, just a misunderstanding. It's all been straightened out. Everything's fine, now."

"Do you want me to come over?"

"Not tonight. You can come tomorrow morning, but you don't really need to. Everything's just fine." He laughs. "Just one of those things that happens, you see."

"Dad, is Mom slipping? Because, it seems to me that she's been pretty consistent for several months."

"No, no. Nothing like that. Like I said, it was just a silly misunderstanding. But we're fine now. Really."

"Okay Dad, whatever you say. I'll see you tomorrow."

Early the next morning, Linda arrives at her parents' house and knocks on the front door. Her mother opens it. "Hello. It's good to see you."

"How are you doing today, Mom?"

"Oh, I'm fine. I was just taking a nap. Please come in, won't you?"

Linda enters and shifts her attention to several strange holes and other indentations along the wall near the dining room. Before she has much chance to consider the implications she's diverted by a loud moan towards the dining room, where she notices a peculiar sight. Wearing a dazed expression, her dad is sprawled on the floor, cradling his head in his hands. Linda rushes to his side and is aghast when she notices a line of blood dripping from his left eyebrow, trailing down the ridge of his nose. After pulling a wad of tissue from her purse she kneels over and dabs at the blood while searching for some answers. "What happened to you, Dad?"

"I'm—I'm not really sure but I think that…I think that the last thing I remember was that I got hit in the head with something." He touches his forehead and winces. "Ouch! And then I guess I just woke up here on the floor."

"Where was Mom?"

"She was taking a nap, I think. It's a bit cloudy, to tell you the truth."

Florence approaches. When she notices her husband on the floor she says, "Oh my gosh, what's happened to you?"

Her father looks up at his wife and offers a sheepish grin. "I guess I must have slipped or something. But I'm all right." He pulls himself up and shakes his arms. "Oh yeah, I'm going to be fine."

Linda glances about the kitchen in search of clues and finds a big one in the form of a twelve-inch cast iron skillet, lying upside down under the kitchen table. She inspects it. Unmistakably, blood and hair are stuck to the bottom. She turns her attention to her mother. "Mom? Did you hit Dad with this frying pan?"

"Of course not. I didn't want to hit anybody. I just wanted to go. I just wanted to get out of here and I'm locked in, you know…"

Her father interrupts, "I'm fine. It'll be okay. I wasn't seriously hurt, so it doesn't really matter what happened."

Linda puts a sympathetic arm around her mother's shoulder. "Mom, you were locked in only to keep you safe. But if you're going after Dad with a big frying pan, you could hurt him."

Her mother shakes her head. "I don't know what you're talking about. I've got to go to the bathroom." She exits the dining room as her husband gets slowly to his feet.

"Look Linda," he says, "she don't mean nothing when she does things. She gets frustrated and throws things once in a while. She doesn't hit me very often and when she does, well, it's just a little love pat."

Linda shakes her head in disbelief. "Look at these holes in the wall here. Are these from the 'misses' you're talking about? Dad, has it been raining frying pans in the house? Any one of these 'misses' could have killed you. This is really hard…I love Mom and want her to get better more than anything. But Dad, I can't lose you. I can't allow you to sacrifice your life. If anything happens to you then what good will come from having kept Mom at home through this?"

"She wouldn't do anything to somebody on purpose. She is still in there someplace, Linda. We just have to find a way to get her out."

"Dad, think this through. We've now got serious safety issues between your safety and her safety. She really cannot stay here in this house any longer like this. We really need to call her doctor right now and get a hospital evaluation set up. Okay?"

Her father frowns. "Well, maybe you might be right there. In the hospital they could give her some new medicines to smooth things out better. That should only take a few days."

Linda picks up a nearby telephone, asking her father, "What's the number for the doctor?"

"It's right over there on the calendar."

Linda makes the call and soon it's all arranged. A bed is secured and a full work-up is scheduled. The only hitch, the doctor is adamant that an ambulance should be deployed to ferry her mom to the facility. "Your mother is too emotionally distraught at this point. Do not try to transport her by car. Use an ambulance."

When Linda brings up the subject, her father absolutely rejects the idea of an ambulance. "Too scary for her," he concludes.

Linda ponders a bit then snaps her fingers. "Okay, how about this, then? Tell you what we can do, Dad. Let's order a limousine, and deliver our mom to that hospital in a style commensurate with her status in this family."

Her father smiles. "Perfect. I'll go help her get ready."

An hour later Linda follows the black limo weaving its way through Hillsboro streets on the way over to Forest Grove. She can't help smiling as she notices her mother's head poking through the open sunroof. The wind pushes her gray locks from side to side while her nervous husband sits nearby. "Damn!" Linda says to herself. "I wish Philip were here to get this on his camcorder. Nobody'd believe it."

CHAPTER TWENTY-FIVE

Remembering Miranda

August 24, 2004 is the two-year anniversary of finding Miranda Gaddis's body. A memorial is held at Gardiner Middle School field in Oregon City.[1] Primarily just family members of Ashley and Miranda participate in the vigil while TV camera crews hover nearby.

The observers sit on bleachers with Linda O'Neal positioning herself among Maria, Lori and Ashley's grandmother. Philip, who wants to record the day for the families, is roaming, aiming his camcorder towards the big posters of Ashley and Miranda, as he snakes his way toward the front. A brisk wind begins shaking the spot-lit portable gazebo that serves as a makeshift stage.

Lori's stepfather approaches and picks up an electric bullhorn then begins his introduction. "Okay, let's get everybody over here. Let's get going. This is about two girls' lives that came to an end. And we're here to find a way to handle it." The crowd claps. As rain begins blowing onto his face, he says, "The emcee for tonight is Miranda's older sister, so she's going to take it from here."

The man hands the bullhorn over to the slender blonde teenager who brushes aside the rain from her eyes. "Hello. We've come here to remember the girls, not to talk about their deaths, but to talk about their lives. Also, about who they were, and where they live in our hearts, right now. Today marks the two-year anniversary of the day they found Miranda and Ashley's bodies. I know that it's been an emotional rollercoaster for all of us. Remembering this will always bring emotions you don't necessarily want to show. So we cannot hide from it and it is never going away. And it has not yet come to an end. We have a long road ahead of us and there are two ways to handle this. Let the situation get hold of us, and go down or grab hold of the situation and take advantage of it. You can't change the past, no matter what you do. But you can take advantage of the present and plan for your future. You can't prevent the events that happen to you or even prepare yourself mentally for them. But with that said, Lori, Ashley's mom is going to talk first."

Despite the now pelting rain, the emotionally stirred audience claps loudly, watching Lori Pond walk from the bleachers to the stage. Philip is only a few feet to her right, holding a strip of plastic over his camcorder while he zooms in on her rain-stained face. She bows her head for a bit then smiles. "I have something I would like to share, something that helped me on days when I was pretty down. 'What if? Life originates with God. Even our personal lives are not our own. Life has nothing to do with fairness, and its values or justification can not be measured by longevity. It is not sad to die young. What is sad is to die and never have lived; to have been alive and never to have seen anything or known God.' We don't feel that kind of sadness for Ashley or Miranda. Ashley and Miranda lived full lives, because they saw the created world through eyes of faith and because they knew the God who made it. Ashley and Miranda were gifts. And the only proper response to a gift is gratitude. Thank you God, for Ashley and Miranda."

By now the wind is blowing fiercely and topples the easel that holds the poster of Ashley. While some male relatives rush to rescue it, Michelle Duffey comes forward and takes the bullhorn.

"I thought about what I was going to say to all of you. My thoughts shifted to what this evening is truly about. It's about remembering two young lives that ended in excessive violence. With that said, although Miranda's life was short, her life experiences, her beliefs, her future goals were already determined. It's still like it's not real to me. It's almost like I'm talking about someone else's child. That's how I have talked so well about it without crying. My daughter,

Miranda who was thirteen, was brutally murdered on March 8th, 2002. Her murder has impacted every aspect of our lives. Violence took a young girl who was a loving daughter, sister, niece, grandchild and friend."

During the long, stormy drive home, Linda and Philip are silent for awhile, absorbing the impact of the memorial gathering. Finally an anguished Linda comments, "It was obvious tonight how much grief still engulfs these families. The mothers' lawsuits haven't gone anywhere. And to top it off, that damned Ward Weaver. I can just see him. He's sitting in the plush surroundings of the state hospital taking long country walks and playing bingo with new buddies, while the families of the victims are still in pain. Damn it Philip, this is not the way it should be. Justice has to be done, so closure can finally begin for those families."

CHAPTER TWENTY-SIX

Psycho?

The next day, August 25, the judge presides over a five minute hearing on the issue of Weaver's mental competence. Lori Pond and Michelle Duffey, who are accompanied by their respective entourages of friends and family, sit stoically in the second row, staring straight ahead and deliberately not making eye contact with Weaver. Linda O'Neal, who attends the proceedings with Philip, can't take her eyes off the murderer and glowers at him.

Suspense surrounds which direction the judge's decision will take the case. If he finds Weaver incompetent, there will be no trial in the foreseeable future. If he determines Weaver's symptoms have been faked, that he was actually mentally fit all along, everything goes back into full prosecutorial motion. The judge wastes no time in stating the court's position. He states the mental evaluation from the State Hospital affirms that Weaver's mental capacity is normal; he is not insane and he is in fact fully lucid. The report's conclusion is emphatic. "Mr. Weaver is able to assist and cooperate with counsel and participate reasonably in his own defense, if he chooses to do so. The reason for his lack of cooperation and participation during his state hospital stay and with his legal counsel is not based on mental disease or defect, although he continues to exaggerate symptoms and feign cognitive and memory deficits."[1]

In response, Weaver's lead attorney, Michael Barker, addresses the judge. "We would agree that Mr. Weaver has regained the ability to aid and assist." Then he reminds the judge that he and his partner have a motion under consideration to be replaced by new lawyers.

The judge sets September 8 to announce a trial date and explains he will respond at that time to their request to be taken off the case. Lori Pond smiles and nods as a scowling Linda shakes her head. Finally, the judge designates September 15 as the day in which he plans to rule on the motion for change of venue in the case.[2]

On the sidewalk in front of the courthouse, several reporters intercept Lori Pond during her exit, pleading for a reactive comment. Reminding them she is still under the cloud of Herndon's gag-order, she nevertheless admits, "I'm glad things are going forward."

During the next two weeks the public and media buzz with speculation regarding the Ward Weaver case. His potential fate becomes a hot topic. Some express frustration with his manipulations. Is it possible, they wonder, that the scoundrel will actually be assigned yet a third defense team? And if so, how much more will the taxpayers have to shell out? If not, when in hell will he finally be put on trial? One TV station launches an "unscientific" public opinion poll that produces a 95 percent affirmative response to the question, "Do you think Ward Weaver is guilty of killing Ashley and Miranda?"[3]

The day before the next court hearing, September 7, Weaver's attorneys surprise everyone involved when with no explanation they decide to stay on the convoluted case after all.[4] This action prompts the judge to cancel the September 8 hearing and declare his intention to set a new Weaver murder trial date during the September 15 change of venue proceeding.

During that hearing, eight days later, the Weaver attorneys come out swinging. They bang the drum about media driven bias. Citing the newspaper and TV stories that were in constant citywide orbit, they argue that the intense media coverage will interfere with their client's impartial trial and impartial jury rights. "The media has broadcast the state's case in exquisite detail," says Peter Fahy.

The prosecutor becomes indignant and asks to be heard. When the judge nods she begins by blasting the whole issue of media publicity surrounding Weaver and places the blame squarely on his past antics. Weaver himself had announced he was the prime suspect months before he was actually arrested. "He helped turn this into a media circus," she says. "He put himself in the public eye. He has repeatedly sought the limelight and the publicity." The prosecutor refers to the September 11, 2001 terrorist attack on the World Trade Center when trying to compare how mass grief can diffuse fairness in judgment. She says Clackamas County constituents are experiencing collective grief over the tragedy.

The judge characterizes Weaver's publicity-hound exploits as having contributed to the media frenzy. "Isn't he going to be responsible for that?" he asks. "It's not the state's fault." Next the judge shifts his attention to the purpose of the assembly when he announces that the change of venue motion is denied.

"Now, as to the trial date, January of 2005," the judge declares. "And jury orientation for the trial could begin January 24, with jury selection starting two weeks later."[5] [6]

At 4:30 PM on Friday, September 17, 2004 Linda O'Neal sits at her desk working on private investigation cases and trying to stop agonizing over Ward Weaver's justice arc which keeps intruding on her thoughts. Her phone rings and she picks up. "Linda O'Neal Investigations, can I help you?"

On the other end of the line, an excited Maria exclaims, "Linda! There's something going on with Ward Weaver."

"What are you talking about, Maria?"

"Well, I don't know for sure what it is, but Lori called me up and wanted me to watch her baby son and daughter, right away."

"What do you think is happening?"

"The prosecutors want to have a meeting with Lori, her attorney and our mom in a couple of hours, so I'm scrambling to get ready for them. She wouldn't tell me anything, and I begged her. But that right there shows me something big is going on, Linda. I don't know what it is yet though. What's your take?"

Linda ponders then says, "Maybe something about the change of venue or…Damn! The judge is set to consider exclusionary stuff. We have to pray some serious chunk of evidence won't be excluded from the trial. Oh my God! So when are you getting the kids?"

"Any minute. They're going to drop them off on the way to the meeting."

"Listen Maria, I want you to call me as soon as they pick the kids up. I want you to call me then so we can figure out what the hell is going on, okay?"

"Okay Linda. I'll call, I promise. Bye."

Linda begins pacing the floor as the hours pass. She can't stop thinking about the new development. Several scenarios race through her mind and questions cascade through her brain. *"Is Weaver pulling a new trick? Have they found new evidence? Is the prosecution's case suddenly fracturing?"* Once again the loudly ringing phone grabs her attention. She races over to pick up the receiver. It's Maria. "Well, what'd she tell you? What's coming down with Weaver?"

"Linda, she wouldn't tell me anything. Nothing at all. They've got her lips zipped. She's my sister, for God's sake! But she won't talk to me."

Linda prods. "How about her demeanor then? Was she upbeat, sullen, neutral?"

"I can tell you this Linda, Lori is excited and for the first time in a hell of a long time, she's not pissed off. She was even smiling. I couldn't believe it."

During the long weekend that follows Linda and Philip spend much time speculating about the ramifications of Maria's revelations. What is going on? It's not like Lori not to call her. Lori and her mother remained tight-lipped and refused to divulge anything to anyone. Sleep is short and far between for Linda and Philip, whose nerves are strained. Then, Monday afternoon, September 20, Maria calls.

An agitated Linda blurts out, "Well, what have you found out? What is it?"

Maria is gleeful. "It's a done deal, Weaver's going to plead guilty."

"So it's finally over? No, they will have to have a hearing. Maybe even two or three hearings." Linda realizes that she is nearly in a trance, as if there were someone else saying these words. It is over? How can this big festering hole in all their lives be over?

"When is the sentencing?"

"This coming Wednesday at 9:00 in the morning, but you guys better come early, because the press will be there and there are only one hundred seats in the courtroom. And tell Dad, no cameras are allowed."

Linda and Philip are among the first on the scene at Clackamas County Courthouse that Wednesday morning.[7] Standing close together off to the side to give each other comfort, they watch the TV news crews circling around, pointing video cameras in all directions. They nod as the dance team girls share hugs before entering the courthouse. Later Lori Pond and her sisters arrive and cross the sidewalk to enter the courthouse. As the crowd in front of the courthouse swells, Linda is startled to hear rumblings of collective discontent about what is about to transpire in the courtroom. A plea agreement will only take place if the defendant agrees to admit his wicked deeds. But the only bargaining chip available to induce Weaver would be waiving the death penalty. They'll let him live if he admits he did it. The bystanders seem to Linda to vehemently disagree with not going for the death penalty. Linda's own opinion is conflicted. On the one hand, the death penalty sends a message, but she feels it's mostly symbolic. After all, Weaver's dad was condemned twenty years ago, and he's still appealing. But from the perspective of the prosecution, the family and the people whose lives are affected most directly, it's certainly the expedient thing to do. "And remember," she tells Philip, "The prosecutor almost always consults with the victim's family in a decision like this. In the meeting Maria told us about, they ironed out all of this. I think we should go in. We've all been waiting so long for this." Linda sighs and rushes ahead.

By 8:45 every available seat in the courtroom is occupied. A TV camera begins to record, the operator panning through the faces. Philip and Linda manage to maneuver themselves into the second row directly behind Mallori Weaver, her attorney and foster mother. Linda grips Philip's hand. Several uniformed police stand rigidly at the back of the room. Linda wonders how Weaver will behave when they bring him in. Everyone waits. Quiet whispers fill the air. At the prosecution table are the three Deputy District Attorneys. At the other table, defense lawyers nervously arrange some papers and check their watches. Linda notices Maria passing out tissues to her sisters who sit beside her and her mother. Then a rear door flips open to allow Ward Weaver, wearing black and white stripes, manacled to a stun belt, to shuffle in, flanked on both sides by uniformed, armed guards.

When the judge strides in and says, "Be seated. Thank you," the session begins.

Linda says quietly to Philip, "Ashley and Miranda, this is for you."

The prosecuting attorney announces, "In case 2-1992,[8] a change of plea in this case to a plea of guilty. The state is prepared to proceed with the pleas at this time."

The judge looks across to the defense table. "Mr. Barker, Mr. Fahy, are you ready to proceed?"

"We are ready, your honor."

"All right." The judge glances coldly at Weaver who stands, shoulders hunched, staring at the floor. "Mr. Weaver, I've been provided, prior to coming onto the bench that you're ready to enter a plea of guilty in this case and pleas of 'no contest' to various parts of the indictment that's been filed here. And on page two of the plea petition, it appears to be your signature. Is this your signature?"

Weaver's voice is so soft it can scarcely be heard. "Yes it is."

"Okay. And you understand, of course that a guilty plea is a permanent act. That when you enter a guilty plea that's not something that you're going to be able to change your mind about at a later time."

"I understand."

"Okay. And other than the fact that what the state's going to recommend includes the fact that they're not going to seek the death penalty, has anyone made any threats or promises to you to induce you to enter these pleas?"

"No sir."

"Okay. Other than the fact that they're not going to seek the death penalty for the aggravated murder charges, you're otherwise taking this action freely and voluntarily?"

"Yes, I am."

"Now you're also proposing…we'll be talking about these individually as we go through them. You're proposing to enter pleas of no contest to certain other parts of the indictment in this case. And, am I correct that it's been explained to you that a no contest plea means that you're not going to contest the fact that the state has sufficient evidence to prove the material elements of each of those crimes beyond a reasonable doubt?"

"Yes sir."

"And I'm going to ask the state after you enter a no contest plea as to those counts in which you're entering a no contest plea, to recite for me the facts that they're relying upon, and if I agree that those facts are sufficient to support a finding of guilty, I'm going to be making a finding of guilty. Is that clear to you?"

"Okay."

The judge pauses briefly and consults a document before resuming. "Again, the final question on many of these things…it's my understanding that you're stipulating and agreeing that as to the two principal counts of aggravated murder, that it will be appropriate for the court to sentence you to two life terms without the possibility of parole and that those sentences will be served consecutively. Is that correct?"

"Yes," Weaver mumbles.

"Okay. And again, that this entire plea agreement is the product of your own free will. Is that right?"

"Yes it is."

"As to count one, the charge of aggravated murder alleged to have occurred on or about the ninth of January 2002, in Clackamas County, Oregon, what is your plea to that charge? Guilty or not guilty?"

"Guilty."

"And by pleading guilty, you're telling me that you personally unlawfully and intentionally caused the death of Ashley Marie Pond, a human being under the age of fourteen years."

"Yes, sir."

"Is there a factual basis for Mr. Weaver's plea to that charge?" the judge says woodenly.

"Yes there is, your honor."

"I'll accept your guilty plea to count one, and then as to count eight, again, what is your plea to the charge of aggravated murder alleged to have occurred on or about the eighth day of March, 2002, in Clackamas County. Guilty or not guilty?"

"Guilty."

"And by pleading guilty to that charge, you're telling me that you personally unlawfully and intentionally caused the death of Miranda Gaddis, a human being under the age of fourteen."

"Yes sir."

"Is there a factual basis for his plea to that count?"

The lawyer responds mechanically. "Yes sir."

The judge takes up another count and once again the courtroom hears the response, "Guilty."

"At this point, Mr. Weaver, as to the plea agreement, you agreed to enter pleas of no contest to the ten remaining counts. And you understand again, that by pleading no contest you're not going to contest that those facts are sufficient to prove the material elements of these crimes beyond a reasonable doubt. Understand that?"

"Yes sir."

"Okay. Then as to count two, what is your plea to an alternative view of the crime, the charge of aggravated murder alleged to have occurred on the ninth of January, 2002 in Clackamas County, State of Oregon."

"No contest."

The Deputy District Attorney nods for the judge's attention then speaks. "With respect to count two, the following factual basis says Ashley Marie Pond did disappear on January 9, 2002. That when she left her home she was fully clothed and her clothing was intact and she was not intoxicated. She had previously accused the defendant of sexually abusing her. When she was found she was discovered to have been intoxicated at the time of her death. And other individuals witnessed the defendant behave in a highly sexualized and inappropriate manner with Ashley Pond prior to her death. And the defendant is accused of attempting to murder Emily Bowen in the course of sexually abusing her."

Judge Herndon turns his attention back to Weaver. "Mr. Weaver, you unlawfully and intentionally, in an effort to conceal the commission and the identity of the perpetrator of attempted sexual abuse in the first degree, committed on or about that same day, that you then caused the death of Ashley Marie Pond. Those are the facts that you are pleading no contest to?"

"Yes sir."

The prosecutor continues her summary of charges. "Between April 5, 2001 and December 1, 2001, Ashley Pond, twelve years of age, was having regular visits to his home during that time frame. Again, a number of individuals observed this especially inappropriate behavior against Ashley Pond. A witness by the name of Donna Clark observed a man who she believes to be the defendant, kissing Ashley Pond in a very sexualized manner. And Ashley has been intentionally murdered by the defendant."

The judge resumes addressing Weaver. "Again, by pleading no contest you're telling me that you're not going to contest the evidence the state has to establish guilt beyond a reasonable doubt to unlawfully and intentionally attempt to engage in sexual intercourse of Ashley Marie Pond, a child under the age of fourteen years."

"Yes sir."

"As to count nine, alleging an alternative theory for the death of Ms. Gaddis, what is your plea to the crime of aggravated murder, alleged to have occurred on or about the eighth of March, 2002, in Clackamas County?"

"No contest."

And so it goes for another agonizing twenty minutes, each count getting its facts stated, with a rote response by the defendant, and a quick summation of why the facts are prosecutable by the district attorneys. The rhythms remind Philip of a bizarre Gregorian chant, the interplay between judge, prosecutor, Weaver and so on continuing to spew out with duplicate cadences. Over and over, the ritual continues through abuse of corpse charges, other sexual abuse counts and additional theories of the crimes. Linda wishes she could remind them all that this monster has viciously cut off the lives of two girls who will never grow to adulthood or have families of their own. She knows that for many hearing these charges, only the calm utterances of horrific facts keep them from letting their emotions take over.

When the judge has finished accepting the pleas, he reminds Weaver that it is now time for the victims' families who have had to bear this hearing in silence to have their turn. He invites any who wish to sit on the witness stand, look at Ward Weaver and speak their minds. Lori Pond is first. Wiping fresh tears, she regains her composure and lashes out, "Our nightmare began January 9, 2002. My family and I deserve closure. This brings closure. A death sentence followed by multiple appeals for years would not bring closure. I met Mary McCarty. Ward Weaver's father killed her daughter Barbara in 1981. Ward Weaver's father has been on death row in California for about eighteen years. Mary McCarty is still without closure. I don't want this for my children or my family or for me. We deserve closure. I want you, Ward Weaver, to admit that you murdered my daughter. Now everyone knows you murdered Ashley to cover up your sexual abuse of her. And I—I..."

Lori's deeply felt emotions overcome her delivery forcing her to take a long pause. Weeping, she attempts to conclude her remarks. "I guess I should have wrote this down and I thought I could do this. I just know that I'm going to live and I'm going to continue on and I may have to do it without my daughter, but I do have other children that I'm going to need to be strong for. And I thank you for this opportunity. I really don't have much more to say except to say thank you for justice."

The judge smiles sympathetically and motions for her to leave the stand. "Okay. Thank you."

The next victim's statement comes from Ashley's nine-year-old younger sister. "Why my sister? We all miss her. Just why? You had a choice to do what you did. She loved you. Why Ashley and Miranda? Nobody knows you took a big part of our life. Do you see what you did to my mom? You did not have to be a bad person but you chose to be one. Why? We do not get it. We have sleepless nights. It is just wrong. I wish sometimes it was a bad dream."

After her, Ashley's other surviving sister speaks poignantly, "Some days I wake up and believe that I will see her face again. But truly, I can't even remember her face at all. I see her death run through my mind like a bad movie over and over again. Mr. Weaver, I hope that you are satisfied that you created this horrible memory for me to live with for the rest of my life."

By now many in the audience, even the men, are sniffling and dabbing tissues to tears. All eyes fall on Weaver, who remains frozen.

After a few moments of hesitation Michelle Duffey sits down in the witness chair. Her comments are laced with the humble outrage she obviously feels so acutely. "As I sit here this morning, looking at your face, I am full of emotions, pain, sorrow, grief, sadness, anger, confusion, shock, a lack of understanding, these are just some of the many feelings I have toward you Ward, and your disgusting behavior. I need some answers. And I'm hoping today you can provide me with some."

The courtroom is totally silent, every spectator straining to hear the wounded young mother.

"First and foremost is the question, why? Why did you kill my daughter Miranda? Why did you kill Ashley? What did they do Ward, that was so bad you felt the need to take these young, innocent lives? I would never have thought in a million years, Ward, you could do something so evil, demented and unthinkable. March 8, 2002, started out like any ordinary morning. I was getting ready for work. My four children were eating breakfast and preparing for school. As I left out the door that morning, I remember kissing my kids, telling them to have a good day, and we exchanged 'I love you's.' Little did I know that it would be the last words I exchanged with Miranda. I had terrible visions and nightmares of the danger she was probably in. I can hear her voice yelling for me. 'Mom, mom! Please help me!' I can hear her crying when I close my eyes. I ask you today Ward, did she suffer? What were her last words? When Miranda's lifeless and decomposed body was found in a cardboard box in your shed, my heart broke. Again, I ask 'why?' Why did you kill her? Why did you kill Ashley and then dispose of her body as if it was a piece of trash?"

Linda weeps softly as she tightly grips her husband's hand. Duffey's statement continues. "Miranda was not trash. Being a survivor of sexual abuse herself, she vowed to always help those who could not help themselves. Or those individuals that seemed lonely. I believe that is why she befriended Mallori. Mallori was lonely, always being picked on by other kids. But Miranda defended her. She talked to her often. They shared secrets. They were friends."

Jayne Patan, Weaver's second wife who had been seated behind Linda in the third row suddenly stands and rushes from the courtroom, not stopping until she is outside in front of the courthouse. A TV news crew descends upon her asking for her reaction. "It was too hard," she complains. "I couldn't sit in there."

"What was the hardest part for you?"

"Hearing Michelle Duffey wanting to know the last words that Miranda said, and if she asked for her mom, and if it was a painful death, all that broke my heart." Jayne begins weeping and as she turns to rush away, she mutters, "I just want to get home to my own child and hold her tight and never let go of her."

Meanwhile, back in the courtroom Michelle's words continue stinging all that hear except Ward Weaver whose face is impassive. "Why? Why Ward, would you bring your own daughter so much grief and pain and sorrow as well? Not to mention the shame she now has for you. And you hope to continue a relationship with Mallori? What makes you think you deserve that? First off, I could never understand nor believe that Mallori would ever want anything to do with you. She is much better than that. She's a good child."

Next, Miranda's sister pleads, yet Weaver seemingly ignores all. "Do you know what it is like to see a mother grieve and mourn the death of her child?" She cries a few minutes, unable to stop, then resumes. "I have. It's very painful. An experience that no child should ever have to witness. What if that was your child? I guess that probably isn't fair to ask, because I'm sure in time you would have killed her too."

Miranda's older sister confronts Ward Weaver. She berates him and says with a broken heart, "I don't understand why Mr. Weaver had to make it drag out so long. He knew he was going to face up to his consequences, but he is a selfish man. He thinks of no one but himself. Look at what he has put his own family through. I don't think him putting himself in the media seemed to help much. Rather, it caused him to appear even more guilty, and caused people across the nation to despise him. This whole time, it's always been about him. But I want him to know, it's not. It's all about justice for my sister, Miranda Diane Gaddis, and her friend, Ashley Marie Pond. How can a man who has done such a horrific crime even look at himself in the mirror and not be disgusted?"

After the victims' statements conclude, the judge and the attorneys consult. Linda tightens her grip on Philip's arm and points toward Weaver. "Did you see that?" she whispers. "While the families were confronting him, he was holding a picture of Mallori. Look! He's still clutching it, in his left hand. I was watching him during the statements, and I only saw Ward Weaver's tears one time for his own daughter. And yet look around, there are tears, throughout the courtroom. Those statements from the children touched everyone. I saw some of the cops who worked on the case for two plus years weeping. And yet, no matter what any of us say, those girls are lost for all time. For what?"

By now Linda's tears are flowing again. "I can't sit here any more." Linda rises to her feet but is quickly pulled back by Philip.

"Don't go," Philip whispers. "The judge is going to say something. I know you'll want to hear it."

"All right Mr. Weaver," the judge says sternly. "I'm about to pass sentence. But before I do, I want to give you an opportunity to respond to your victims. What do you want to say?"

Weaver shakes his head and glances down. "Nothing, sir."

Linda is outraged and mutters. "The asshole is going to refuse to confess the whole truth. He could have given these mothers the answers they so desperately want, but by refusing, he still thinks it's a game he can control."

Overhearing her comment the people nearby stir and mutter in agreement.

The judge stares at the defendant for several seconds in silence. Finally he speaks. "When I listen and look at the magnitude of what you've done here, you know, I really just see nothing but evil, Mr. Weaver. I think that everyone probably shares in the hope that there is a special place in hell for people like you."

The courtroom becomes pin-drop-quiet as if the spectators are holding their breaths, knowing that in the judge's final pronouncement the entire tragedy will draw to its painful end.

Weaver continues to stare at the floor. Judge Herndon shakes his head with disgust. "The sentence of the court will be as to count one, as to the aggravated murder of Ashley Pond. You'll be sentenced to life in the Oregon Department of Corrections without the possibility of parole. As to count eight, the aggravated murder of Miranda Gaddis, I sentence you to life in the Oregon Department of Corrections without the possibility of parole.[9] These sentences are to be served consecutively." The judge bangs his gavel. "This court is now adjourned."

Within minutes, the judge leaves. Ward Weaver is taken back to prison. For awhile, no one in the courtroom moves. And then, slowly, all those who have loved and all those who have empathized with Miranda and Ashley file out of the courtroom in silence.

EPILOGUE

In a large crowded auditorium, Linda O'Neal stands behind an oak lectern. She pauses between sentences, takes a brief sip of water and resumes her talk. "I am so gratified that at long last the families of Ashley Pond and Miranda Gaddis were granted a semblance of closure when Ward Weaver received two consecutive life sentences. Weaver will never have the opportunity to abuse another child again. But what do we do about the other Ward Weavers still slithering around, seeking their small victims? Though Weaver's confession, his plea, brings one segment of the tragic story of the Oregon City Girls to an end, for the families involved, Weaver's conviction is just a whistle-stop, because life continues. And it doesn't just continue for the principals involved, it also continues for each of us, every day across our world.

"Although this particular tragedy took place in Oregon City, during the same time frame that surrounds the Ashley and Miranda debacle, there were nine hundred, six thousand cases of confirmed child abuse in the United States. And a whopping 10 percent of those cases were specifically sexual child abuse, the type of abuse for which Ward Weaver became infamous. Now what that means is two thousand four hundred eighty-two cases of child abuse are committed per day. That's a hundred cases per hour. Now listen carefully, because what I have to say next is staggering. The actual number of incidents of abuse is estimated to be three times the number of reported incidents. We're talking about nearly three million incidents. Put another way, one every ten seconds!

"Now what does this mean to you and me personally? We know that one in four girls falls victim to sexual abuse by her eighteenth birthday. When you include boys, the statistic is equally alarming. One in six is sexually abused by his eighteenth birthday. Please, glance around. Look at each other. Those statistics apply universally. Don't raise your hands or anything, but I'm positive that one fourth of you ladies right now are remembering an incident that happened to you. And in most cases, the perpetrator got away with it, didn't he?"

Murmurs buzz in the audience. Many stare solemnly toward Linda, who continues. "So now, what does this really mean? This means that if you live on a residential block somewhere, one child near you is either being abused at this time or has been sexually abused. That's on your block. If you live in an apartment building, the odds are that some child living on the same floor of your apartment building is being sexually abused at this moment. Nine out of ten people, when surveyed on the subject, report that they regard child abuse as a serious problem. Yet only one in three actually reported the child abuse when they were confronted with a situation. Where does that leave us? You? Me? Our neighbors?

"Well, if nothing else, we need to find meaningful ways to improve on that ratio of one to three who actually report the abuse. Now that's do-able. That's something each of us can accomplish in our individual environments. We don't need government grants. We don't need outside intervention to do the one thing that each of us has the power to do. And that is, when we suspect abuse is occurring, report it."

A blond woman with rimless glasses in the front row raises her hand. Linda motions toward her. "You have a question?"

"According to what you told us earlier, three separate reports had been made to child welfare about Weaver's abuse of Ashley, and in spite of that, she ended up buried in a barrel under a concrete slab, undetected for five months. So practically speaking, what real good does reporting abuse do if they won't take it seriously at the other end?"

"Ashley's case has led to reforms in the way Oregon now handles abuse reports. Within weeks of the bodies being discovered, the governor appointed a special commission to examine the official blunders that your comments address. Several changes have been adopted that have improved how abuse reports are processed."

Linda pulls a stapled set of pages from her nearby briefcase, puts on her reading glasses and reads from the document. "'DHS will immediately refer to both the local law enforcement agency and to the appropriate DHS office, of all child abuse referrals taken. This change will be effective immediately. These referrals will be done during the same business day that they are received.'

"'All child abuse referrals taken on weekends and after hours will be reported immediately to the appropriate local law enforcement agency and the appropriate DHS office. DHS will continue to screen and assess these cases after referral to law enforcement agencies.'

"At the time Ward Weaver's abuse of Ashley was reported, and I'm now referring to the reports of Donna Clark, Claire Stevens and a Clackamas County Assistant District Attorney, there were no written protocols for the bureaucrats to follow on third party child sex abuse reports. Third party child abuse is when someone outside the home is the abuser.

"An erroneous assumption on the part of DHS existed creating huge cracks in the system, one of which unfortunately helped doom little Ashley Pond. DHS assumed that abusers from outside the home were less of a threat to a child because the child has a parent between the child and the abuser. But remember this, child molesters spend as much time deceiving the adults around children as they do deceiving the children themselves.[1] 'DHS policy and field operations have developed model language and set out time frames for branch implementation of third party child abuse policy.'" Linda returns the pages to her briefcase and studies her audience.

"How do we know when abuse is occurring?" Linda pauses dramatically. "Let me rephrase the question. When should we begin to suspect that abuse is occurring? The most frustrating thing about sexual abuse perpetrated on innocent children? It rarely takes on some identifiable manifestation. That's why it's such a horrendous problem. In physical abuse it's a no-brainer. Bruises, a black eye, sometimes even broken bones. Broken spirits aren't as easily detected and children vary widely in their reactions to being molested, so let me briefly toss out a few basic things to be looking for and I hope, maybe we can save more children in danger."

Linda bends her podium microphone slightly and takes a step back, gesturing widely. "The most obvious? Look for changes, any inconsistent change in behavior. Those changes might signal some significant disruption, but the behavior change by itself won't reveal specifically what's up."

A ponytailed man in the aisle seat of row four raises a hand. Linda nods. "Yes?"

"What kind of changes do we look for?"

"Well, for instance, young children might have increased difficulty in cooperating with previously accepted routines. Kids no longer using diapers might inexplicably regress and have problems using the toilet. A favored toy may suddenly be adamantly rejected at bedtime.

"If you find yourself concerned even without finding specific evidence of sexual abuse, then to be on the safe side, why not consult your family physician, pediatrician or other professional. If it turns out there was no sexual abuse, all the better. I know it's a bit of a hassle, some would even characterize it as 'over-reacting,' but I assure you that if abuse is occurring, a lifetime of apologizing later will not make up for failing to rescue that child while that abuse is going on."

A shouted comment from the back of the room is heard. "My little boy was molested by his cousin when he was only seven," she says. "And we knew that something sexual had happened, because he started talking about things we had always never talked about in front of him, sexual stuff."

Linda thrusts her right hand forward and offers a "thumbs-up" hand signal. "Good for you to notice and the more quickly we notice, the more quickly we can intervene to save our little ones from predators. What this young woman brought up is a common red flag, particularly with smaller children: inappropriate interest in, or knowledge of sexual acts. You must be attuned to your child's development. It's typical to be embarrassed when sex stuff pops into life too early. Don't get defensive. If your child is behaving in a sexually inappropriate manner, you should drop everything and talk with the child. It may be that he or she is telling you that it is time for some birds and bees talk. But on the other hand, she might be telling you that someone has violated her, maybe not physically yet, but they are working on it."

A bronze-skinned woman in row two shakes her head despondently. "It's not realistic," she declares. "Most of us work full-time and there are so many things you want us to pay attention to. I don't know about the rest of you, but I'm not even with my kids most of the day."

Linda taps the top of the podium. "When you become a parent, you sign on to be the protector. Sure it seems impossible sometimes. But, you have no choice if you want to keep your kids safe.

"There are several other classic signs that can alert you to a possible sexual abuse situation. Nightmares and bed-wetting, or drastic changes in appetite are all possible symptoms. What about sleep? Look for disturbances, even small ones. Sometimes a previously boisterous, confident kid becomes clingy.

"If you have a school-aged child, keep your eyes on his or her every grade, not just report cards, but daily work. If grades start slipping, well, it's just another of the possible warning signs. To be safe, investigate. Pay attention to how they handle normal activities. If interest seriously wanes for seemingly no reason, again, check it out. Take the same approach with any sudden overly compliant behavior, especially if your child's normal demeanor is assertive or aggressive."

A balding man in row seven stands, then shouts his question. "Of all the things to look for, which one would you put at the very top?"

Before replying, Linda looks off in the distance, pondering. Then she focuses on the audience. "Actually I think the most important thing to look for is something I haven't even mentioned yet. It's fear, fear of any particular person or family member. You'll know when they're scared and if they're scared of somebody, there always is a reason, always. Dig into it to make certain it's not abuse."

Linda takes several silent seconds before resuming. "Look, these are crucial precautionary steps we all must take if we are to have any chance at stemming the epidemic of child molestation that is running rampant in our community, our state and our nation. I can't tell you it will be easy, because I know it won't be. Think about the odds for a minute. One in ten men has molested. One in ten! And I'm so sorry to admit this, but molesters have only a three percent chance of ever being apprehended. I'm sure every person in this audience personally knows someone who has molested and who was never punished for it." Linda solemnly shakes her head. "You want to know why? Let me repeat from earlier: only a minority of us will ever report sexual abuse."

A young mother from row eleven waves her hand frantically. Linda notices her. "You seem to have a problem. What can I help you with?"

The woman hesitates and then speaks rapidly. "What if you suspect a person might be up to no good with your kids, but you aren't sure. I mean, are there things we can look for?"

Linda nods. "Yes there are. And I'm talking about basic, common sense things. Some of those things you already know, but may not be paying attention to. Now mind you, not all child sex offenders are going to demonstrate every characteristic, but you should notice adults who seem preoccupied with children. And I'll admit that measuring degrees of preoccupation can be problematic. But you must, if protecting your child is a priority. Look at single adults involved with children-oriented activities. Some have lofty goals but a few are troubled, potential abusers. Paid workers and especially volunteers. Adults who make their livings in kid activities who also spend their limited free time being with kids even more. Pay close attention to them. Along those same lines, pay attention to adults who volunteer for various youth groups yet aren't parents of any of the participants. Some love children and want to be part of their lives; others are predators.

"There are adults who create incidents of seemingly innocent physical contact with little kids. Maybe they are horsing around, wrestling, mock shoving and tickling. How many children get scooped up to sit on non-parental laps, or get cuddled or caressed, or even getting kissed and hugged. Is that innocent? Maybe it is. Not every adult who tickles a little kid is a certifiable child molester, but this is enough of a warning signal to promote your awareness. Nearly a quarter of all children will be molested sometime before their eighteenth birthday, the vast majority by someone they know and perhaps, trust—like Ward Weaver with Ashley."

A grey-haired woman from row five gestures for Linda's attention. "I'm a grandmother. I work as a teacher's assistant in a third-grade class and I can't tell you how many times the little ones will initiate close contact with the adults around them. It's like many of them are 'affection-starved.' Sometimes we have to push them away and it breaks my heart to see the effect that kind of rejection can have. But we are forbidden to have close, touching-type contact with students."

"That's a tough situation," Linda says. "But it all boils down to common sense. As intelligent people, you must trust your common sense instincts. Have you ever seen an interaction between an adult and a child that immediately made you alarmed? You find yourself thinking, 'That's just not right.' If you observe anything going on that triggers a funny feeling, follow-up.

"Frankly, I blame a lot of these conflicts on societal preoccupation with being 'politically correct.' If questionable adult behavior makes us suspicious, we immediately chide ourselves for having evil thoughts about somebody. Maybe you think it's hard to believe he or she has the capacity to hurt a kid. And yet, there is not one of us who would not call the police if we saw a bear or mountain lion walking down the street. We do not chide ourselves thinking that bear hasn't hurt anyone yet or he has a right to walk the streets. We instinctively 'know' that a bear walking down the street is a dangerous situation regardless of our political persuasion on the environment. An adult's behavior that triggers your instinct for protecting those around you is no different."

A dark-haired man from row twelve interrupts with a shouted comment. "With all due respect ma'am, there is no way the average mother or father can size up every single adult that crosses his or her children's paths. It's an impossible chore."

"One in four," Linda shouts back to the man. "Remember the statistics. By age eighteen, one in four will have been sexually assaulted. And one out of ten men—ten percent of the total—are doing the offending. And, surprisingly, one in twenty-five women are pedophiles. So even if it seems hopeless, we've got to keep up our vigilance. Just like the government is asking with regard to the terrorist threats.

"Here's a tip, be on the look out for adult males who, when they are around groups of children, adopt child-like antics for their behavior. You know, running, jumping, giggling, teasing and general silliness. Ask yourself about adults who allow kids under their control or in their company to do questionable things or adults who want to take your children on special outings too frequently. And here is the zinger, be wary when they plan activities that would include them being alone with children. Give a second look to adults who do not have children of their own, and yet seem to be very up to speed on all of the kid culture stuff, the current fads, the currently hot music, the video games in vogue, the TV shows they watch. And most importantly, be wary of any adults that your child develops especially strong affection for, for reasons that just don't make a lot of sense to you. Along those same lines, pay close attention to the motives of childless adults who seem remarkably able to infiltrate your family and social functions and ironically seem always available to watch your kids for you when you need a breather."

A short-haired woman from row seventeen raises her arm high. Linda gestures for her to speak. "Hell!" she exclaims desperately. "I mean, I listen to all these characteristics, and many of them fit people I know are good folks who just love children. How do I tell the man from the boogie man?"

Linda nods. "Trust your instincts, create a newer sensitivity. I'm quite aware that not everybody who is a sexual child abuser is going to necessarily demonstrate all of these behaviors, but I'll make this guarantee, 99 percent of those abusers fit into at least some of those behavior categories. Look at Ward Weaver."

From row three a blond crew-cut man raises a hand. Linda acknowledges him. "Yes, sir."

"Are you saying Weaver fit your standard profile?"

Linda shakes her head slowly. "The best answer I can offer is:

sure, he certainly has some of these traits. But not enough of them obviously to fit the FBI profile. For instance, remember the trait of acting like children around children? Or allowing children to do questionable things. Weaver even allowed children to drink alcohol in his home, demanding pledges from each that they would always keep the secret from their parents. The autopsy on Ashley Pond discovered a minimum of five ounces of alcohol in her body. Who do you suppose was the source for that booze? Other traits? Weaver certainly knew their music. He installed a big TV, had a fancy stereo system that used to pound out hip-hop tunes long into the evening. He was always very physical with the pre-teen girls that perpetually hung out at his place. You know, wrestling around, tickling and dancing with them on the living room rug. Up to the very day the cops dragged him off to jail for raping and trying to kill his son's girlfriend, many of the kids were deeply enamored of Weaver. To them he was one cool guy."

The man from row three responds. "But why then, didn't he fit the FBI prototype created earlier, so they should have become more suspicious and nailed him?"

Linda pauses briefly to prepare a reasoned answer. "That's a tough one, all right. They were looking for a serial killer, not a child molester that killed to conceal his crimes. Weaver in many ways was responsible for the synthesis of a whole new profile that they're still chewing on to this day. Weaver did not fit into their traditional profiles and that's what allowed him to keep the FBI at bay for so long. They are sticklers for profiles. With Ward Weaver, they were looking at the wrong profile. He was a sweet guy to the youngsters. He was a devoted single father, raising a young teenaged daughter. He even played father figure to many of her friends. But beneath that facade he was scheming all the time, slowly grooming little girls, for that eventual moment when he'd strike.

"There are seven steps that child molesters use to groom their victims for the 'kill.' Remember these steps so that you can stop the coordinated attack that these monsters use on the most vulnerable of our children.

1. Once they have selected a potential victim, they withhold attention from the victim while showering attention on members of the victim's peer group. This accomplishes two goals. The first is that it separates the victim from the group. Secondly, it makes the child crave attention from the perpetrator.
2. The predator will then praise the victim. That makes the child now worthy of attention. It does not matter what this behavior is so long as the child learns to garner attention by behavior that pleases the groomer.
3. The pervert moves on to a reward, usually something that is slightly improper such as alcohol or perhaps a secret second helping of dessert that no one else gets.
4. The molester will make this reward a secret just between the two of them. The molester will tell his victim that he will be in trouble if the kid tells on him.
5. He or she will test the victim's willingness to keep the secret and then reward for not telling by involvement in more questionable behavior.
6. They will bind the child to the molester by convincing him or her that it is the sharing of this "bad behavior" that makes their relationship special. The molester will tell the child that they both will be punished if anyone finds out.
7. He or she will strike and then make the child feel responsible for the safety of the victim's family or peer group by threatening to harm those people if the victim ever tells or refuses sex.

"And so it goes until 'we, the people make the protection of the most vulnerable in our society our highest priority.'" Linda glances at her watch before continuing. "I see that my allotted time is almost up, but one other thing I want you to know is that you do not have to do it alone. There are several fine organizations that want to help us protect our children.

"One of the finest is Darkness2Light. You will find one of their pamphlets on the table outside as you leave here today. Another helpful organization is Child Watch International. Both of these groups as well as many others can be found by checking sources on the Internet.

"Today, as you step out of this building to go about your lives, you will be struck by the brightness of the world outside. For Ashley and Miranda's sakes, enjoy living. Enjoy your children. I hope you'll take with you not only the information you've learned today, but my warning: If you want to protect those children, be aware. Never, never stop. And don't forget to trust your suspicious feelings; Ashley and Miranda are counting on it."

Afterword

Shortly after the coroner took the body of Ashley Pond from Ward Weaver's home, people began approaching the chain link fence that police had erected around the property a few days earlier.

Slowly and tentatively at first, the adults and children began hanging teddy bears, toys and handwritten signs and notes on the fence. The number of people visiting the site grew dramatically over the next few hours and by the next day, August 26, 2002, much of the fence was covered with the offerings, obscuring the view of Weaver's former home.

The police allowed the spontaneous memorial wall to remain for several summer days, during which it became a shrine to Ashley and her fallen friend, Miranda Gaddis, and a destination for thousands of people in Oregon and the surrounding region. "Ashley + Miranda we love you," read one sign. "We will never forget you," read another.

The first time I saw a spontaneous memorial marking a child's death on the news, I thought it was a freak show. I assumed it was created by attention seekers looking to get on TV. Why else, I thought, would people bring teddy bears and cards to a place where someone they didn't even know had died?

I changed my mind after spending time with the people who created and visited the memorial. As the reporter who first interviewed Weaver and named him as the prime suspect, I had a personal stake in the events. But I quickly realized the people who created the memorial did, too.

After talking with dozens of them, I became convinced they were not looking for attention. Instead they struck me as being genuinely moved by the tragic deaths of the two young girls and compelled to express their sympathies to the families. Some parents used the occasion to teach their children cruel but valuable lessons of life-don't trust strangers or even so-called friends you don't really know.

And it struck me these people did know Ashley and Miranda. Not personally, but enough to understand the difficult, short lives they had led. Part of that was through the coverage that I and other reporters had given the story, including the family photos and home movie scenes that had accompanied so many TV stories. Many people recognized themselves and their families in their images.

From then on, I've never dismissed spontaneous memorials again. I now recognize them as genuine expressions of our common humanity, and the sadness we feel when even a single life is cut short.

- Jim Redden
The Portland Tribune

Acknowledgements

We gratefully acknowledge and thank our parents, John and Florence Billings and Tenny and Margaret Tennyson, givers of life and love.

Linda Watson, our co-author's wife, our first reader, who gave of herself as editor and sounding board.

Rick Watson's daughter, Christine Thompson, who read our book three times in one weekend and called it a "page turner."

Heartfelt thanks to my sister, Karrie, my friend and constant encourager, for reading our book. You are always an inspiration to me!

Susie and David Burns, my best friends and balcony people whose love and support is infinite. Susie, your editing was perfection. David, I hope everyone buys your newly released novel, *Day Follow Night*. It's an epic journey and a great read.

Trisha, my beautiful daughter, you are the best of me. Thank you for your input after reading the first draft.

Jonathan and Damon, our sons, thanks for putting up with us while we were writing the book and often distracted.

Peggy Linden, my first and oldest friend, who always accepted me exactly the way I was. We shared everything including mothers with Alzheimer's disease.

Jim Redden, you are a man of integrity and your constant pursuit of the truth as well as your superb articles in the *Portland Tribune* clearly led to the arrest of Ward Weaver. Thank you from the bottom of my heart for taking the information I gave you and running with it.

Ron and Mary Laitsch, our agents and first contacts in the publishing world. Thanks for your unflappable confidence that our book was, indeed, going to become something special.

Tiller Russell, Curt Miles and Loren Mendell, of *Planet Grande Pictures,* three of the best, the brightest minds and the nicest fellows one could ever hope to be involved with. Your professionalism resulted in a splendid documentary. Thanks for reading our first draft manuscript before shooting commenced. Your intelligent, thoughtful critiques were incorporated into later drafts.

Des Connall, Wayne Mackeson, Gayle Kvernland and Adam Dean, the very first attorneys that I worked for. I learned from the BEST how to be the BEST.

Dan Golden and Adam Schaefer, the guys at our Office Depot service counter. You went way beyond normal boundaries and gave of yourselves to provide us beautiful quality despite the massive amount of copying associated with writing a book.

We wish to thank published authors: Ed Goldberg, Aviva Layton, Harley Sachs, but especially Bill Johnson for reading and critiquing our first draft. Your reviews helped us significantly in the rewrite phase.

Thanks to Audrey Dixon for her constructive criticism that brought our projects to fruition.

Janine Robben, a reporter, for her kind words upon reading our first draft and her search for the truth.

George Clark, with whom I became partners after a chance meeting. Thanks for believing in the project and for adapting our book into your movie script *After the Rain*.

International Search and Rescue Expert Harry Oakes and his dog Valorie for continuing to pursue the truth despite rejection.

Mary Nunencamp: you and your husband's work in educating the public about pedophiles is inspirational. I hope to follow in your footsteps. Thank you for caring so much about the children.

Dr. Joan Dunphy and her team at New Horizon Press, please accept our thanks and appreciation for your efforts to produce a successful book. Extra special thanks to Chris Nielsen, for all of your support for new authors.

Special thanks to all of the family and friends of Ashley Pond who took the time to talk to me about Ashley...especially Ashley's aunt, Maria, who asked for my help to solve the mystery of the disappearance.

-Linda O'Neal, Philip Tennyson & Rick Watson

Endnotes

Prologue

[1] 911 call entered into evidence January 21, 2002 by Detective Viola Valenzuela-Garcia.

[2] Janine Robben, 911 call transcript, *Portland Tribune*, August 2, 2002.

Chapter 1

[1] Detective Viola Valenzuela-Garcia, Oregon City Police Department Report, January 15, 2002.

[2] Detective Viola Valenzuela-Garcia,Oregon City Police Department Reports, January 10, 2002 and January 25, 2002.

Chapter 2

[1] Detective Viola Valenzuela-Garcia, Oregon City Police Department Reports, January 15, 2002, January 25, 2002.

[2] *The Oregonian*, December 8, 2002.

Chapter 3

[1] Taped interview with Suzie*, September 29, 2002.

[2] Stephen Beaven, *The Oregonian*, January 24, 2002.

Chapter 4

[1] Stephen Beaven, *The Oregonian*, January 24, 2002.

[2] Stephen Beaven, *The Oregonian*, January 27, 2002.

[3] Stephen Beaven, *The Oregonian*, January 27, 2002.

[4] Stephen Beaven, *The Oregonian*, January 24, 2002.

[5] Anna Song, *KATU-TV* Documentary, December 27, 2002.

Chapter 5

1. Detective Jay Weitman, Reports, January 25 - February 15, 2002.
2. Detective Downing, Oregon City Police Reports, January 29 - February 19, 2002.
3. Special Agent Christopher Davis, FBI Report, January 31, 2002.
4. Detective Viola Valenzuela-Garcia, Oregon City Police Report, March 1, 2002.
5. Bryan Densen, Stephen Beaven, Noelle Crombie and Sarah Hunsberger, *The Oregonian*, December 8, 2002.

Chapter 6

1. Detective Greg Fryett, Oregon City Police Report, March 9, 2002.
2. Janine Robben, *Portland Tribune*, August 27, 2002.
3. Detective Foster, Oregon City Police Report, March 20, 2002.
4. Stephen Beaven and Sarah Hunsberger, *The Oregonian*, July 13, 2002.
5. Stephen Beaven and Noelle Crombie, *The Oregonian*, July 11, 2002.
6. Jim Redden, *Portland Tribune*. June 14, 2002.
7. Detective Hutterball, Oregon City Police Department Report, March 12, 2002.
8. Affidavit of Probable Cause to Obtain Search Warrant, pgs. 11, 12,
9. Channel Two Documentary.
10. Janine Robben and Jim Redden, *Portland Tribune*, July 5, 2002.
11. Noelle Crombie, *The Sunday Oregonian*, August 25, 2002.
12. Jim Redden and Janine Robben, *Portland Tribune*, August 13, 2002.
13. John Walsh, *America's Most Wanted*, March 16, 2002.
14. David Stroup, *Clackamas Review Oregon City News*, May 2, 2002.
15. Stephen Beaven, *The Oregonian*, April 23, 2002.

Chapter 7

1. National Center for Missing and Exploited Children was mandated by Congress in 1984. Jill Smolowe and J. Todd Foster, *People Magazine*, June 3, 2002.
2. Janine Robben and Jim Redden, *Portland Tribune*, July 5, 2002.
3. Stephen Beaven, *The Oregonian*, March 28, 2002.

Chapter 8

[1] Erin Barnett, Noelle Crombie, Stephen Beaven and Sarah Hunsberger, *The Oregonian*, September 8, 2002, September 22, 2002.

[2] Stephen Beven and Noelle Crombie, *The Oregonian*, September 28, 2002

Chapter 9

[1] Michelle Caruso and Nicholas Maier, *They're Killing our Children*, pg. 88. 2002.

[2] Janine Robben and John Stevens, *Portland Tribune*, August 30, 2002.

Chapter 10

[1] Stephen Beaven and Tracy Jan, *The Oregonian*, August 25, 2002.

[2] Kim Christensen and Stephen Beaven, *The Oregonian*, September 1, 2002.

[3] Linda O'Neal interview with Jayne Patan,* January 2, 2003.

[4] Janine Robben, *Portland Tribune*, August 27, 2002

[5] Interview with Jayne Patan,* January 2, 2003.

[6] Detective Viola Valenzuela-Garcia, Oregon City Police Report, July 12, 2002.

Chapter 11

[1] Detective Viola Valenzuela-Garcia, Oregon City Police Report, May 7, 2002.

[2] Detective Smith, Oregon City Police Report, March 22, 2002.

[3] Stephen Beaven and Sarah Hunsberger, *The Oregonian*, July 13, 2002.

[4] Taped interview by Linda O'Neal with Ron Shumaker.

[5] Noelle Crombie, *The Oregonian*, August 25, 2002.

[6] Michelle Caruso and Nicholas Maier, *They're Killing Our Children*, pg 99-103. 2002.

[7] Oregon State Police and FBI interview with Kathryn Diaz,* March 21, 2002, and Oregon City Police interview with Mallori Weaver, March 8, 2002.

[8] Linda O'Neal interview with Kathryn Diaz*.

9 Sarah Hunsberger and Erin Barnett, *The Oregonian*, September 4, 2002.

10 Noelle Crombie, *The Oregonian*, August 31, 2002.

11 Detective Viola Valenzuela-Garcia, Oregon City Police Report, January 21, 2002.

12 Sarah Hunsberger, *The Oregonian*, August 27, 2002.

Chapter 12

1 Janine Robben, *Portland Tribune*, September 6, 2002.

2 Taped interview with Claire Stevens*. October 13, 2002.

3 Stephen Beaven, *The Oregonian*, January 24, 2002.

4 Bryan Benson and Noelle Crombie, *The Oregonian*, October 10, 2002.

5 Kim Christensen and Stephen Beaven, *The Oregonian*, September 1, 2002.

6 Detective Viola Valenzuela-Garcia, Oregon City Police Report, June 4, 2002.

7 Detective Viola Valenzuela-Garcia, Oregon City Police Report, July 11, 2002.

8 Detective Viola Valenzuela-Garcia, Oregon City Police Report, June 10, 2002.

9 Detective Viola Valenzuela-Garcia. Oregon City Police Report, June 6, 2002.

10 Affidavit of probable cause for issuance of search warrant August 21, 2002 (2-99)

11 Detective Huot, Oregon City Police Report, June 6, 2002

12 Detective Viola Valenzuela-Garcia, Oregon City Police Report, June 4, 2002.

13 Detective Viola Valenzuela-Garcia, Oregon City Police Report, June 10, 2002.

14 Detective Viola Valenzuela-Garcia, Oregon City Police Report, June 17, 2002.

15 Detective Viola Valenzuela-Garcia, Oregon City Police Report, June 4, 2002.

16 Canby Police Department Report. July 30, 1993.

[17] Detective Viola Valenzuela-Garcia, Oregon City Police Report, May 23, 2002.

Chapter 13
[1] Detective Viola Valenzuela-Garcia, Oregon City Police Report, January 10, 2002.
[2] Detective Viola Valenzuela-Garcia, Oregon City Police Report, June 26, 2002.
[3] Taped Interview with Claire Stevens*.
[4] Jim Redden, *Portland Tribune,* June 16, 2002.

Chapter 14
[1] *The Oregonian,* December 8, 2002.
[2] Jim Redden, *Portland Tribune,* August 27, 2002, July 2, 2002.
[3] Jim Redden, *Portland Tribune,* August 27, 2002.
[4] Stephen Beaven, *The Oregonian*, July 11, 2002.
[5] Janine Robben and Jim Redden, *Portland Tribune,* July 5, 2002.

Chapter 15
[1] Stephen Beaven and Sarah Hunsberger, *The Oregonian,* July 13, 2002.
[2] Detective Viola Valenzuela-Garcia, Oregon City Police Report, January 21, 2002 and February 8, 2002.
[3] Jim Redden, *Portland Tribune*, August 13, 2002.

Chapter 16
[1] Affidavit of Probable Cause to Obtain Search Warrant, pg. 3.

Chapter 17
[1] Oregon City Police Department Reports, August 13, 2002.
[2] *KATU Channel 2 News,* August 13, 2002.
[3] *KATU-TV* News coverage.
[4] Janine Robben, *The Portland Tribune,* August 20, 2002.
[5] Janine Robben, *The Portland Tribune,* August 27, 2002.
[6] David Stroup, *The Oregon City News,* August 28, 2002.

7 Noelle Crombie, *The Oregonian*, August 27, 2002.

8 Detective Viola Valenzuela-Garcia, Oregon City Police Report, September 11, 2002.
9 Sarah Hunsberger, *The Oregonian*, November 15, 2002.

Chapter 18

1 Janine Robben, *Portland Tribune*, August 27, 2002.
2 Detective Greg Fryett, Oregon City Police Report, September 24, 2002.
3 Detective Jay Weitman, West Lynn Police Department Affidavit, August 29, 2002.
4 Family accounts, Philip Tennyson's video, etc.
5 Sarah Hunsberger, Noelle Crombie and Stephen Beaven, *The Oregonian*, August 30, 2002.
6 Detective Greg Fryett, Oregon City Police Report, August 30, 2002.
7 Detective Greg Fryett, Oregon City Police Report, September 4, 2002.
8 Janine Robben, *Portland Tribune*, September 24, 2002.
9 Detective Jay Weitman, West Lynn Police Department, Affidavit, September 18, 2002.

Chapter 19

1 Detective Viola Valenzuela-Garcia, Oregon City Police Report, September 11, 2002.
2 Detective Viola Valenzuela-Garcia, Oregon City Police Report, January 10, 2002.
3 Stephen Beaven and Sarah Hunsberger, *The Oregonian*, September 28, 2002 and Sarah Hunsberger, *The Oregonian*, October 1, 2002.
4 Doug Beghtel Photo, *The Oregonian*, September 10, 2002.
5 Noelle Crombie, *The Oregonian*, September 14, 2002.
6 Detective Greg Fryett, Oregon City Police Report, September 23, 2002.

[7] Detective Greg Fryett, Oregon City Police Report, September 24, 2002.

[8] Oregon City Police Report, September 28, 2002.

[9] Oregon City Police Report, September 28, 2002.

Chapter 20

[1] Stephen Beaven and Sarah Hunsberger, *The Oregonian*, October 4, 2002 and October 5, 2002.

[2] Sarah Hunsberger, *The Oregonian*, October 1, 2002.

[3] Noelle Crombie, *The Oregonian*, February 27, 2003.

[4] Noelle Crombie, *The Oregonian*, December 11, 2002.

[5] Steven Carter, *The Oregonian*, December 12, 2002.

[6] Noelle Crombie, *The Oregonian*, January 27, 2004.

[7] Detective Greg Fryett, Oregon City Police Report, October 11, 2002.

[8] Detective Fryett, Oregon City Police Report, October 11, 2002.

[9] Emily Tsao, *The Oregonian*, September 25, 2004.

[10] Jim Redden, *The Portland Tribune*, December 27, 2002 and Stephen Beaven and Noelle Crombie, *The Oregonian*, November 8, 2002.

[11] Jim Redden, *The Portland Tribune*, December 27, 2002 and Stephen Beaven and Noelle Crombie, *The Oregonian*, November 8, 2002.

[12] Stephen Beaven and Sarah Hunsberger, *The Oregonian*, November 23, 2002.

[13] Sarah Hunsberger and Stephen Beaven, *The Oregonian*, November 26, 2002.

[14] *The Oregonian*, December 30, 2002.

[15] Oregon City Police Department Report, January 13, 2003.

Chapter 21

[1] Philip Tennyson home video.

[2] Sarah Hunsberger, *The Oregonian*, January 10, 2003.

[3] Anna Song, *KATU TV,* February 23-26, 2003.

[4] Clackamas County Sheriff's Department Report, February 24, 2003.

[5] Janine Robben, *Portland Tribune*, April 8, 2003.
[6] Noelle Crombie, *The Oregonian*, March 31, 2003.
[7] Noelle Crombie, *The Oregonian*, March 28, 2003.

[8] Noelle Crombie, *The Oregonian*, March 28, 2003.
[9] Stephen Beaven, *The Oregonian*, February 7, 2003.
[10] Emily Tsao, *The Oregonian*, June 23, 2004
[11] Sarah Hunsberger, *The Oregonian*, August 23, 2003.
[12] Noelle Crombie and Sarah Hunsberger, *The Oregonian*, January 10, 2004.
[13] Lori Pond, taped conversation, April 23, 2003.

Chapter 22

[1] Noelle Crombie, *The Oregonian*, June 11, 2003.
[2] Noelle Crombie, *The Oregonian*, July 31, 2003.

Chapter 23

[1] Clackamas County Sheriff's Department Report, October 7, 2003.
[2] Kelly Day, *KPTV*, October 29, 2003.
[3] Jim Redden and Janine Robben, *Portland Tribune*, November 4, 2003.
[4] Jim Redden and Janine Robben, *Portland Tribune*, November 4, 2003.
[5] Noelle Crombie, *The Oregonian*, November 7, 2003.
[6] Jim Redden, *Portland Tribune*, November 18, 2003.
[7] Noelle Crombie, *The Oregonian*, November 11, 2003.
[8] Psychological Evaluation by State Hospital, July 26, 2004.
[9] Noelle Crombie, *The Oregonian*, January 7, 2004.
[10] Noelle Crombie, *The Oregonian*, January 13, 2004.
[11] Clackamas County Sheriffs Department Report, January 11, 2004.
[12] Emily Tsao, *The Oregonian*, March 4, 2004.
[13] Emily Tsao, *The Oregonian*, April 30, 2004.

Chapter 24

[1] Emily Tsao, *The Oregonian*, June 23, 2004.

2 Emily Tsao, *The Oregonian,* June 23, 2004.
3 Emily Tsao, *The Oregonian,* July 24, 2004.

Chapter 25
1 Philip Tennyson, home video recording, August 24, 2004.

Chapter 26
1 Psychological Evaluation by Oregon State Hospital, July 26, 2004.
2 Sarah Hunsberger, *The Oregonian*, August 25, 2004.
3 KATU-TV Newscast, August 25, 2004.
4 Jim Redden, *Portland Tribune*, September 10, 2004.
5 Emily Tsao, *The Oregonian*, September 8, 2004.
6 Emily Tsao, *The Oregonian*, September 17, 2004.
7 Sarah Hunsberger, *The Oregonian*, September 22, 2004.
8 Transcript of Court Proceeding, September 22, 2004.
9 Emily Tsao, *The Oregonian*, September 23, 2004.

Epilogue
1 Cheryl Martinis, *The Oregonian*, September 22, 2002 .

* Names have been changed for reasons of privacy.

Deadly Masquerade
A True Story of Illicit Passion, Buried Secrets and Murder
by
Donita Woodruff

Hungering for a second chance and the bustle of the big city, Donita, a young single mother, decides to move her family from a small town back home to Los Angeles. Hurting from previous romantic relationships, Donita is hesitant to start anything new until she meets academy award nominee David Allen - successful, handsome and charming. The two are swept up in a whirlwind romance. Life seems too good to be true, but even wedding bells can't hide her new husband's secrets. Suddenly, Donita and her children are caught in a world of vicious lies and double lives, where nothing is as it appears.

Mysterious phone calls, a questionable ex-lover and an unsolved murder all begin to unravel in Donita Woodruff's true life account, *Deadly Masquerade*. When the perfect man reveals a sordid double life, Donita has one choice - to take matters into her own hands. Risking it all, she investigates the evidence of a twenty-year-old homicide, only to discover a dangerous game of cover-up that leads right to her front door. Trusting no one in this rogues game, she must hide what she knows to bring the killer to justice and protect her children.

Deadly Masquerade is a suspenseful page-turner full of skeleton-in-the-closet secrets and deadly liasons, with a twist so bizarre and shocking, it could only be true!

Donita Woodruff has been interviewed extensively by both print, including the Associated Press and the *National Enquirer*, and television- ABC, NBC, *The Montel Williams Show*, CNN World News-media for her role in the capture of fugitive killer Freddie Turner. Her true life tale of survival and triumph led her to write her first book, *Deadly Masquerade*. She lives in California with her two children.

A New Horizon Press True Crime Release:
0-88282-266-7 $24.95 HC

Real People/Incredible Stories

Murder at the Office
A Survivor's True Story
by
Brent C. Doonan

They had been co-workers. They had been friends. Mark Barton seemed personable, friendly and trustworthy when he began working at Brent Doonan's day-trading company, All-Tech. Then he began to lose money.

Heavily in debt to All-Tech, Barton left and secretly opened another day trading account at Momentum Securities, across the street. Once again Barton ran up huge debts and quickly owed Momentum over six figures. Then he vanished. When Barton reappeared, it was to repay his debt in a way no one could have expected. In a blaze of bullets and blood, Barton killed four Momentum employees and wounded seven others. He then calmly crossed the street to All-Tech, paid his old friend Brent a visit and shot him five times. He went on to kill five more people and wound an additional six in the worst incident of workplace violence in history.

As Barton's fury was unleashed, Brent made an amazing escape. After barely making his way to an upstairs office, strangers cradled his shattered body as they waited for help to arrive. They all prayed. And they saw the light in Brent's eyes fading.

In the days that followed, the incident became *Time Magazine's* cover story and made headlines nationwide. Reporters proclaimed that day-trading was not a panacea, but a powder-keg. Their assertion seemed to be that anyone could be Mark Bartion and that the day-trading business was the true danger. But was this true or was Barton a sociopath whose violent tendencies were only lying in wait?

Though Barton was gone, he left many victims, both alive and dead. Brent tells the shocking true story of the Atlanta Massacre and his very personal, inspiring recovery fueled by perserverance and strength

Brent Doonan, graduated from Indiana University with a B.S. in Finance and Real Estate. He was the co-founder and president of All-Tech Direct, Inc. in Atlanta Georgia, and appeared in interviews on *The Today Show, NBC, ABC* and *Fox News.* Currently, he lives in Wichita, Kansas and works as the finance manager for Doonan Truck and Equipment.

A New Horizon Press True Crime Release:
0-88282-272-1 $21.95 HC

Real People/Incredible Stories

Trail of Blood
A Father, a Son and a Tell-tale Crime Scene Investigation
by
Wanda Evans in Collaberation with James Dunn

When Jim Dunn got the heart-stopping call every parent dreads: "Your son has disappeared," on a Sunday night in 1991 and then saw his son's blood splattered apartment, it set into motion a six-year nightmarish odyssey of desperate searches. Ahead were moments of frantic hope, growing despair and finally acceptance that Scott was dead, despite the fact that his body was not found.

As Dunn worked with Lubbock, Texas police investigators and followed his own leads, mounting evidence pointed to Scott's live-in girlfriend and her new lover. However, Dunn learned there was a seemingly insurmountable problem to getting justice for his son: Texas law insists on a body before prosecuting anyone for murder and Scott's body was nowhere to be found.

Frustrated, Dunn turned to members of the little-known Vidocq Society, highly experienced criminologists and forensic experts who crack the coldest "unsolvable" or "unprovable" cases around the world. Vidocq member Dr. Richard Walter, a forensic pathologist and criminal profiler, consulted Scotland Yard, studied DNA evidence and blood spatter patterns and then pointed out who he deduced had killed Scott and why. The D.A. agreed, but said his hands were tied: Scott's body still had not been found. However, when Walter set forth a unique theory based on the fact that there was enough of Scott's blood in the room to prove murder, the DA brought the case before the grand jury. Six years after his disappearance, Scott's girlfriend Leisha Hamilton and Tim Smith, a love-smitten neighbor, were tried and convicted of Scott's murder.

" A Brilliant and utterly gripping mix of crime-scene investigattion and courtroom drama. As good as CSI gets, as far as actual forensics, combined with a family tragedy that awakens compassion for the surviving victims." - Connie Fletcher, Booklist, March 1, 2005

Wanda Evans, a noted journalist, writer and speaker, has been published in many venues, including Reader's Digest, Good Housekeeping and Southern Living. A former columnist for the Lubbock Avalanche-Journal, she lives in Lubbock, Texas where she is working on two political biographies.

James Dunn, a former sales and marketing professional and CEO of the software company Comprehensive Marketing, is an active member of the Vidocq Society and Parents of Murdered Children. He is a financial planner, lives in St. Marys, GA, with his wife and continues to hope for the day he can bury his son.

A New Horizon Press True Crime Release:
0-882822-261-6 $24.95

Real People/Incredible Stories

Faces of Evil
Kidnappers, Murderers, Rapists and the Forensic Artist Who Puts Them Behind Bars
by
Lois Gibson and Deanie Francis Mills

Every day, Lois Gibson is able to put power, control and a sense of justice back into the hands of victims of violent crime, heinous rapes, kidnappings and murders. Gibson, herself the victim of a violent rape, uses her skills to coax from the memories of victims the most intimate details possible and with the stroke of a pencil, reconstructs the faces of their tormentors. These eerily accurate portraits have been directly responsible for the capture of over 700 vicious criminals for which her skills are noted in the *Guinness Book of Records*.

Faces of Evil is Gibson's riveting story of how she became the world's most successful forensic artist, interwoven with her thirteen most suspense-filled cases. Gisbon takes you with her inside the gritty atmosphere of forensics, putting you behind the scenes of terrifying enigma after enigma and into the victims' mind set as they seek vindication. Follow the nine-year-old girl who sees and helps catch her mother's killer, the pregnant blind woman who identifies and aids in the capture of her rapist and the hero cop whose deathbed description leads police to his killer.

This is a fascinating true crime book like no other; mixing chilling crime scenes with the inspiring story of one woman's passion for justice.

Lois Gibson is a twenty-two-year veteran forensic artist with the Houston, Texas police department. Recently profiled in *People Magazine*, Oprah Winfrey's *"O"* magazine, *Reader's Digest, Dateline NBC* and *Unsolved Mysteries,* she regularly appears on *America's Most Wanted* and is also the holder of the Guinness World Record Certificate in Forensic Art. Gibson has a B.A. in Fine Arts from the University of Texas at Austin and is a Professor at Northwestern University as well as being affiliated with the FBI and U.S. Marshall's Service. She resides in Houston, Texas with her family.

Deanie Francis Mills is a widely published writer whose work appears in *Redbook, Good Housekeeping* and *Parent* and is the author of *Torch* (Penguin Putnam) *Tightrope* (Dutton Signet), *Losers Weepers* (Putnam Berkley) and *Ordeal* (Dutton) She resides in Hermleigh, Texas with her family.

A New Horizon Press True Crime Release:
0-88282-258-6 $24.95

Real People/Incredible Stories